RADICALISM UNVEILED

Religion and International Security

Series Editor: Lee Marsden, University of East Anglia

In the twenty-first century religion has become an increasingly important factor in international relations and international security. Religion is seen by policy makers and academics as being a major contributor in conflict and its successful resolution. The role of the Ashgate series in Religion and International Security is to provide such policy makers, practitioners, researchers and students with a first port of call in seeking to find the latest and most comprehensive research on religion and security. The series provides established and emerging authors with an opportunity to publish in a series with a reputation for high quality and cutting edge research in this field. The series produces analytical and scholarly works from around the world that demonstrate the relevance of religion in security and international relations. The intention is not to be prescriptive or reductionist in restricting the types of books that would be appropriate for the series and as such encourages a variety of theoretical and empirical approaches. International security is broadly defined to incorporate inter and intra-state conflict, human security, terrorism, genocide, religious freedom, human rights, environmental security, the arms trade, securitisation, gender security, peace keeping, conflict resolution and humanitarian intervention. The distinguishing feature is the religious element in any security or conflict issue.

Other titles in the series:

The Ashgate Research Companion to Religion and Conflict Resolution
Edited by Lee Marsden
978-1-4094-1089-8

Religious Transnational Actors and Soft Power
Jeffrey Haynes
978-1-4094-2508-3

Religion, Conflict and Military Intervention
Edited by Rosemary Durward and Lee Marsden
978-0-7546-7871-7

Radicalism Unveiled

FARHAAN WALI

Routledge
Taylor & Francis Group

LONDON AND NEW YORK

First published 2013 by Ashgate Publishing

Published 2016 by Routledge
2 Park Square, Milton Park, Abingdon, Oxfordshire OX14 4RN
711 Third Avenue, New York, NY 10017, USA

First issued in paperback 2016

Routledge is an imprint of the Taylor & Francis Group, an informa business

British Library Cataloguing in Publication Data
Wali, Farhaan.
  Radicalism unveiled. -- (Religion and international
  security)
  1. Radicalism--Religious aspects--Islam. 2. Radicalism--
  Great Britain. 3. Religious fanaticism--Islam. 4. Hizb
  al-Tahrir. 5. Muslim youth--Great Britain--Attitudes.
  I. Title II. Series
  320.5'57'0941-dc23

The Library of Congress has cataloged the printed edition as follows:
Wali, Farhaan.
  Radicalism unveiled / by Farhaan Wali.
     pages ; cm. -- (Religion and international security)
  Includes bibliographical references and index.
  ISBN 978-1-4094-6371-9 (hardback)   1. Islam--Great Britain.
2. Islamic fundamentalism--Great Britain. 3. Radicalism--Great Britain.
4. Muslims--Great Britain. I. Title.
  BP65.G7W35 2013
  320.55'70941--dc23

                                                            2012044659

ISBN 13: 978-1-138-24957-8 (pbk)
ISBN 13: 978-1-4094-6371-9 (hbk)

Contents

List of Tables

Chapter 1
Penetrating the Clandestine Veil

Hizb ut-Tahrir[1] (henceforth, HT), a radical fringe group, has managed to inspire countless young people in Britain to turn away from the bedrock principles of this country, infusing them with religious fanaticism. For over three decades HT has operated relatively unchallenged within British society, yet relatively little has been published about how this movement evolved and why its appeal among some young Muslims continues to grow. The rise of global terrorism, particularly in the wake of 9/11, promoted fierce scrutiny of the Muslim community here in the UK. However, heightened security measures and stricter legislation did not prevent four home-grown terrorists from killing and injuring hundreds in Britain's largest terror attack. Unsurprisingly, radicalisation has taken centre stage. Tony Blair, in the aftermath of the 7/7 bombings, identified young British Muslims as being particularly at risk from radicalisation, a sentiment echoed across media and academic channels alike (The *Guardian*, 10 November 2005). Young British Muslims have been singled out as a problem group, because extremist elements are increasingly gaining a foothold among their disgruntled ranks, making it even more important to understand their needs. Despite the fact that a better understanding of radicalisation has been achieved, there is a great deal missing in our knowledge about the emergence of HT in Britain, making it vital to discover why some young people are attracted to the organisation.

Encountering HT

On 13 August 1995, at the age of 16, I attended a rally in Trafalgar Square. I did not know at the time of the storm that such an event would trigger, nor could I have predicted the social upheaval that would result from it. The '*Rally for Islam*', as it was entitled by the organisers, was a pioneering event.[2] Surprisingly I witnessed the existence of different, and to some extent conflicting, identities of young Muslims. In particular, these were well educated British-born Muslims, from similar ethnic and socio-religious backgrounds. Yet they consciously appeared to reject all aspects of Western civilisation as morally corrupt and inherently wrong. What

---

1   According to Hizb ut-Tahrir's official manifesto, the group is defined as an 'Islamic party that was formed in 1953 [by Taqiuddin al-Nabhani in the West Bank] with the objective of working to re-establish the Islamic way of life and to carry Islam to mankind (Anon. 2000, p. 76).

2   The '*Rally for Islam*' was organised by Hizb ut-Tahrir (HT).

stood out with significant clarity was the apparent re-structuring of identities into a single religious perspective, which appeared to be inspired by a collective group identity. This perceived homogeneous identity appeared to melt the individual identities into a collective one, embracing the different types of identity among the spectators. I was shocked by the great devotion shown by these young Muslims to religion, especially as I was raised in a secular household, making this difficult to understand. In encounters with other young Muslims, I perceived them to be thoroughly integrated into British society. It was this contrast that provoked in me a great deal of interest in understanding the processes involved in the making of a radical identity.

My Journey In and Out of HT

When I began to look at HT, it became apparent that I was setting out to generate knowledge and insight of a social reality that I had already experienced in my youth. For this reason, I had a set of subjective assumptions about the radicalisation process, as I had already experienced HT radicalisation. Thus, in essence my investigation of HT was not starting from scratch, but rather from pre-existing knowledge. It became clear that I could not avoid using my own personal experiences of HT, and thus I needed to identify a way of utilising this experience rather than pretending it did not happen. So, I needed to find a way to compare my raw data with my own experience as a member of HT and share it with the respondents. In particular, 'conscious partiality', as articulated by Mies (1983), stood out as a key way to maintain a real and flexible counterbalance between object and subject, which I did not want to separate in an artificial manner. In other words, as someone who has experienced HT radicalisation, I am also my own source of knowledge. As du Bois (1983, p. 111) explained, the centrality of experience means the knower is part of the matrix of what is known. The process of 'partial identification' with HT activists made it necessary to move away from 'value-free objectivity' as a methodological starting point (Mies, 1983, p. 123). This is because I cannot simply assume ignorance of those being studied, and regard them simply as objects, especially since this would deny my own experiences of HT membership.

Before delving into my observations, I want to contextualise my motivation for writing this book by drawing upon some of my own experiences as a former member of HT. My early youth was greatly shaped by my feelings of social dislocation. In particular, I struggled to construct a coherent identity during my adolescence. I tried to develop a position that would relate my teenage life to what I had experienced before, in an effort to gain meaning. I was raised in a very secular household, in fact, religiosity was not emphasised in any way. As I matured, I could not develop a unified understanding about all the diverse aspects of my life. Religion and ethnicity were disconnected from my social identity, preventing me from establishing a unified identity. Also, I found it difficult to make sense of my ethnicity, especially since I lived in a predominantly white area. Despite rejecting my ethnicity, I still felt socially dislocated from the white working class friends I had made at secondary school. There were two reasons for this sense of exclusion. Firstly, I was raised in a middle class household, which brought me into conflict with my white working class counterparts, especially as I struggled to relate to their social world. Secondly, despite gaining some degree of acceptance amongst my white friends, I could not fully overcome their negative perception of belonging to a different ethnic group. This consequently reinforced within me the sense that my identity was artificial.

At college I was confronted, for the first time, with a multicultural environment, which to some degree forced me to re-evaluate my negative stereotypes about race and ethnicity. This new social situation allowed me to re-invent myself; however, it was extremely intimidating and overwhelming. I felt isolated and slightly insecure, so I went in search of the 'familiar'. Thus, I came into contact with HT recruiters when I started to attend Friday Prayers, and they introduced me to HT radicalism. I had never considered myself connected to a global community and thus I was never emotionally moved by the plight of Muslims. However, this changed when I was exposed to the rhetoric of HT. I slowly began to think in terms of 'us and them'. At this point my identity was struggling to adjust, because the new ideas being offered to me were impossible to work into a smooth and consistent whole. HT rhetoric projected a homogenous identity – one is Muslim and not British or Pakistani. However, I considered my identity evenly distributed, even when I became a member, it was a mix of positions.

After several years of wrestling with my own contradictions, I decided to join the group. This was not a free choice; significant coercion was used in order to manipulate me into joining the organisation. Although, there was no physical pressure, the coercion was clear if you did not join HT then you were 'sinful and God would condemn you to the pits of hell for an eternity' (Faheem, Member). By virtue of ignorance, I was placed in a state of guilt for not working for the party aim, and thus I felt compelled to join. After a lengthy delay, I was placed into a *Halaqah* (private study circle) with six other individuals and a *Mushrif* (Teacher) was appointed to indoctrinate us into HT culture. This is considered a key stage and an instrumental part of group radicalisation. During this period, intellectual pressure is applied, forcing the novice to bend towards group expectation. In particular, the *Mushrif* was very keen to establish a joint construction of reality, amongst us, in order to create a new cognitive perspective. The *Halaqah* provided a conceptual framework, with which connections had to be made to our own social realities. To remove extreme individual differences and independent thought the *Mushrif* forces novices to agree with and carry the ideas presented in *Halaqah*. The novice is seen as intellectually inferior, especially if he or she displays independent thinking. In my *Halaqah*, I remember that most of the novices conformed to the *Mushrif*'s judgements in order not to appear different. Although, this alignment of ideas is consciously arrived at, it does denote the acceptance of influence.

On the surface, a recurring feature of HT rhetoric is *Mabda* (ideology), which is the basis of organising and mobilising the fraternity. In reality, this is not true, as I experienced. HT enforced ideology onto its members, demanding they obey the commands of the party hierarchy. When I became a member, I wrote a letter to the then Amir (leader), Abdul-Qadeem Zullum, asking him about the limits of the party's authority. According to Zullum, 'it is *wajib* [obligatory] on the member to obey his *Masool* in all circumstances except if the *Masool* requests a *haram* [forbidden] action is clear that it is *haram* e.g. leaving a *Fard* or doing a *haram* such as *Zina* [adultery], drinking alcohol etc.' (Answer and Question, 2002). This clearly indicates HT authority has wide reaching influence and control, which is applied at the discretion of the hierarchy. Furthermore, *Istinkar* (rejection) of HT is *haram*, because 'the aim of Hizb ut-Tahrir is to carry the Islamic *dawah* [mission] and resume the Islamic way of life, its work is ... to change *dar al-Kufr* [land of non-Islam] to *dar al-Islam* [land of Islam] ... to reject this work or free oneself of the responsibility of this work by rejecting the Hizb is prohibited by *Sharia* [Islamic Law]' (Admin File, p. 130).

When the novice begins to convey the thoughts of HT effectively, as if they were his own, then he is considered for membership. However, the novice must show desire for membership by imposing himself on the organisation, which serves as the first indicator for their readiness. During this period, I remember that novices competed with each other to gain the recognition of members. At the time, this staged rivalry provoked some controversy among the novices, as they questioned the morality of such a policy. Senior members felt it was totally acceptable for novices 'to compete in this fashion for good deeds' (Faheem, Member). However, the atmosphere became rather polluted by individuals trying to outdo others, but for the hierarchy it showed psychological dependency for HT and a desire for membership.

I recall being summoned, without any explanation, on an early Sunday morning by a senior member. I arrived at the location to find several members already present, among them was the *Naqib* (area leader) and *Masool* (local leader). To my surprise, they offered me membership into HT, which I reluctantly accepted. Jalauddin Patel, who was the *Naqib* of West London at the time, explained that in order to become a member, I must take *al-Qasm* (the Oath).[3] In fact, the swearing of the oath is a requirement for all prospective members, as to be assured of his sincerity and loyalty. After a few weeks, I soon realised the full ramifications of the oath, which in reality meant I belonged to HT. However, I do not believe my personal identity gave way completely to the group identity. When I was exposed to group pressure, for example, I realised

---

3   The Oath (*al-Qasm*): Everyone who joins HT has to be (1) 'a faithful guardian of Islam; (2) adopt the opinions of this Hizb ut-Tahrir, its thoughts and its constitution by word and deed; (3) trust its leadership; (4) execute its resolutions even if they differed with my opinion; and (5) to exhaust all my efforts to achieve its objective as long as I am a member in it' (*Al-Qasm*, Hizb ut-Tahrir, 20 August 1998)

that in public situations I conformed to HT. However, privately I disagreed with the group. As a member, I found it impossible to operate without independent thought and free will. As I became submerged in party activism, my concerns heightened. Consequently, I broke HT protocol and started to voice my concerns openly. Initially, I tried to create a conflict among the majority by challenging their norms, but I found it difficult to provide an alternative norm for them to consider because they only referred to HT ideology.

I started to question the coercive nature of HT, as *Masools* seemed to operate with impunity. Moreover, because I challenged the party leadership concerning its practices, I was subjected to an investigation. The findings of the investigation found that I had not been acting in compliance with the directives of the UK leadership, and thus I was subject to reprimand in accordance with the party code of conduct. In order to assess my loyalty, the leadership informed me 'the *Masool* has the power to prevent any member from contacting his friends if the *Masool* thinks this will cause harm to the party'. This allowed HT to control my interactions, especially with other members and it prevented me from contacting other Islamic scholars. The leadership issued a final warning:

> ... he must completely abstain from any violations or anything that affects the party or its thoughts and that he must adhere completely to the party, its thoughts and have complete trust in the party, its thoughts and its *Masools*. And if he does not adhere to all of this then he should be informed of his 'ihmaal taam' [complete removal] (Letter from Central Leadership, 2002).

I refused to comply with this request and subsequently was dismissed from HT. Although, this is a short glimpse into my narrative with HT, it does show that I experienced huge social change. In particular, I struggled to blend and mix different identity-types together into a complete whole, which initially pulled me towards HT radicalism. Within HT my identity was totally refashioned. Even though, the sense of belonging I attained in HT overshadowed other social attachments, it was not anchored by ideology. In fact, I had little connection to HT ideology; instead I was attracted by the homogenous nature of the organisations fraternity. The members emerged from social realities and backgrounds that were very similar to mine, but after I left HT, I wanted to know whether these young people were drawn to the group by similar motivations. On the surface, HT activists appear driven by one single overriding variable, namely ideology, but I wanted to go much deeper. Therefore, I sought to contextualise HT membership. This meant giving voice to HT narratives in a way that would allow me to understand the changing experiences and worldviews of HT activists, what they saw as important, and how they dissected their past and present experiences.

Ethnographic Approach: Penetrating the Veil

The topic of radicalisation is highly contested amongst social theorists, who continue to strive for answers to such questions as, who are radicals? Are there common characteristics associated with radicals? Do radicals vary among themselves; and if so, how do they differ? A cursory survey of the literature has indicated that no single variable, or theory, exclusively explains why radicalisation occurs. Therefore, understanding the impact radicalisation has had on some young Muslims required investigating a specific radical Islamic movement, namely HT. In my early encounters with members of HT, I noticed, on the surface, they appeared thoroughly 'westernised' in relation to dress, language and leisure activities. However, these young men had become radicalised, turning against liberal and secular values. I wanted to find out what processes contributed to this change. The work of fellow researchers appeared to be characterised by their fascination for radicalisation, from a distance. The primary reason for this neglect can be attributed to access, because groups like HT operate in a secretive manner. So, this begs the question, how does one study HT?

Although there has been significant study of radicalisation, little research has used an empirical approach to study this phenomenon. After reading major works, and through personal contact with some of the main theorists and researchers engaged in the debates, I noticed a number of problems concerning the lack of access to primary encounters. This is because radical Islamic groups, like HT, operate in a clandestine fashion and use morally unacceptable behaviour to achieve their goals, making it difficult to record their activities in real settings. Also, the social world of radicals was not properly constructed, providing only a partial picture of the radicalisation process. Initially, in order to overcome these barriers, I needed to navigate around the problem of accessibility. None of the existing approaches I had studied gave sufficient insight into this problem. For this reason, I adopted an ethnographic approach, because it provided me with an opportunity to study the activities of group members in their natural surroundings.

This approach allowed me to study the activities of HT members, to see how they make sense of their surroundings. A cursory appraisal of previous approaches to radicalisation showed that most theorists rejected 'participant observation' of radical groups, because it was adjudged impractical and unworkable. However, after spending several years interacting with members of HT through participant observation, I was able to interpret their social world, giving me an insight into how they became radicalised.

In essence, I gained an understanding of why some young Muslims are attracted to HT, from their point of view. This is important because some researchers have a tendency to make assertions on the nature of Islamic organisations based on artificial situations. Post (1991), for example, equates mental illness to the antecedents of radical behaviour among individuals and groups. This generic observation is based on unscientific generalisations, because biographical data from radical groups like HT is not readily available. However, my access to HT put me in the unique position of being able to gather the biographical databases required for the development of a valid scientific approach. Thus, participant observation allowed me to gather more detailed information, accessing the meaning of events and social interactions as understood by HT. This allowed me to get close to my respondents, which provided me with a visible picture of HT activities and the everyday experiences of members. So, I spent several years attending HT events and activities. This provided me with insight, as a participant, of the inner workings of the organisational structure. This, furthermore, made my fieldwork easier because I was not considered an outsider, and was given open access to members and to HT culture.

Integrating 'Objectivity'

To begin with, what distinguishes this book from other scholarly work on HT is my involvement with HT. However, it is precisely this involvement in HT which raised a set of methodological concerns. Firstly, how could I maintain 'objectivity' and 'neutrality' in my fieldwork? As touched on earlier, I resorted to feminist methodology as a way to anchor my observations. This meant the value-free objectivity, 'of neutrality and indifference towards research objects', had to be replaced by 'conscious partiality' (Mies, 1983, p. 122). In keeping with this approach, HT activists were not looked upon as simple research objects but as mirror images of me. As a result, HT members slowly lost their initial suspicion that I might misuse and exploit their histories. This allowed for an open exchange of information, as I took the side of HT activists, partly identifying with them, and in a conscious way created space for critical dialogue and reflection (Mies, 1983, p. 123).

This 'conscious partiality' enabled me to voice my own experiences of HT membership, which led to an open and contextualised knowledge of subjective experiences. Secondly, despite adopting less conventional approaches to objectivity, I was fully aware of the lack of social distance between myself and the respondents. As an ex-member of HT, I had already been involved in what I was studying. This meant I shared similar patterns of ethno-religious socialisation and life-experiences as the respondents. However, this is not a problem, as Mamak (1978, p. 168) observed:

> I found that my academic training in the methodological views of western social science and its emphasis on 'scientific objectivity' conflicted with the experiences of my colonial past. The traditional way in which social science research is conducted proved inadequate for an understanding of the people I was researching.

In this respect, the traditional scientific perspective that views the researched as mere objects of data collection are out-mounded for this analysis, because to penetrate clandestine actors required personal connection and involvement. However, as

Alder and Alder (1987, p. 8) point out, when investigating a clandestine group the 'researchers must assume social roles that fit the worlds they are studying'. In general, scholars studying HT tend to lack insider perspective of HT activism, as they cannot penetrate the clandestine veil of the organisation, hindering their ability to formulate meaningful conclusions. However, I did not require immersing myself into the culture of HT to gain an insider's experience of the group, as I had already gained knowledge through my own experiences. This gave me a unique perspective and standpoint on HT. Therefore, using 'conscious partiality', I sought not only to hear the life histories of HT activists, but to also observe and compare their social reality and experiences to my own.

Therefore, from the commencement of this book, I was aware I could not divorce my personal involvement with HT. In actuality, my subjectivity was intimately embroiled in my observations, as it guided my choice of topic and it influenced the selection of my approach. Consequently, I was concerned that my subjectivity may skew my reading of the social reality of HT activists. For this reason, I took steps to prevent this from happening. Firstly, I only selected HT activists whom I did not know, so when they revealed their life histories to me it was unknown. In theory, HT activists have an autonomous psychology, possessing a wide range of personality traits that are different and unique. For that reason, I did not enter my fieldwork with a preconceived profile of HT activists. Instead, I wanted to rely heavily on the data I collected. This meant utilising appropriate methodological techniques, namely interviews and surveys, to solicit complete and meaningful data that could be used to construct a picture of HT radicalisation. Secondly, since the research focused on unravelling the back stories of activists, I disclosed from the outset my involvement with HT. Therefore, as complete objectivity was considered impractical, I made every effort to acknowledge and integrate my subjectivity within a contained methodological standpoint.

Although, my own experiences provided the backdrop for my study, it became clear that I needed to place HT activists at the centre of my research. Constructing knowledge around the life experiences of activists within a fringe group, like HT, made it incumbent to tailor my approach around the sensitivity of the respondents. This enabled me to objectively interpret my observations, while acknowledging my prior involvement in what I was studying. As mentioned, I decided to use my previously gained knowledge to enhance my research. In this respect, my experiences as a former HT member gave me a distinct standpoint, which is not available to other social scientists who have attempted to study HT. For this reason, I actively used the knowledge of my former membership to interpret the social world of HT activists. I integrated my knowledge of HT in a number of ways into my research. Firstly, I used it to cut through programmed and robotic rhetoric often spouted to 'outsiders'. Secondly, most of the respondents I interviewed shared similar social experiences and backgrounds to me, which allowed me to ask more penetrating and targeted questions. These two points are very important, as respondents can easily sabotage any attempt to research them (Evans-Pritchard, 1940, p. 13). This was unlikely to occur in my research as I was already inside the social world of HT. Therefore, my personal involvement in HT gave me an open gateway to explore the lives of HT activists, without it I would not have been able to scratch the surface of HT. My experiences placed me in an advantageous position from which to build knowledge and construct a more accurate image of HT's social world.

Studying HT: Scholars and Literature

It is clear from my standpoint that I think a substantial amount of scholarship on HT in Britain has not contributed to a penetrative study. Instead the publications and research I have surveyed continue to explore HT from its 'exterior' rather than its 'interior'. I define 'exterior' research as an attempt to explore the internal world of HT radicalism, but without a penetrative method of accessing primary data sources. A number of articles have been furnished using 'exterior' research, especially in the aftermath of the 2005 London bombings, which attempt to explain the appeal of HT to young British Muslims. However, these studies often lack access to HT members, forcing them to resort to either interviewing ex-members or using secondary literature. In order to shed light on the appeal of HT, scholars must engage with 'live' and 'active' HT narratives. The use of narrative research has revealed the 'dialogic' nature of HT identities in which historical and psycho-social constructions of HT identity are investigated through the voices of HT activists, in respect to their experiences as young middle class Muslims. In other words, one cannot hope to explore the appeal of HT without the use of 'interior' data sources.

As stated earlier, although in the last decade scholars have assembled a colossal body of knowledge on radicalisation, much of this has seldom investigated HT. A chief explanation for this oversight has been the impenetrability of HT, because of its clandestine and secretive nature. Nonetheless, there have been several noteworthy contributions, making it imperative to review these studies and place them within my research context. Firstly, Taji-Farouki's influential piece written in 1996, 'A Fundamental Quest', is the closest attempt by a western academic to unlock the mysterious nature of HT. Her study sets out to document the chronological evolution of HT in the Middle East, providing insight into the formative period of the organisation and its founder. At this point, I feel it is important to bring to light some methodological observations, which I have drawn out of her study to inform my own work. Firstly, the piece employs a historical methodology by which Taji-Farouki used internal HT documents and leaflets to construct a historical picture of the inception of the movement. How she acquired and accessed these sources is somewhat sketchy. She does not explain her methodology in her book, which raises significant questions about how she gained access to internal HT material. Secondly, the piece is not concerned with the socio-cultural factors related to HT radicalisation; instead it is a factual exploration of the emergence of HT in the Middle East. For this reason, the study does not claim to investigate why some young British Muslims are joining HT in Great Britain, making it crucial to develop new insight into the evolution of HT radicalisation in this country.

In contrast to this scholarly work, the autobiographical narrative written by Mohammed Mahbub Husain (Ed Husain) has been championed as a noteworthy insight into HT in Britain, yet this ignores the many contextual deficiencies and inaccuracies in the piece. Before I elaborate on these issues, it is worth briefly noting that autobiographical information relates and contains data about the self (Brewer, 1986). With that said, the book written by Ed Husain is based on his alleged encounters with members of HT, in the early 1990s. These short encounters form the basis for his analysis. Yet, as he confirms, he was never a member of HT (Hussain, 2007). This is highly significant as his observations would have been greatly restricted by organisational and structural confidentiality. HT operates behind a set of rigid administrative codes, which are only accessible to members. In practical terms, this means he had no way of determining how HT operate and execute their plans. Secondly, the narrative is exclusively based on autobiographical declarations, which cannot be substantiated and offers little scientific value. This brings into question the quality and validity of his assertions, as no scientific approach was employed to acquire the data. It is vital when dealing with information that has been fashioned by a researcher's own experiences to use specific techniques to maintain analytical integrity and rigour (Berryman, 1999). However, the *Islamist* is not an academic examination of HT and radicalisation, rather it is simply a piece of work based on Husain's own assumptions and experiences. In that regard, the usefulness of the piece is greatly reduced.

Beyond the work of Taji-Farouki, scholars have displayed a passing interest in HT. A major body of the literature contributing to the discourse on HT in Britain relates to unlocking the nature and causes of HT radicalisation. Before I reflect upon some of these contributions, it is clear that the individual is greatly influenced by his or her social reality and experiences. Hence, my personal experiences and the data collected from the respondents has shown personal experiences play a defining role in the radicalisation process. For this reason, my review of the literature begins with the generic concern that scholarship on HT of previous years has not contributed to unlocking the inner world of HT. This is because scholars have not gotten inside HT, and thus my overview of the literature will ultimately expose this methodological oversight as the primary reason for a lack of knowledge regarding HT.

I want to start with the piece written by Parveen Akhtar, '(Re)turn to religion' (Abbas et al., 2005, pp. 164-76). The author theorises that HT radicalisation is grounded within a complex spectrum of religious awakening, in which religion provides an ideological identity. Though fascinating, Akhtar cannot substantiate theory with empirical fact. In reality, the author makes no attempt to consult primary sources and extract data that may support their assertions, which detracts from the content and value of the piece. In particular, the author seeks to 'examine the reasons why Hizb ut-Tahrir appeals to young Muslims' without articulating or giving voice to lived experience (Abbas et al., 2005, p. 173). The author claims 'studying the group in isolation cannot account for why its qualities suddenly appeal to a generation of British Muslims' (Abbas et al., 2005, p. 174). This statement perpetuates a number of misconceptions. Firstly, HT has not procured mass appeal amongst young British Muslims. In fact, they have only gained support amongst a homogenous group of young middle class Asian Muslims. Unfortunately, despite claiming to 'contextualise Hizb ut-Tahrir', the author appears unaware of HT's middle class appeal. This makes it essential to study the narratives of HT activists, which the author fails to do, in order to gain insight into the appeal of HT.

The analysis offered by Lewis (2007, p. 119), in his book *Young, British and Muslim*, provides some interesting insight, especially as the author acknowledges HT as 'a useful window into the recruitment techniques, appeal and ideology of radical Islam'. However, the author overly relies on the testimonies of ex-members. In particular, he places significant credence in the narrative offered by Shiraz Maher, an ex-HT activist who joined after 2001. The account given by Shiraz aligns HT radicalism to the '*Biradri* system' (cited in Lewis 2007, p. 122). This standpoint ignores the social reality and sociological base of HT membership. As my data will show, those young people attracted to HT often emerge from secular middle class households, and thus are not socially embedded within the traditional paradox of the '*Biradri* system'. It can be analytically risky to depend solely on narratives from ex-activists when trying to ascertain the appeal of HT. This is because the attitudes of active members will strongly differ from ex-members, skewing ones research if they rely on a pre-selected population (for example, ex-activists). Another problem with using ex-members is the phenomenon of 'faking' (Beere 1979, p. 385). When I conducted interviews with ex-HT activists, I quickly realised through my ability to corroborate their narratives with my own experiences that most tended to consciously distort and give socially pleasing responses.

Similarly, a piece written by Sadek Hamid attempted to assess whether HT had influenced the development of radical Islam in Britain. In particular, the author sought to answer 'why British Muslim youth join HT' (Hamid in Abbas et al., 2007, p. 149). The author makes some crude conclusions, for example, he believes 'young people were attracted to HT entirely due to their slick appearance, and their ability to be well-spoken and seemingly possess religious knowledge at the same time' (Hamid in Abbas et al., 2007, p. 150). Despite providing no empirical evidence for this claim, it is worth deconstructing this socially constructed misrepresentation of HT. Firstly, within the closed circuit of peer group relations, which is often the setting for HT radicalisation, young people are attracted to the familiar. As I will discuss in my fieldwork chapters, young HT activists were drawn to HT recruiters by sharing the same social upbringing and critical life-experiences. Secondly, this account ignores the psychological and sociological triggers of radicalisation, reducing the phenomenon to the radical group. Thirdly, the author articulates HT radicalisation within a traditional-modern paradox, believing HT offer young people a modern re-tailored conception of religion. This ignores the non-religious triggers of HT radicalisation, as my data will show religion is not necessarily a precursor for joining HT. Overall this article lacks empirical substance, unfortunately Hamid does not have any physical access to HT and thus attempts to craft a picture of HT from some anonymous ex-members. These singular accounts offer little substance in relation to why these men became radicalised (for example, what is their social background and experience). The literature is overwhelmingly dominated by articles looking to explain the phenomenon of HT radicalisation from a distance. Subsequently, they do not offer any empirical data to corroborate theory as scholars struggle to penetrate HT, which greatly weakens their usefulness.

Exploring Trajectories

As I have already mentioned I joined HT in early 1996 when I was at college. The observations I made during my membership provided me with a unique source of background information. When I left HT in early 2002, many issues from my experiences continued to affect my thoughts. In particular, I could not understand why HT seemed to attract only a homogenous group of young middle class South Asians. From a personal perspective, I attributed leaving HT to several factors, but perhaps the most significant issue was to do with why I joined in the first place. I was recruited into HT at 16. At that age I had not developed a stable identity nor had I experienced life, and this made me very impressionable. Therefore, I felt it important to address this matter in my study, which required gathering new data through lengthy fieldwork, participant observation and in-depth interviews. Although I had spent several years with HT, fieldwork experience as an outsider would enable me to contrast my experiences with qualitative research. This was very important because I wanted to avoid disrupting my findings by looking at things from a purely personal perspective. However, I did not want to completely ignore my previous experiences, so I used that familiarity to make data collection easier. As a former member, I was fully aware of the backgrounds of HT members before I started my fieldwork.

My research began in a participatory manner, because I wanted to monitor members' activities, thinking that this would provide insight into the social world of the radical. However, in documenting the types of group interaction it soon became apparent that there were other, much more important issues to be examined in relation to the causes of radicalisation. It became clear that I needed to conduct interviews, in part to examine some of the ideas that were emerging from the ethnography. It was self-evident that HT is not only made up of many separate individuals, but that some of those individuals are alike to one another, and so can be differentiated from other members. Thus, trying to paint a portrait of a typical HT member in as accurate and vivid a manner as possible is extremely difficult. In the end, then, detailed interviews were undertaken, in some instances, more as conversations in a series of natural settings. Rather surprisingly, on many occasions the ethnographic work and interviews became joined at the hip, particularly when members of group conversations began, without any triggering, to reflect on their own and each other's life histories. Thus, the interviews conducted with the male respondents revealed a rich source of narrative concerning the routes taken into HT. These qualitative accounts concentrate on life narratives: to be exact, their social background and upbringing, with attention given to the context of radicalisation (for example, how and where they encountered HT).

This research had one key goal, to determine why some young Muslims join HT. In a broader sense, I discovered a reciprocal relationship exists between the radical and the social world, which provides a pretext for radicalisation. As stated, my reference points were several powerful and insightful biographical accounts of HT members. I chose these case histories, while interacting with HT members in their natural settings, because they exemplify some important theoretical points and provided a rich source of narrative concerning the pathway into radicalism. After interviewing 28 male respondents, my findings have uncovered some common themes. A recurring theme, which emerged in the accounts from my respondents, is that of identity; and how their current identities seemed greatly dependent on their past and present experiences. The goal of my research was to map out the 'turning-point moments' in the lives of HT members who have undergone a life-altering experience. Consequently, each of the radicals I interviewed exhibits a distinct social world of lived experience. Therefore, the accounts I have selected may seem somewhat dramatic, but they offer me a glimpse into the construction of a radical in different social settings and from rather different perspectives.[4]

Accessing Female Members

When I began this study I chose to look at male and female HT members together. After consulting the literature on Muslim women (Hussain, 1984), however, I realised that a combined approach would reduce the importance of gender. Conducting a short review of the literature on Muslim women, I quickly identified some distorted views about their role. Wade and Souter (1992), for example, asserted that Muslim women are unable to lead a normal, functional life because of religious and cultural constraints. This implies that Muslim women cannot pursue educational and career interests, as they are bound to a patriarchal culture. Although I do not fully accept this position, it is very important to look at the issue through the experiences of the female HT members. My research has pointed to several important themes, such as family upbringing, ethnicity, class and gender. As a result, I have looked closely at these and other topics.

---

4   In addition to a series of standardised interviews with ordinary HT members, I conducted in-depth interviews with the former leadership of HT. These documented conversations were designed to explore issues related to the emergence of HT in Britain, identifying the key pioneers.

In order to access and collect data from female members, I needed to find a way to bypass strict HT segregation rules between the sexes.[5] For this reason, I decided to set up a *focus group*, because this would allow me to study female members in a more natural and comfortable setting than that offered by individual interviews. I assembled a group of female members to discuss and comment from personal experience on the issue of why they joined HT. This allowed me to gain a wider understanding of the women's shared experiences of everyday life and the influences within other social settings. The focus group provided a rich source of data, which allowed me to find out why certain issues were salient. I did encounter some problems with this research method, however, when talking about indoctrination. The responses of each participant were not independent and a few of the more dominant female members skewed the discussion about indoctrination. Although this discussion became less reliable, the women did express their own definitive individual views openly and confidently.

Control Group

In order to understand why some young British Muslims join HT, while most others do not required establishing a 'control group'. This entailed convening two group discussions. The first grouping comprised exclusively of non-affiliated young British Muslims from similar social backgrounds as HT activists, who seemed just as zealous about religion and politics yet engage in non-radical activism. This control group was very important to my research, as I wanted to avoid the common mistake of solely focusing on those who have become radicalised. This is quite crucial. If I only concentrated on HT activists, then I would not be in a suitable position to work out what made them so dissimilar from those who did not join HT. In particular, I managed to track down young Muslim activists (not affiliated to any organisation or group), but who had been approached by HT recruiters. It was interesting finding out why HT radicalisation proved to be unsuccessful on these young people, despite sharing similar social backgrounds and realities. The second control group involved ex-HT members; I wanted to discover what had led them to leave the organisation, because the roots of their change and departure are equally as important as those who do not join HT.

Sociological Study of HT

After I conducted interviews with male and female members, it became incumbent upon me to verify this information. I sought to determine whether the views and experiences expressed by my respondents were representative of the

---

5   Strict HT policies regulate the mixing between the sexes, which is forbidden in relation to group activity.

wider HT population. Therefore, I quickly recognised the inescapable necessity for administering a series of surveys. More importantly, the surveys became a key mechanism for unlocking the social base of HT membership. I needed to understand the nature of social embeddedness of HT members. In other words, HT members are fixed and rooted within multifaceted social realities that define and confine their social identities. Thus, from a social perspective, my study has demonstrated that most HT member's identities are fashioned from their social experiences and backgrounds – the place of their families in the class structure in which they grew up, university and peer groups, the significance of ethnicity and race, and the cultural gap between the first and second generations that defines what is expected of children outside of the home. This sociological analysis provides an alternative way of looking at the developments that have taken place amongst the membership of HT in Britain. Traditionally, sociologists are interested in identifying the relationships between social structures and processes, as they place greater emphasis on individuals moving from one social setting to another (Erikson, 1950). Therefore, in my sociological chapter, I sought to expound and distil upon the key sociological features of HT membership – such as class, age, gender, ethnicity and race, and religion etc. By focusing on these interrelated components, I was able to formulate a quantitative image of HT's membership, which included: demographic composition, socio-economic status and origin, recruitment areas, attitudes towards family and religion.

Statistics for the total number of members in Britain cannot be independently verified, as the group operates in a clandestine manner. Aminur, a member from South London, suggested that the British branch consists of 'approximately two thousand members'. While Abdul asserted that the group has an ever-expanding membership, which currently stands at 'five to six thousand'. During fieldwork, I noticed that this discrepancy in numbers was widespread. Many members tended to embellish the size and successes of HT, while others underrepresented the party's growth in order to remain off the radar, so to speak. This uncertainty made it very difficult to carry out a sample survey, because it was necessary to define the target population from which a sample was to be drawn. In theory, there are several methods that could be used to determine sample size: (1) national lists for small populations; (2) replicating a sample size of comparable studies; and (3) using published data (Lyman and Longnecker 2008, p. 277). Firstly, it was not feasible to make the entire population my sample, as I cannot locate all HT members. Secondly, no empirical data currently exists on HT membership, making it impossible to draw upon other studies. Thus, I needed to determine another way for calculating the sample size.

In trying to consider the dynamics of my target population, I was aware HT is relatively homogenous. However, I still wanted to analyse my data in multiple ways, for example, differentiating between genders, age groups, and so on. After consulting various HT documents, I found the administrative file of HT. This is a secret document that outlines the way in which the group must be structured and organised. I promptly realised that the file could be used to calculate an appropriate sample size, which would reflect the population being studied. In order to describe this process, I need to first explain some basic issues related to the *At-Takattul Al-Hizbi* (party structure). Firstly, the *Wilayah Committee* (executive) is a group of elected members entrusted with safeguarding the values, the ideological principles and the strategic direction of HT (Anon, 1965). Secondly, the day-to-day activities of the organisation are delegated to the Local Committees. It is important to bear in mind that for a particular area to be constituted as a Wilayah, there must be no less than fifteen members, enabling the construction of a Wilayah. Forming the Wilayah Committee (WC) requires the number of its members to be five until the number of members exceeds two 250. Then the number of Wilayah Committee members will be distributed in relation to the scale of members in the area. This is determined by the presence of an extra 50 members, which will equate to one member in the WC. If the number of members exceeds 500, then for every extra 500 members there will be one member installed on the WC.

On 13 March 2004, HT announced the results of the UK Wilayah Committee elections. More importantly, since nine male members were elected to the WC, I was able to estimate the target population, which equates to 900 members.[6] In theory, this calculation could be extended to encompass novices, but this would increase the chance of error and inference. Indeed, a larger sample that includes novices will only make things worse, because it will distort the credibility of the sample. In order to apply a consistent sampling technique, it was necessary to establish a large sample. If the population of members is 900, then a good sample is 200 because it equates to 22.2 per cent of the population. The survey encompassed two main sections: the first part was interested in demographic questions and upbringing. The second section of the survey was designed to obtain data on location of recruitment, social experiences, religiosity and peer groups. Thus, in all cases, I surveyed 95 male and 91 female members.

---

6   Nine female members were also elected to the women's WC

Chapter 2

The Origin of Hizb ut-Tahrir

Historically, HT was one of the most vocal radical Islamic movements in Britain, becoming a galvanising force among some young Muslims. HT emerged as the pioneering radical Muslim youth movement during the early 1990s; it was dubbed 'Europe's fastest growing Muslim group' (*The Observer*, 13 August 1995). It infiltrated university campuses in a concerted effort to create an Islamic awakening among the placid student population. As a result, it quickly gained media-wide notoriety for its combative public activity and evangelical style of recruitment. The national press branded it a 'fanatical group of Muslim extremists' (*Daily Mirror*, 4 March 1994). The rise to national prominence, in part, was achieved due to their sheer determination to take full control of university campuses and to build a strong recruitment base among second generation South-Asian British Muslims. However, it is difficult to rationalise this success, especially since the movement was inspired by historical events which occurred after World War II in the Middle East. In my search for explanation, it became clear that I had to begin my investigation by looking at the historical triggers that inspired the inception of the movement in 1952.

Origins of HT: Taqi al-Din al-Nabhani

According to Taji-Farouki (1996, p. 114), the inception of the movement 'lies in the response...to the break-up of the Ottoman Empire, the fragmentation of its territories into nation-states, the creation of Israel and the impotence of Muslim societies in the face of neo-imperialism'. These historical events induced Taqi al-Din al-Nabhani to respond by establishing a new political party, HT. Nabhani was a relatively unknown scholar with little political experience, except for the time he spent under the tutelage of the famous Sheikh Izz ad-Din al-Qassam. After completing his studies at Al-Azhar University in 1932, he returned to Palestine, even more disgusted with the continued supremacy of western imperialism. However, it took the establishment of Israel to entice Nabhani to greater activism. His early writings and political views were greatly influenced by *al-qawmiyya al-`arabiyya* (Arab nationalism). In 1950 he published his first book entitled '*Inqadh Filastin*' (Saving Palestine) followed by '*Risalat al-Arab*' (The Message of the Arabs). Initially, he sought to establish a legitimate political party, making a formal request to the Jordanian authorities on 17th November 1952, in accordance with the new constitutional guidelines (Taji-Farouki, 1996). Nabhani (2001, p. 1) described the new group as 'a political party with Islam as its ideology and the goal of resuming an Islamic way of life by establishing an Islamic State, which will implement Islam and propagate it worldwide'. However, his request was denied, because his political party operated on a platform that was considered incompatible with the newly conceived Jordanian constitution. Nevertheless, the movement continued to operate, expressing a collection of revolutionary ideals aimed at re-establishing the *Dawlah Islamiya* (Islamic State). As a result, the Jordanian authorities sanctioned a strict decree proscribing HT and declaring its activities unlawful. However, this did not stop the movement from gaining considerable support, as it established new cells throughout the Muslim world.

Deconstructing HT: Ideology, Aim and Strategy[1]

The *Mabda'a* (ideology) of HT was conceived by Nabhani within a specific historical and political frame. Nabhani was disgusted with the continued supremacy of western imperialism, which he sought to vanquish by reviving the Muslim populace. 'The Western culture was the dagger drawn by the West in the face of the Islamic State and by which it fatally stabbed her' (Nabhani 1953a, p. 4). This heightened fury towards western culture plays a significant role in the construction of HT ideology. Nabhani's cardinal ideological beliefs seem to be greatly inspired by two fairly narrow responses. The first, as Davis (1984, p. 134) has identified within Islamic radicalist thought, is to a perceived 'culture conflict' with the west. The ideology of HT is deeply laced within the dogmatic narrative of confrontation. The 'west' is identified as a significant source of conflict. Nabhani perceived secularism, for example, as purely a western construct that was alien to Islam. The disintegration of the *Dawlah Islamiya* (Islamic State) was exacerbated by the influx of western secular ideas which challenged the role of Islam in state practice. The second conforms to Dekmejian's (1988, p. 4) observation that most Islamist groups express their revivalist programme in response to 'internal decay'. These two rather predictable facets of Nabhani's rhetoric and discourse are greatly perpetuated across the spectrum of Islamist movements.

Ideology of Confrontation

The development of HT ideology can be traced back to the colonial and post-colonial period. It was articulated in response to the perceived cultural and

---

[1]   According to HT's manifesto, HT is a 'political party whose ideology is Islam, so politics is its work and Islam is its ideology. It works within the *Ummah* [Muslim Nation] and together with her, so that she adopts Islam as her cause and is led to restore the Khilafah and the ruling by what Allah revealed' (Anon. 2000, p. 1).

political dominance of the West, and thus was contrived within a specific framework of confrontation. Firstly, Nabhani framed the conflict with the West into a religious dichotomy, as the inevitable clash between '*Iman*' (belief) and '*kufr*' (disbelief) (Nabhani, 1953c, p. 23). This, as Kurtz and Turpin (1999, p. 641) explained, gives the confrontation a 'larger-than-life' dimension. Secondly, as the interaction with the West matured, Nabhani sought to fabricate a distorted narrative of confrontation with the West, depicting it as monolithic and dangerous. In particular, Nabhani was particularly concerned with the Western cultural and intellectual invasion of Muslim society. As he warned:

> The Muslims failed to realize the contradiction between the Islamic and European concepts. Another cause was their failure to distinguish between science, industry and inventions which Islam encourages Muslims to acquire, regardless of the source, and culture and ideology which can only be adopted from Islam (Nabhani, 1953, p. 173)

Nabhani was deeply critical of the Arab response to the internal decay, especially those who espoused the intellectual superiority of western culture and ideology. This is because Nabhani manufactured a dogmatic cultural polarisation between Islam and the west. He viewed Islam as a complete system of human governance that deciphers all facets of human identity, and thus the world is thereby composed into a single frame of competing cultures, between '*Haq*' (Truth, Islam) and '*Batil*' (evil, non-Islam) (Nabhani, 1953c, p. 18). Therefore, anything that emanates from the ideology of western society is *Batil* and thus must be excluded from Muslim society and identity. The demonising of Western culture allowed HT to establish a framework of action in which Muslim people could reinforce a perception of shared Muslim identity.

Thirdly, Nabhani identified the transformative effects brought about by those Muslim intellectuals and reformers who have been 'seduced by Western culture' (Nabhani, 1953, p. 1). These intellectuals are viewed as a corrosive force within Muslim society. Therefore, HT ideology was counter-poised not just to the West, but also to some Muslims within the Arab world, and thus HT had created a 'multi-faceted other' (Ismail 2006, p. 37). Mohammed Abdu's views were wholly condemned by Nabhani, for instance, as they promoted western ideology through the backdoor.[2] Abdu strongly believed secular ideology was being introduced far too rapidly into a religiously orientated society, and thus advocated a more gradual reformation of Islamic faith in the public sphere (Hourani, 1998).

---

[2]   Mohammad Abdu was an early 20th century Egyptian reformer, who sought to bridge the intellectual gap that had been created between the West and the East, through reason and rationality (Hourani, 1998).

Reconstructing History: Muslim Decay

The theme of internal decay constitutes an important fragment in HT ideology, which merits further exploration. As mentioned, Nabhani's intellectual outlook was to a great extent provoked by colonisation. This encounter awakened his consciousness regarding the plight of the Arab world, which he felt had sunk into the 'abyss of decline' (Al-Nabhani 2002d, p. 1). As Dekmejian (1995) noted this type of reaction is often embedded within the religious revivalist paradigm. In other words, HT ideology is rooted in generic cycles of revivalism that were a response to perceived crisis and internal decay. To begin with, Nabhani sought to understand why the Arab world had lost its high standing, seeing that 'for many centuries the world of Islam was in the forefront of human civilisation and achievement' (Lewis 2002, p. 3). In pursuing an answer to this question, Nabhani acknowledged that the internal decay had commenced well before the first colonialists had stepped foot on Arab soil. Thus, Nabhani made the history of Islam and Muslims his initial point of departure. The socio-political contexts in which Nabhani engineered his ideology were to some degree preceded by his assumptions that the continuity of the Islamic historical narrative had become disrupted. For him determining the exact formula for the processes that resulted in the internal decay were considered integral to producing a coherent and workable model of revival for the contemporary Arab world. The evolution of Nabhani's radical thought in large part corresponds to Esposito's (1983) theory of Islamist revivalist movements. Esposito in Islam and Politics (1983, p. 30) outlined the need for the Islamic radical to construct the 'totality of Islam'. This entailed extending Islam's continuity and history, from the idealised period of the Prophet Mohammad to the present, in a way that merged the political and spiritual. As Esposito (1983, p. 32) explains, the reactionary development of 'pre-modern revivalism' to the socio-political decay is a key component in ideological construction. For Nabhani, the process of comprehending 'what went wrong', lead him to articulate the precise causes for the intellectual decay in relation to the idealised.

The Muslim world did not reach such a cataclysmic state of unconsciousness, it was asserted, through a single lapse rather it was due to many historical factors accumulating over a lengthy period of time, which according to Nabhani was caused by the correct understanding of Islam being eroded (Nabhani, 2002d). This 'moralising discourse' grew from Nabhani's discontent towards a general state of decay amongst Muslim society, which he felt had become far removed from the idealised condition as laid down by Mohammad. Voll (1982) provides a seminal deconstruction of how Islamic radicals, like Nabhani, perceive continuity in Islamic history, which greatly informs their ideology and strategy. Voll (1982, p. 4) makes two highly significant observations: firstly spiritual incentive guides the revivalism and second the past plays a notable part in directing contemporary behaviour and action. Nabhani's revivalism sought to recapture the strength of Islam by providing a simple framework for understanding the earlier historical periods.

For Nabhani, the Muslim decay came about due to the 'mighty weakness that overtook the minds in understanding Islam' (Nabhani 2002b, p 1). This lack of understanding arose as a direct result of detaching the spirit of the Arabic language from the authority of Islam. The Arabic language is bestowed with indispensable attributes when attached to the Quran, which according to HT is the language of Islam (Nabhani, 1953b, p. 1). When the Islamic State spread across vast quadrants it failed to establish the vitality of the Arabic language. Consequently, the Arabic language began to be ignored and became absent from the State's apparatus, especially during the Ottoman rule. Progression was suspended, as the extraction of divine rulings through the process of *Ijtihad* (extracting new rulings) became neglected (Nabhani, 1953, pp. 167-8). 'The understanding of Islam from its sources does not come about but in Arabic and the extracting of the divine rules cannot be accomplished except in Arabic' (Nabhani, 1953a, pp. 186-7). This very simplistic reading of Muslim decay, greatly underplays the complexity of Islamic historiography. Some historians believe that a reliable and authentic rebuilding of Islamic religious tradition cannot be exclusively extrapolated from Muslim source material alone (Crone, 1987, p. 204). Crone (2003, p. 7), for instance, asserts that religious tradition from Muslim sources is a 'monument to the destruction rather than the preservation of the past'. Nabhani's skewed appraisal of Muslim history reflects his overreaching tendency to manufacture a narrative that fits his socio-political agenda. This reconstruction of narrative about Muslim decay is embedded within his personalised reading, and thus little consensus exists concerning this 'historicisation'.

Merging Religion and Politics

Within the academic literature concerning the evolution of Islamic radicalism, significant weight has been attributed to the socio-political causes of this rather disturbing trend. Nabhani was not immune to the wider debates taking place across the Arab World. HT ideology was certainly contrived within a particular framework of understanding and in relation to competing intellectual responses to the socio-political decay: such as, (a) Arab reformers and modernists; (b) Arab nationalism; and (c) other radical Islamist movements (for example, Muslim Brotherhood). These intellectual movements, including HT, were essentially the native response to two distinct social phenomena – colonisation and independence.

Arab reformist and modernist movements emerged rapidly during the early colonial period, but this intellectual tradition faded, to some degree, and generally had mixed influences on the post-independence period. These movements initially sought to attest Islam's compatibility with western civilisation in response to colonial assertions of its backwardness (Armstrong 2001, p. 162; Ismail 2006, p. 44). A shift towards modernisation projects eventually proceeded, which sought to resurrect the Arabian Peninsula by following 'western achievements' (Dabashi, 1993, p. 326). Secular ideals and institutions were seen as the intellectual backbone of Western modernity, and despite its introduction into an excessively religious setting, began to take root. Even though a number of these developments took place before Nabhani, it is clear that these events shaped his understanding of Arab history during the 1950s. In particular, he was trying to formulate a new manifesto that could transcend the national and regional context of the Middle East. In order to achieve this grand vision, he grounded his political readings of the period within a dogmatic Islamic framework. Nabhani perceived Islam as a divine doctrine which gives individuals systematic answers to a whole range of human quandary. So, it is no surprise that Nabhani believed 'political thought' is the 'highest types of thought' (Nabhani, 1956, p. 1). But for this conception to be realised within a newly formulated manifesto, Nabhani needed to merge Islam with politics. In this regard he said: 'the Islamic Aqeedah (doctrine) is a political idea ... distinguished from other Aqeedahs and ideologies in that it is spiritual and political' (Nabhani, 1956, p. 1). This rendering of Islamic belief, as an all-encompassing system, naturally signified opposition to secularism. Secularism, in the sense of separating the spiritual and political realms, became an alien concept to HT. Consequently, as Nabhani (2002a, p. 6) noted, Mohammad established the first *Dawlah Islamiya* (Islamic state), a state in which divine rules were amalgamated within a political dimension and reality, resembling theocratic states in Christendom.

This demonising of Arab nationalism was greatly reactionary to the historical and modern developments taking place around Nabhani. Yet, his rejection of Arab nationalism can be traced to his rather simplistic reading of the decline of the Arab people and nation. As mentioned, Nabhani's early writings were monopolised by two distinct questions: why the Arab world declined and how can it be revived? The process of deconstructing Arab decline necessitated understanding what made the Arabs great in the first place? In simple terms, he concluded that Islam was the primary catalyst for the Arab ascent. Pre-Islamic Arabia was a backward wasteland in which lawless tribes fought in protracted feuds (Crone, 2003). Therefore, the advent of Islam liberated the Arab, as it unified tribes under a single banner and provided an ideological platform to seek progression. This logic eventually saw Nabhani discard Arab nationalism in all its guises. He concluded that the Islamic thought had to have complete clarity, for it to be pure, and thus nationalistic revivalist theories were totally incompatible with Islam. Arab nationalism, as a movement, sought to establish an Arab revival upon an ambiguous basis that was non-Islamic, which became transparent with the rise of the Ba'th party, in Damascus during the 1940s, as they promoted religious secularism and nationality as an integral whole (Nabhani, 1953c, p. 1).

Socio-political factors provide important contextual insight into the evolution of radical Islam. For Nabhani, witnessing the social disintegration of his homeland and the establishment of Israel certainly had a transformative effect on him in terms of his ideology. These events transformed the geo-political map of the Middle East, and so it is not surprising that HT ideology evolved from this socio-historical frame. Firstly, HT ideology was configured against the backdrop of regional socio-political shifts and various dislocations. Socio-political dislocations were linked to all facets of state functionality which were purported as clear and definitive signs of the failure of man-made ideology. Essentially, HT ideology was crafted in response to these perceived problems. This socio-political reading of the inception of radical Islam is somewhat skewed towards the outcomes of the milieu caused by modernisation: such as urbanisation and industrialisation, disaffection of people towards the failures of incumbent Muslim rulers. In particular, Ayubi (1991, p. 179) believes the evolution of radical Islam can be explained through the 'paradigm of frustrated expectations' in relation to the failure of modernisation. For HT, the failure of Muslim nation-states to resolve the frustrations of its citizenry provided fertile soil to plant their radical ideology. As Anderson (1997, p. 23) explained, radical Islam manifested itself as a result of the milieu created by Muslim governments. In sum, the socio-political context surrounding Nabhani played an instrumental role in the development of his ideology and activism.

The 'Utopian' Ideology: *Dawlah Islamiya* (Islamic State)

For HT, the *Mabda'a* (ideology) is considered the 'soul of its existence' (Nabhani, 1953d, p. 1). Consequently, HT has adopted Islam as its ideology. From this ideology emanates a host of systems that deal with all of man's perceived problems (Nabhani, 1953c, p. 18). As Mannheim (1936) pointed out, ideology is a means through which individuals make sense and interpret their social world. According to Nabhani (1953c, p. 13), an ideology 'is a rational doctrine from which a system emanates'. In its practical formation, the ideology is fashioned from an intellectual ideal that generates a host of conceptions, which in theory supply detailed solutions to temporal and metaphysical problems. The doctrine has been defined as an all-encompassing theory that is established upon 'a comprehensive idea about the universe, man and life' (Nabhani, 1953c, p. 13). Theoretically, this conclusive idea leads to a comprehensive set of solutions resulting in progressive ascent for humankind. As Bloch (1986) suggested, ideologies contain within them the notion of supremacy and utopianism. Consequently, ideology imposes itself into all facets of human existence, making it excessively overbearing and dangerous.

The term ideology appears frequently in the philosophical principles of Nabhani; however the term has evolved a distinct ethos that defines HT theology. Theology, in the sense of supplying the basic tenets of Islamic faith and practice, became integrated with politics which gave rise to HT ideology. This rendering of HT ideology possesses significant problems. In particular, the ideology is only a theoretical model, which is a revised interpretation of the Islamic tradition that has encapsulated modern dimensions. Many theorists have displayed strong scepticism towards theories that proclaim to be all encompassing, as unrealistic and unworldly (Heywood, 2003). HT ideology exists simply in theory, which a group of individuals seek to establish, and thus according to these individuals it is a workable theory that has a real dimension to it. Nahbani stipulated the essential importance of a method that implements the ideology, as he states without it 'the idea (ideology) would turn to be a hypothetical and fanciful philosophy in pages of books without any effect in the life' (Nabhani, 1953c, p. 13).

This ideology cannot be enacted or brought into practice since the *Dawlah Islamiya* (Islamic state) was destroyed in 1924, and therefore HT ideology is only a conceptual model embedded within the minds of its members. Despite the *Dawlah Isamiya* being a highly vague and idealised concept, it has become entrenched within HT ideology and rhetoric. HT was established with one overriding aim to re-establish the *Dawlah Isamiya*, which is considered the practical instrument of implementing HT ideology. The state envisaged by Nabhani was greatly inspired by two contradictory state systems: (1) Mohammad's Islamic State in Medina (632 CE); and (2) the modern nation-state system. Essentially, he extracted the key mechanisms of the nation-state and gave it an Islamic twist. However, this to some degree is an over simplification, as Nabhani's ideology advocates the institutionalisation of Islamic laws and values through the state. HT sought to revive the Islamic world based upon a new ideology that could recapture the idealised message of Mohammad. In fact, Nabhani perceived Mohammad as a divinely appointed statesmen and prophet, with no formal distinction between religious and political practice. In sum, the utopian nature of HT ideology makes it radically counter-opposed to the west, as HT only accept one conception of Islam and thus this boundless version of Islam transcends theology to impact all aspects of socio-political life.

Labelling HT Ideology

What kind of label best defines HT ideology: political or violent? On the surface, politics appears to be the central defining feature of HT ideology. This might be a somewhat contentious description, since HT ideology is also shaped by religious proclamations (for example, Shariah law) and to a much lesser extent violent militancy. It is therefore problematic to reduce the complex ideology of HT to a single thread, such as politics or violence. Clearly, HT cannot exist without theology, but politics brings HT ideology to the physical world. The convoluted nature of HT ideology makes it difficult to classify its ideology into a single bloc, and thus requires me to list the lines of distinction between violent and political ideology. Firstly, HT does not promote violence as a means to secure power and re-establish the *Dawlah Islamiya*. This is an important demarcation between HT and other violent radical ideologies (for example, Hizballah or Al-Qaida). Groups espousing violence as a means for creating ideological change are wholly condemned by HT. As asserted by Imran Waheed, in the wake of the 7/7 London bombings: 'The entire Muslim community has made its position on the London bombings clear – these actions have no justification as far as Islam is concerned' (*worldpress.org*, 12 September 2005).

Secondly, violent radical ideology is often rationalised in accord with the paradigm of conflict: namely between *Dar al-Islam* and *Dar al-Kufr* (land of Islam and land of infidels). Violent ideology emanates from groups sanctioning armed struggle against regimes that implement non-Islam, because sovereignty belongs to God. HT is critical of such movements, especially those who endorse material struggle, as they failed to differentiate properly between 'Dar al-Islam and Dar al-Kufr'. Nabhani felt Muslim society resembled Mecca at the time of Mohammad, because the rules and systems were non-Islamic, making the Muslim world 'Dar al-Kufr'. Therefore, HT activism and ideology must be performed through 'political action and not by material means' (Anon. 1994, p. 9).

HT, above all, considers itself to be a political party (Anon. 1994, p. 3). This means its ideology is skewed towards radical politics. This inference of 'radical' is quite important, since HT are not 'passive radicals'. Firstly, HT, as the principle actor, identifies and portrays their ideology as 'radical'. In other words, they do not seek gradual reform nor do they participate within the political process, rather they advocate radical transformation. Secondly, HT believes their approach is in keeping with Mohammad, who as Lewis (1988, p. 2) suggests: (The Prophet) 'as rebel has provided a sort of paradigm of revolution – opposition and rejection, withdrawal and departure, exile and return'. This representation of Mohammed as a political radical, allows HT to express their ideology in the language of Islam, despite following a purely political project (for example, pursuit of political authority). What then of violence? This is a complex and problematic question, from which I would like to focus on one key issue. As mentioned, HT does not endorse violence or armed struggle against Muslim governments. However, upon the establishment of the *Dawlah Islamiya* HT advocate Jihad against all non-Islamic nations in order to institute Islamic law across the globe. Thus, HT accepts violence within their ideological framework, but in terms of activism they are non-violent. Subsequently, from this perspective, I would argue that HT augments varying forms of politics, theology and violence into its ideology at different stages of its activism.

Chapter 3

Exporting HT to Britain

In subsequent chapters, I explain how HT, with its middle class social base, is not orientated to attracting young working class Muslims to their radical cause. This greatly limits their mass appeal. HT members exclusively prioritise non-welfare politics, as their economic interests are secured and thus, on the surface, ideology plays a fundamental role in recruitment and activism. This begs the question, how and why the ideology of Nabhani had an influence on the behaviour and minds of a specific demographic of British Muslims (namely middle class South Asians)? Trying to work out how and why HT successfully recruited a large homogenous cluster of young Muslims will invariably be the focus of the following chapters. At this stage, I have two rather simple, but ambitious, aims: (a) Firstly, I want to understand the background of HT's historical development in the UK, and (b) I hope to use some of the large body of academic literature on radicalisation to dissect the actions, actors and activities of HT in Britain.

After looking over the extensive literature, it was clear radicalisation had come sharply into view as a subject of scholarly debate and enquiry, but I realised the development of HT had received little attention. Taji-Farouki's (1996, pp. 171-87) contribution still remains the most noteworthy research on HT, despite the fact she only devotes a handful of pages to the UK branch. She believes the appeal of the movement within a national context lies in its ability to offer disgruntled young Asian Muslims a 'simple message' (Taji-Farouki 1996, p. 177). This message advocates the supremacy of Islam in two distinct ways: firstly as an ideology that addresses all human problems and secondly through the reestablishment of the Caliphate which enacts the ideology. This rather simplistic assessment of HT attraction fails to engage with more critical questions, such as why increasing numbers of indigenous Asian Muslim youth became radicalised by HT. The reason for this lack of engagement can be attributed to when the research took place, namely in the early 1990s, and thus radicalisation is of little interest to her. Also, the context of the piece centres on a historical narrative of the movements inception in 1952 and its subsequent development in the Middle East. Consequently, only a cursory overview of HT activism in the UK is provided, but Taji-Farouki (1996, p. 186) does acknowledge the need to explore further 'the British experience' of HT, as it forms a 'fascinating chapter in HT's career'. Interest in HT activism has been somewhat reignited with the 2005 London Terror attacks. Several minor contributions have been made, but these pieces frequently lack empirical depth. In particular, two specific features are often missing: (1) insight into HT's evolution in Britain, and (2) empirical data concerning HT radicalisation (for example, sociological data on demographic support, biographical accounts of radicalisation and interviews with senior members etc.). For these reasons this book is an attempt to explore the contextual factors that contribute to HT radicalisation in Britain.

Trying to put together a historical narrative of HT was very challenging, because locating the relevant members would be extremely problematic since most of them had left the group. After several discussions with some senior members, I was able to identify a list of members – who were considered the pioneers, namely Farid Kassim and Omar Bakri Mohammed. Arranging interviews proved to be a long process, as in most cases, I had to use wider contacts and networks to establish contact with the members. Before conducting the interviews, I realised the best way to elicit information was through unstructured interviews and in-depth conversations. Thankfully, this technique proved very effective, seeing that I gained considerable insight into the activities and strategies as they were formulated and applied. However, surprisingly, the accounts did not match. In fact, both men provided me with two opposing chronologies. In some ways this disparity was understandable since the men recounted and drew upon divergent social and political realities. Thus, trying to locate the truth was not an easy task.

Farid Kassim: The Starting Point for UK Activism

The unexpected rise of HT during the early 1990s came as a shock to some Western academics (Taji-Farouki, 1996). In reality, their growth and development had been underway since the early 1980s, which had been orchestrated by a few home-grown affiliates. Farid Kassim became the first indigenous member of the UK branch, as he stated: 'There is nobody in Hizb ut-Tahrir (UK) that was around when I was, when it began' (Kassim, Interview 26 June 2004). Farid was born and educated in the United Kingdom, with part of his secondary school education at the acclaimed Furzedown grammar school in Battersea. Although Farid emerged from a middle class background, it was immediately noticeable that he did not want to indicate which social class he felt he belonged to growing up. His refusal to talk about class, and his subsequent attempts to devalue his middle class upbringing, indicated that his political sympathies did not lie with his own class. Indeed, his family had extended ties to the Labour Party; his maternal grandfather was a well-respected member of the Labour Party.[1] This legacy had a substantial influence on Farid, and by the age of 16 he became a member of the Labour Party. Reflecting on this period, Farid commented: 'I sincerely thought that I could make a difference within the Labour Party ... believing that society could be alleviated by greater distribution of wealth' (Ibid., 26 June 2004). In spite of this, his political outlook started to change, and he adopted a more Marxist ideology. This newfound ideology, in many ways, was not amenable with his middle class status. This

---

1   Donald Algure, Farid's maternal grandfather, was a well-respected member of the Labour party. He was a significant figure during the 1960s for transport and health within the Labour movement.

somewhat subtle contradiction was brought out in the interview, as it became clear that he exhibited symbolic signs of withdrawal from activities linked to his class culture. Despite his family's income and background, he continued to identify with the radical left.

By the end of 1980, Farid enrolled at Nottingham University, completely unaware of the life-altering experience that awaited him. As he commented: 'I was a student at Nottingham University, and I embraced Islam there, from a member of Hizb ut-Tahrir' (Ibid., 25 June 2004). This chance encounter had formally introduced him to a small group of transient members, belonging to the relatively unknown HT, who were studying at the same institution. These enigmatic characters were enrolled as foreign students, holding citizenship of a host of Middle Eastern countries, which enabled them to conduct activity in a clandestine manner. They were primarily responsible for Farid's eventual conversion to Islam, as he described in vivid detail:

> Before I embraced Islam I was an agnostic, I thought of myself as a Communist … He [member of HT] approached me in a very puristic way, in terms of the *Aqeedah* [doctrine] of Islam. He really opened my eyes, showing me how you should think, not in terms of thinking logically or scientifically, but thinking rationally. So, after a lot of discussion, I embraced Islam … it [Islam] gave my life meaning. (Ibid., 26 May 2004)

This period proved to be a significant turning point in his life. Farid had become greatly invigorated by his discovery of HT, as he explained, 'When I first started with Hizb ut-Tahrir I felt excited, it brings light to you, which you want to bring to the *Ummah* [Muslim community]' (Ibid., 26 May 2004). Clearly, a central part of this overall experience is about finding, or searching for, meaning. Farid struggled to gain a deep sense of purpose with his involvement in left wing politics, because he found it tough to be committed to the achievement of material goals. In contrast to this, HT provided him with a definite ideology, which was far less orientated to the attainment of material or economic advantage. This gave Farid a new way of looking at the world around him and an appreciation of how it can be changed. Thus, swapping his political and ideological allegiances was a relatively easy affair, since he had been strongly opposed to the major values of capitalist society.

The Educated Middle Class

A cursory look at HT membership will reveal it embodies a kind of radicalism that is typically middle class in nature. As Esposito (1998, p. 167) notes, this is not entirely surprising since radical actors are often economically privileged and well educated individuals who have become disenchanted by western society. Likewise, the study conducted by Glynn (2002) of Muslim groups in Tower Hamlets observed that non-radical organisations attracted a disproportionate number of educated middle-classes. While trying to chart the way HT developed, I was struck by the need to ask whether early members were drawn from the ranks of the educated middle classes. The answer to this question was somewhat complex, as it greatly hinged upon Farid's recollections. To start with, Farid acknowledged enlisting the help of a small band of students, allowing him to initiate a starting point for wider campus activity. As he states: 'we all came from very similar economic backgrounds' (Ibid., 26 May 2004). The attraction of middle-class youths to HT was greatly advanced by their identification with Muslim students who shared their own middle-class background and experiences.

From discussions with Farid, it was clear that he made deliberate and frequent reference to the context of Islamic activism on university campuses. In particular, native students felt deprived of a voice. So, the few individuals who had been co-opted by Farid became increasingly frustrated by the absence of scholarship, as transient members solely directed their activity towards Arab nationals. However, this difficultly would eventually be overturned by the persistence of Farid, who negotiated a source of culture from transient HT members. As he stated:

> We were frustrated, we wanted knowledge, and we knew that there were some guys from Hizb ut-Tahrir, they had a great command of politics and a great command of intellectual issues, they talked about issues in a radical way, but they were all Arabs ... so we pushed them hard. They convinced us of the method to establish the *Khilafah* [Islamic State] and the need to revive Muslims. So from that they could see our interest, and we were intellectuals. There were a few non-Arab speakers in Nottingham, and we were very enthusiastic to get the culture. So, they appointed one brother to go through *Dowla Islami* (Islamic State) ... this was the first time, certainly in Britain, any non-Arab had got culture from Hizb ut-Tahrir.

This account indicates that the core recruits considered themselves to be 'intellectuals'. Although the term is highly ambiguous, in this context, it was almost certainly used to describe a Marxist view. In a Marxist context, 'anti-establishment intellectuals' are often seen as those individuals continuously occupied by political and intellectual struggle against the state (Jennings and Kemp-Welch 1997, p. 69). In a broader sense, intellectuals should not be classified in relation to their profession, but rather by the values they uphold and propagate. More significantly, as Hoffer (1982) points out, an intellectual's involvement with radical politics is often a symptom of personal anxieties and disaffection. On the surface, as Taji-Farouki (1996, p. 177) notes, the attraction of HT lay in its outwardly perception of being considered 'intellectually sophisticated' by early recruits. By projecting themselves as radical intellectuals HT were able 'to exploit the growing cultural chasm between such youth and their tradition bound-elders' (Taji-Farouki 1996, p. 177). In other words, HT took advantage of disaffected youth who were struggling to develop a stable identity, as they found themselves ensnared by their parents' sub-continent values and issues. If this is true, then it is important to understand why some young Muslims felt discontent.

It was noticeable that the majority of early activists emerged from similar social realities. A variety of educated, middle class Muslim students were making the conscious choice to join the group. Many of these activists were drawn to HT, not by Islam, but through a variety of political and social issues. The reason for this is explained by Halliday (1999, p. 896), who suggests: 'Islam may, in some contexts, be the prime form of political and social identity, but it is never the sole form and is often not the primary one within Muslim societies and communities'. The new HT recruits sought to structure their ethnicity, nationality and religion in a manner that brought them into conflict with British society. Trying to decipher the pathway early recruits took towards HT can be somewhat problematic, since on the surface ideology is suggested as the sole trigger for their activism. Two overriding markers can be identified concerning Muslim activism: Firstly, if Islam is interpreted as a doctrine that amalgamates the temporal and spiritual, then it is natural for it to seek expression beyond the private realm. For Farid, 'the party ideology exposed the fallacy of man-made law', which meant HT mobilised recruits to focus on the public sphere (Ibid., 26 May 2004). Secondly, by focusing on the public sphere HT recruits became acutely aware of socio-economic deprivation and corruption, making much of their activism a very real response to these perceived injustices. Consequently, the outcome after joining HT appears to be increased in-group solidarity and empowerment.

Farid suggested the instability of the political landscape during the early 1980s provided a natural source of activism and recruitment. In fact, student activists were greatly animated by the plight of the Muslim world, and HT was seen as the champion of the oppressed and exploited. The global situation concerning the Muslim world during this period was undergoing immense transformation: the Iranian revolution (1979); the Iran–Iraq war (1980-1988); and the continuing war in Afghanistan (1979-1989) generated an increase in Islamic militancy. Farid attempted to describe the contextual reasons behind the rapid evolution of HT, as he saw it:

> Think about it politically, at that time, the Iranian Revolution had taken place. The war in Afghanistan was happening ... So Muslim students were talking about these issues, but groups like the Islamic Foundation had a namby-pamby approach. So, when we would talk we'd speak out openly against what happened in Iran and Afghanistan, although we were a bit careful, because people were very naïve ... but we made an impact ... these became Muslim issues. We sought to elevate Muslim thought by attacking concepts like nationalism (Ibid., 26 May 2004).

HT's ideology certainly provided a new basis for self-identification and empowerment. As Ballard (1996) explained, a rather palpable example of Muslim mobilisation was the preferred usage of the label 'Muslim' compared with other ethnic identifiers, which reflected their feelings of marginalisation from the majority culture. HT ideology, which for recruits was synonymous with Islam, became paramount to their identity because it was considered the solution to all worldly problems and provided a road map to 'political mobilisation'.

This historical overview of campus activism during the early 1980s is somewhat difficult to quantify in relation to the rise of HT. Farid insisted a key motivating force behind student mobilisation was Muslim conflict, which he defined within an international context. However, the events he described gradually wound down during the middle of the 1980s, when HT started to gain a presence on campus.[2] Although, these global conflicts were widely unpopular across campus, the supporters failed to mobilise the student body. More significantly, they lacked tactical direction, contributing to their inability to expand or recruit. Despite these obvious shortcomings, Farid strongly believes the supporter's deliberate focus on international issues, at the expense of local problems, helped create a starting point for national activity. As I will show later, this is one of the major issues of contention between Farid and Omar Bakri.

Farid mentioned that local problems, which he described as pragmatic, dragged HT away from its global ideology and message. Therefore, those attracted to local affairs are often driven by materialistic concerns, and thus not disposed to idealistic politics (Parkin, 1968). In contrast, rival Muslim groups, like Young Muslims, *Jamaati Islami* and the Islamic Foundation, were operating from a pre-defined position that centred on developing their role within the immigrant Muslim communities. Professing this as a critical error, Farid described how their oversight had negated Islam as a global entity, and this to some extent explained the initial inroads HT made among Muslim students. The Muslims from the sub-continent have a broad association to the culture of their origin. However, they have an equal affinity to the global *Ummah*, and, as a consequence, they were deeply affected by the continuing war in Afghanistan and the conflict between Iran and Iraq. It was argued, by Farid, HT was the only significant political actor, as other groups were largely concerned with localised issues, giving HT full supremacy to articulate the Muslim student response to global events.

Lack of Islamic Activism

The beginnings of HT in Britain can be traced back to transient members and the small group of indigenous Muslims who became affiliated to the movement. After the transient members returned home, the home-grown affiliates began to initiate activities on their own. This period marked a significant turning point for the indigenous affiliates, as the student population was gradually becoming more politically active, notably characterised by the sudden emergence of opposing

---

2   The Gulf War (1991), according to Farid, proved to be a very big catalyst in mobilising student activism.

Islamic movements, like the Young Muslims in Whitechapel, Jam'iat Lhyaa' Minhaaj Al-Sunnah (JIMAS),[3] and to a lesser extent HT. For these three fledgling organisations, it marked a new stage in the history of Muslim activism in the UK. As Farid explained:

> ... By about 1985 I had travelled to London, and if you're talking about Hizb ut-Tahrir in Britain then you need to understand the scene at that time you had Jimas, Young Muslims and Hizb ut-Tahrir. So, we were three new groups just starting out, so it was a really interesting time in the Muslim community at that time ... so they perceived us as being a competitor, although I didn't, but they did. The Islamic activity at that time was very different; you had very few circles and lectures. At that time we started to get more people into *Halaqah,* and *Halaqahs* started to grow, then later on more people came in (Ibid., 26 May 2004).

It is understandable that Farid did not consider HT as a realistic competitor, as they only had a few affiliates, yet these organisations immediately perceived HT as a credible rival. The reason for this agitated response to initial HT activity concerned the scope of political discussion that they introduced to the landscape, which was previously lacking a political dimension.

Farid prior to his arrival in London had made intermittent visits; in particular during the summer of 1984, he attended the 'third Islamic exhibition' at the University of London. This conference saw a host of Islamic scholars debate the contemporary problems of the Muslim world. Farid's initial observations of the event were positive, as conferences of this nature are important. However, after further reflection he became deeply sceptical, especially as it was convened with the support of Muslim leaders, which undermined the very essence of the event. In an article in the newly launched *Al-Fajr* magazine, they articulated their position, as the following passage demonstrated:

> Indeed we challenge those dignitaries and participants who attend such conferences to speak the truth; both to the leaders and our people. The fact is that all the rulers of the Muslim countries do not intend or wish to solve the problems of the *Ummah.* Their participation in Islamic conferences is nothing more than pretentious, merely to satisfy the people of their countries who strongly feel for the teachings of Islam. (*al-Fajr Magazine,* October 1986)

Furthermore, Farid and his associates attended the annual winter gathering of the Federation of Student Islamic Societies (FOSIS), convened in December 1984 under the auspicious title of 'Reconstruction of the Muslim *Ummah'.* Once again, HT affiliates empathised with the delegate's enthusiasm and optimism, yet as Farid commented, 'Conferences of this nature failed to get to grips with the

---

3   JIMAS is a UK based Muslim charity organisation that was established in 1984 (for more information refer to: http://www.jimas.org/aims.htm).

vital problem' (Kassim, 26 May 2004). The group continued their observations of Islamic activity, attending other such events, which revealed a recurring theme of failure to address the vital issues. This has critical importance because it places the pending expansion into a better context, as HT members were exploring gaps in the discourses taking place at the time.

Organisational Problems and Lack of Scholarship

Farid was established in London, yet this did not restrict his 'shuttle diplomacy' across the country. In particular, on a small stay in Bristol he was able to establish a group of contacts who soon became the platform for activity in the west of England. Preceding this, Farid had successfully established a number of contacts and a stable cell had been convened in Cardiff. The UK affiliates were meticulously erecting contacts and cells, in an endeavour to expand the interior platform of HT. The foundations of the UK branch had been established by indigenous affiliates, which owed greatly to Farid's extraordinary enthusiasm and dedication. Although young Muslims joined the group in growing numbers, it became more difficult to control and organise the affiliates. Farid, for example, mentioned that a central theme discussed by senior officials during the 1980s was concerned with how to organise the UK activity.

> The founding *Amir* [leader] of Hizb ut-Tahrir never envisaged that Hizb ut-Tahrir would be firmly rooted in Europe or will have any structure in Europe …
> As Hizb ut-Tahrir was developing during the 1980s, growing in size, it became an issue of how do we structure and organise ourselves. The *Halaqah* and the party culture is the bedrock of Hizb ut-Tahrir, so it was a new subject for the party. We tried to make analogies with *Masab ibn-Amir* [Medina], but neither of these quite fit our reality. Also, it wasn't a global village, back then, and thus it was a new subject for the party. (Ibid., 26 May 2004)

HT ideology does not establish any protocols for the group structure to exist outside of the designated area of work (*Majal*). Therefore, as HT began to expand throughout the 1980s, it became an issue for the affiliates to address the question of organising the party body. This vital component had to be incorporated into a developing body of individuals, yet the tools required to accomplish this goal were greatly lacking. HT was still a small dysfunctional group of individuals who lacked the ability to transcend to the next stage. This disordered approach to the organisation of the fraternity left Farid extremely frustrated, as he stated:

> To be honest with you when talking about the enthusiasm we had. I used to moan about the Hizb in Britain, we're not moving, not doing anything, were not making contacts etc...There was no structured approach, but from the late 1980s we started to structure ourselves really properly. We took advantage of

the people we had to organise it properly, to organise circles, lectures, Regents Park Mosque circles were established [1987]. We had the old red and white *Khilafah Magazine,* which we used to produce once every two weeks. (Ibid., 26 May 2004)

Clearly, they were in need of expertise in the art of organising public activity. This disparity appeared to be rectified by the arrival of experienced members from the Middle East by the late 1980s.

Omar Bakri Muhammad: Radicalism and Scholarship

The Islamic political landscape would be forever transformed by the arrival of Omar Bakri Muhammad, on 14 January 1986. Omar Bakri Mohammed was born in Syria, into an affluent upper middle-class family. According to Bakri, he was sent to al-Kutaab Islamic school where he studied the Islamic core sources. As a teenager, Bakri joined the Muslim Brotherhood. However, by the age of 17 he had joined HT in Lebanon, growing increasingly critical of his association to the Muslim Brotherhood, which had fragmented into a politically apathetic organisation leading to the holistic erosion of its cardinal principles (Ibid., 2 June 2004). Since his arrival in the UK, Bakri had been shrouded in controversy, yet his central goal to establish a global Islamic State, 'starting here in the UK', remained the same (Ibid., 2 June 2004). Surprisingly, the British press had given Bakri extensive coverage, enabling him to voice his extremist rhetoric. This made Bakri a divisive figure among the Muslim community, but what is less clear is how he helped engineer the birth of Muslim youth radicalism. On his immediate arrival he established regular public circles at the Muslim Welfare House (Finsbury Park), 'concerning *Fiqh* and other political issues', which were conducted exclusively in Arabic (Ibid., 2 June 2004). The arrival of Bakri provided Farid, and his small band of affiliates, with a new sense of constructive purpose and a stable outlet for scholarship.

Activism in Britain: Bakri's Perspective

It is interesting to note on his arrival in the UK, Bakri made several observations of the state of Islamic activism that sharply contrasted with those made by Farid. He was initially very sceptical, as his early perceptions were formed from media reports and the general Muslim public. As he stated:

When I come to Britain ... I find Muslim talking about *halal* meat that's [the] main discussion about Islam with non-Muslim. I was surprised really, they were discussing minor issue, like [the] circumcision of woman, is that Islam as a way of life? Islam is great civilisation for 1300 years of rule, in the end we don't want Islam to be about the circumcision of woman or *halal* meat.

This rather simplistic overview of Muslim interaction with the British state is quite interesting because it reveals how Bakri views Muslim demands for acceptance in British society as a negative development. Early Muslim migrants made little demands on the state for acceptance since they subscribed doggedly to the myth of returning to their homelands. More significantly, Bakri fails to acknowledge the need for Muslims to advocate demands in response to the host country's unwillingness to recognise Muslim religious practice in the public sphere. As Ansari (2004) notes, this forced Muslims to generate closer communal connections in order to overcome segregation, which left them a sporadically integrated community.

Furthermore, Bakri was greatly restricted by language and geography, making these preliminary observations difficult to substantiate. Despite these obvious limitations, Bakri was partially correct in his appraisal of the lack of radical activism in the UK. This inability to project political Islam into British society left a lasting impression on Bakri, since he was deeply cynical of the recurring themes of discourse that he had encountered. In particular, the Muslim community lacked intellectual and political leadership. This form of leadership is very different from the traditional and modern cultural leadership that is often found in Muslim communities. In particular, traditional leaders found it extremely difficult to communicate with newer generations as they often lacked basic linguistic competency and thus struggled to relate to young people. More significantly, young Muslims found it hard to gain access to local and national political structures because the older generation monopolised local institutions. For this reason, Bakri immediately singled out Muslim students, because they were perceived to be at the forefront of social protest and change. Also, they had no outlet within the community to express their socio-political interests, which arguably reinforced their alienation from both community and society. Bakri proclaimed 'the future of the Muslim community' was the youth, because from within their ranks revival would take place (Ibid., 25 June 2004). As a result, Bakri immediately enacted a plan to culture British Muslims. This provided Farid and his small band of affiliates with a new sense of constructive purpose and a stable outlet for scholarship. Thus, Bakri's arrival heralded the launch of a sustained campaign on the Muslim youth of Britain.

Bakri developed a strategy to target university campuses, as this offered HT a natural way to contact the youth. They quickly began visiting universities across the country, forming societies and holding talks. Initially, the activity was instigated in a very simple and informal way, as Bakri explained:

> … we put stall[s] outside just [a] table, Farid and me. I get anyone who speak[s] Arabic, while anyone English speak[s] to Farid. And we convince them Islam is supreme way of life, Islam [is] total submission to God, Islam [is] unique way

of life and it duty to call for Islam to implement Islam. So we say be proud of your *Deen* [Islam], we [Muslim] were great civilisation because we establish Islam, there is no Islamic state today ... So, people start to sympathise with us, we should do something, we can do a lot, we can form societies, so they start to form societies and we enter into universities. Now we have students inside. (Ibid., 2 June 2004)

This enabled them to recruit novices at these universities, providing them with a permanent link to these institutions. This groundwork formed the method of introductory activity, which was replicated nationwide allowing the men to generate active cells. HT during this period operated almost exclusively on university campuses, in order to build and indoctrinate a large body of student activists. HT radicalism was built on two key recruitment triggers: external plight and internal identity. The construction of internal empowerment provided HT with the means to draw disaffected Muslim students to its ranks. Glynn (2002) noted, Islamic organisations provide identity reinforcement and connection to an idealised past. As she states: 'Islam is something to be proud of, with a great history and international presence as well as religious promises of future glory, which can all transport its followers from the grey confines of the inner city' (Glynn 2002, p. 980). This approach enabled HT to recruit novices at universities, providing them with permanent links to these institutions. This groundwork formed the method of introductory activity, which was replicated nationwide allowing the men to generate active cells. HT during this period operated almost exclusively on university campuses, in order to build and culture a large body of activists. This secretive period of recruitment was essential, because it allowed the movement to make contact with the student population and turn some of them into activists who believed in the ideology of HT.

Focusing on Britain: Targeting Muslim Youth

It was asserted by Bakri that young Muslims were deprived of intellectual leadership concerning political Islam. Bakri immediately went about defining a way to target Muslim students. He started discrediting minor topics, namely issues about *halal* meat, and focused on the discord of Western society and ideology. More significantly, Bakri wanted to single out the 'educated younger generation', as he felt the older generation would be reluctant to embrace HT's radical ideology. Lewis (2007) makes an interesting observation about recent trends amongst educated British born Muslims, who appear to be actively making space for themselves in civil society with Islam. Thus, it was not surprising Bakri assigned such emphasis to this specific sub-demographic of young educated Muslims. In contrast, in the case of the first generation, Bakri felt they were wedged firmly within the confines of their immigrant culture, which they had transported from their countries of origin. 'All they wanted [first generation] was money, roof over their head, some *halal* meat and a place to pray, that's all' (Ibid., 2 June 2004). The young recruits felt HT could provide them with a way to oppose the negative culture of the first generation, as they fused religion and culture together. In contrast, young recruits were mindful of the distinction between 'Islam' and 'culture', and thus acceptance of HT ideology meant they were explicitly rejecting ethnic cultural traditions (such as dress and marriage practices). Bakri explained that immigrant parents failed to understand, or were incapable of empathising with, their children's experiences in Britain. As he described: 'They just work and go home ... they isolated themselves from British society' (Ibid., 2 June 2004). Dwyer (1999) suggests, those young Muslims that seek greater identification with Islam often use it as a means to repel parental cultural norms and control. Through espousing religious authority HT recruits were able to define their identity away from cultural interface. In this respect, HT ideology allowed recruits to construct a positive framing of their identity, which gave them a way to adapt to British society, and thus religiosity was only a paradoxical outcome. Thus, Bakri swiftly identified race and identity as integral issues for young British Muslims.

It was clear to Bakri that young Muslims struggled to balance their Western identity with their cultural and religious values. Young Muslims often develop multiple identities, which shape their attitudes within different social contexts. This perpetuated what Bakri described as the 'Bobby and Abdullah syndrome' (Ibid., 2 June 2004). The inability to adapt to changes and resolve problems during socialisation created a hybrid identity. At home the Abdullah persona would revert to an ethnic association, speaking the language of his forefathers and adhering to their customs. However, beyond this remit the Bobby persona would materialise; he would drink, go clubbing and be a fully integrated member of British society. Some social theorists contend that this duality signifies the formation of 'dynamic mixed cultures' (Cohen and Kennedy 2000, p. 363). In theory, a hybrid identity allows individuals to interact with opposing cultural mores, creating new identity options. In spite of this, Bakri asserted that this hybridisation could not be preserved and in due course stimulated identity problems, which prevented assimilation. As he commented:

> This is where [universities] I met Bobby, because when he starts to rave and dance with them [non-Muslims], they call him *Paki,* now that's a crisis. He sacrifice[d] everything, then you call me *Paki* ... we tell him no you are Abdullah; you belong to [a] great nation, to the *ummah* [nation] of Islam. So, we invite them, we integrate them to our beliefs not to integrate with their [non-Muslims] beliefs. They're supposed to accept to integrate with our way of life not integrate with their way of life, it's completely opposite. Come with us let's interact, so no isolation, no integration, there is only interaction, let's interact with the belief we carry and be proud about it, be proud to be Abdullah and Muslim. (Ibid., 2 June 2004)

This rather revealing extract shows, in a nutshell, according to Bakri, the fallacy of assimilation into British society. To start, it seems pretty clear having a preference towards the host identity is regarded as artificial, since non-Muslims are believed to be inherently ambivalent towards minorities. Furthermore, the mixing of identities is prone to contradictions since the ethno-religious culture cannot be reconciled within new cultural settings, like university. Bakri constantly stressed the importance of universities and colleges, because these local environments allowed HT to locate disaffected young people. Parkin (1968) has suggested that socially alienated people are more inclined to the appeals of radical movements. In general, for ethnic minorities, identity and race are very powerful markers that can affect psychological well-being. Thus, it is not surprising that local issues were used to generate party cells.

Assuming the recollections of Bakri are accurate, one could surmise that greater emphasis was placed on local issues and events. In fact, throughout the interview, he made it clear that HT strategy focused on the social realities of young British Muslims. Although, international issues were important to him, Bakri prioritised the local in order to inspire an Islamic awakening. This meant targeting problems that young Muslims experienced growing up in Britain, and giving them an Islamist spin. As he described:

> So, when we carry Islam in British campuses or [in] society, we invite non-Muslims as [a] spiritual belief if he accept ok, Allah guides, if not then as political belief. So he can solve his own economic and political problems. So we start to pick on [the] problem[s] in society and give solutions from Islam, racism, housing problem, moral decline, mortgage, homosexuality, this *dawah* [was] carrying Islam as [an] intellectual belief, and with the help of God we [were] very successful. (Ibid., 2 June 2004)

This approach gave HT the illusion of being able to define and solve individual problems. They catered their message to young educated Muslims. Global phenomena, like the Iran-Iraq war, had little, if any, impact on HT recruits. In reality, by talking about local Muslim issues, HT was able to directly agitate a person's immediate interests. Bakri makes reference to a range of localised problems, which broadly relate to the religious, social, political and economic fields of life. In essence, HT activists shared the experiences of young British Muslims, but their socialisation was rooted in a more middle class framework. As a result, HT appealed to middle class Muslims, because its activists sought out relationships that reflected similar social backgrounds.

Trying to understand the social bases of membership for HT is not an easy task, so I decided to ask Bakri why such a large number of middle class Asians joined HT. Surprisingly, he was willing to engage this issue, unlike Farid. Although Bakri was reluctant to limit HT recruitment to a particular social class, he accepted the fact middle class Asians formed the largest pool of activists. Bakri had several explanations for this attraction. To start with, he suggested students found the intellectual message of HT very appealing. As he asserted, 'we attract them [middle class Asians] to our concepts, because [its] new for them … and they [are] educated so they want to discuss with us' (Ibid., 2 June 2004). In other words, the educated middle class had a greater appreciation of the intellectual spirit of HT, which they presumably felt was superior to their own. So, despite HT members acquiring middle class status they still felt frustrated by discrimination and racial prejudice. Therefore, individuals who feel socially isolated from society are more typically drawn to radical movements, especially if it brings about greater class solidarity.

Bakri espoused a shared sense of belonging as another possible reason for why middle class Asians seemed more inclined to HT radicalism. More significantly, Bakri talked about the social realities of campus life, namely racism and alienation, which left a mark on many Asian students. According to Bakri, the students he encountered were 'lost', having 'no personality of their own' (Ibid, 2 June 2004). These middle class Asians were stripped of their identity, as Bakri commented, 'their identity is corrupt, you feel pain, because the Western culture created racism, you have [the] Western personality, [this] must be taken out'. Consequently, Asian students had a tendency to seek out HT members, as Bakri suggests, 'They come to HT for true brotherhood … *kufr* [non-Muslims] cannot give this' (Ibid., 2 June 2004). There are two simple justifications for this type of attachment: biological necessity and 'preference for similarity'. Firstly, certainly among the members interviewed, the overwhelming majority of HT activists emerged from a similar social background and upbringing. Several studies have shown a strong link between peer group friendships and class background (Howe, 2010). Thus, it is not surprising to see recruits finding solidarity according to social cleavage, as they share interests and lifestyles.

The final, and perhaps most noteworthy, cause of skewed HT recruitment related to agitation of localised problems. Bakri confidently proclaimed working class Muslims were motivated by 'bread and butter politics'. In contrast, middle class HT members, he suggested, were more inclined to intellectual concerns because they were not materialistically orientated. In other words, middle class recruits are not usually motivated by economic conditions, rather they appear more inclined to idealistic causes. More significantly, Bakri claimed that they agitated young people's needs and interests. This could mean HT tapped into the psychological needs of middle class Asians. Some historians, like Kulikoff (1988), believe class identification helps individuals to reinforce their place in the wider society. As a result, young activists exerted their collective class identity through HT, which offered them a way to develop a coherent ideology that met their social needs. This may partially explain why middle class Asians showed greater attraction to the socio-political issues raised by HT. But were these issues manufactured deliberately by HT to target middle class students? Although, Bakri accepted social needs were agitated by HT, he refused to simplify recruitment within a class paradigm. Yet, if HT, as he acknowledged, targeted the social realities of middle class students, then it is fair to attribute recruitment to aspects of class manipulation. Bakri himself declared that the politics of middle class students was different from those of the working class. Throughout the interview, he suggested that working class parents placed added emphasis on seeking out immediate economic reward. This created two opposing social realities and value systems, which, in turn, made it easier to recruit middle class Asians as they were more responsive to idealistic messages.

In the last two chapters, I have looked at two historical episodes. It was vital to understand the emergence and consolidation of HT in Britain since its inception in the Arab world. HT from its commencement had a skewed political outlook, which can be attributed to its founder, Al-Nabhani, who had been deeply affected by European colonisation. HT adopted a dogmatic and confrontational ideology, in which the world was dichotomised into us and them. Not surprisingly, this 'othering' of non-Muslims can be vividly seen in the narrative of Omar Bakri and Farid Kassim, who both have a twisted perception of British society. However, trying to understand the appeal of HT in Britain is not an easy task, especially since the movement has only carved out its membership from a particular social demographic: namely young middle class Asians. Taji-Farouki (1996, p. 177) equates this to a 'growing cultural chasm' between the younger and older generations. This may be true, but the depth of HT appeal and radicalisation stretches much deeper. In particular, a recurring thread in the narratives of both founding members was ideology, which was seen as the precursor for youth involvement and engagement. According to Bakri, young middle-class Muslims were plagued by all sorts of social problems and difficulties (such as racism, alienation, identity crises and so on). This, as Bakri candidly revealed, allowed HT members to exploit the social realities of educated young Muslims at British Universities. In particular, HT ideology was visualised as the only solution to all human problems. For young recruits, this created a strong attachment to HT ideology, as novices equated their social deficiencies and dilemmas to western society and culture. In this context, HT was seen as a means to counteract the west and the social frustrations they had experienced.

There were several noteworthy debates taking place amongst the members about HT activism in the UK. This was to be expected since HT had not set or defined any clear protocols for activism outside of the Arab world. One such debate, namely between internationalism and localism, had been underway since Bakri arrived. This created a number of internal tensions and conflicts, as members struggled to find agreement. Throughout the early 1980s, HT was engrossed by international events, which seemed natural given that they wanted to generate a global revolution. In spite of this, Bakri's arrival marked a sizeable shift in strategy towards Britain. In other words, he wanted to engage in an 'intellectual and political struggle' against the British way of life. It was not surprising, therefore, to find that HT *dawah* was rarely divorced from political and social events throughout the 1990s. More significantly, events like the Gulf War and Bosnia were localised. As exemplified in one local leaflet entitled: *'Bosnia today Bradford Tomorrow'*. HT rhetoric, as orchestrated by Bakri, prioritised the problems faced by young middle class Muslims (for example, identity crisis, racism and social alienation).

At the initial stage of recruitment, these issues provoked greater sensitivity as they aroused feelings of personal dissatisfaction. In contrast, international events were detached from the recruit's reality, and only after joining HT did activists become agitated by Muslim global plight. More significantly, HT recruitment was relatively low during the late 1980s and early 1990s, but rapidly grew once Bakri shifted emphasis to localised issues and problems.

One of the key conclusions to draw from this chapter is the types of young people attracted to HT. There are complex and diverse factors driving radicalisation, making it very difficult to define a theory that provides a single answer. However, an intrinsic component of HT radicalisation appears to be the homogeneity of its social base, which is drawn almost exclusively from young middle class Asians. Trying to formulate a hypothesis for the mobilisation of this specific social demographic is critical. As Bakri asserted, this group of young people reacted to social discrimination by joining HT. This is somewhat difficult to resolve. Firstly, as Ansari (2004) points out, the first generation opted for accommodation, placing them outside the majority culture framework, which denied them recognition. However, this contextual reality seemingly dissolved with the emergence of the second generation, who are struggling 'to discover how to be a Muslim as a minority in a non-Muslim society' (Lewis 2007, p. 6). Stratham (2003) equates the rise in overt religious affiliation amongst some Muslims to two interconnected social realities: (1) Islam seeks to assert itself within the public realm, and (2) Muslim identity formation is an acute response to social deprivation and discrimination. In regards to the latter, Muslim self-consciousness is often reinforced by negative media stereotypes. The public vilification of Muslim belief and practice tends to lead to introverted responses: 'Muslim communities closing ranks' (Samad 1996, p. 97). Similarly, Ballard (1996) believes the marginalisation of Muslims from the majority culture has triggered a reaffirmation of religion. This is because young Muslims perceive their religious identity to be under constant threat, and not their ethnicity, resulting in greater mobility towards Muslim identity. This movement away from ethno-identity labels is exacerbated by the declining attachment to South Asia, as a cultural and linguistic reference point.

Therefore, it is not surprising to see HT actively trying to contest the legitimacy of British Muslim identity. This was made apparent on 24th August 2003, when HT arranged a conference entitled: '*British or Muslim*'. The conference consciously sought to circumvent integration by re-structuring Muslim identities into a single collective religious identity. So, this begs the question, what is radicalisation? Events such as the 7 July 2005 London bombings and the assassination of Dutch filmmaker Theo Van Gogh push social theoretical explanation to its boundaries. These disturbing incidents all involve Muslims, who refer to Islam as the major source of their actions and behaviours. But is this an accurate definition of radicalisation? In the next chapter we seek to explore this further.

Chapter 4
Defining HT Radicalisation

Within the social sciences a robust debate has been underway since 11 September 2001 concerning the causes and consequences of radicalisation. In a British context, however, the debate has been focusing on Muslim identity and the role of radical Islamist groups. Janet Williams, the commanding officer of the Muslim Contact Unit (Metropolitan Police Special Branch), declared that 'radicalisation' was the single biggest threat to national security (BBC, 22 June 2005). Tony Blair, shortly after the London Bombings (2005), proscribed a number of radical Islamist movements.[1] This was designed to tackle the processes of radicalisation that appeared to be taking place among young British Muslims. Within this context, I seek to explore the processes of radicalisation, focusing on the issues that have allowed HT to radicalise some young Muslims in Britain.

A few years ago, I attended a panel discussion on the broad issue of Islam and the West, at a community centre in Tooting, South London. Taji Mustafa, the media representative of HT in Britain, asked the audience, 'When exactly did 'radicalisation' become a dirty word?' He argued that, 'what the government maligns as radicalisation is in fact politicisation ... Young Muslims are taking an interest in global politics and getting engaged in non-violent discussion and campaigning, which is surely a good thing?' This attempt to revise the parameters of 'radicalisation' is a strong indicator of radical groups, like HT, trying to be seen as legitimate political activists. After the gathering, Adam (member, 29) suggested it was a 'government trap to redefine Islamic politics'. As a former member, I was not surprised to hear points of view like this, as activists are trained to defend HT. In particular, I recall attending a member's meeting after the 9/11 terror attacks, in which the UK leadership instructed the fraternity to 'manufacture positive and negative stereotypes' in order to dilute the threat HT pose. Ultimately, the aim of such actions was to avoid any form of legal sanction against HT in the UK. In the end, however, these comments illustrate the need to define 'radicalisation'.

In the course of writing this book, I have explored many different ways of framing the subject of radicalisation, and I believe social psychology is a good starting point. This is because social psychology, as can be inferred from its description, combines the ways in which both social and mental processes determine identity (Rom and Lamb, 1986). Radicalisation, in a social psychology context, refers to a considerable departure from traditional ideals, constituting a full and real change at the root of the personality (Popplestone and McPherson, 1988).

---

1   Al-Ghurabaa and the Saved Sect became the first UK-based Islamist groups to be banned under laws outlawing the glorification of terrorism (*BBC*, 17 July 2006).

This definition offers a good starting point, but this definition needs amending because it is incomplete and far too general in its scope and application. For instance, the same definition of radicalisation could be given to those who undergo a religious conversion. According to Rambo (cited in Eliade, 1987, p. 77), there are two transformations that are central to the conversion process: 'total change in all other aspects of life, and a new awareness of the well-being of others'. In general, the act of religious conversion might have a similar end result to radicalisation, but these two forms of identity change are not identical.

Despite accumulating a vast array of new data regarding HT members and their backgrounds, it is still extremely difficult to pinpoint precisely why some young Muslims join HT, since radicalisation is a 'complex process that does not follow a linear path' (Pargeter 2006, p. 737). Therefore, if HT radicalisation takes place amongst a disproportionate number of young middle class Asians, then I must understand the trajectories of these individuals and sketch out commonalties. The evidence for this will be shown in the course of following chapters. My immediate concern here is to provide a definition of HT radicalisation before any serious study of the topic can be made. Firstly, I prefer to use the idiom *HT radicalisation*, instead of more generic terms like *Islamic radicalisation*. This is because from social constructivist theory, 'framing' of radicalisation draws upon a collective phenomenon that is essentially contextualised to two key agents: the group and the individual. Thus, the definition of HT radicalisation I have crafted can be separated into three distinct parts: (1) a new cognitive perspective is engineered that is (2) internalised, so that (3) a new collective HT identity is created (fostering a feeling of empowerment and solidarity).

New Cognitive Perspective

The most fundamental part of HT radicalisation is the deep process of indoctrination, which provides a new cognitive perspective with which to view the social world. At this point, I want to briefly look at cognitive theory, in order to clarify its meaning in the context of radicalisation. Social cognitive theory defines behaviour as a reciprocal interaction between an internal emotional state and triggers that are available in the environment (Bandura, 1977). Social psychologists have long tried to identify the key cognitive and motivational changes that occur within individuals when they become group members. The radical group is the primary setting for the creation of a new cognitive perspective, because members are willing to 'bend towards group expectation' (Newcomb, 1952, p. 221). This explanation shows the strong interplay between individuals and groups, which enables the group to change the cognitive perspective of members. Wiktorowicz's (2005, p. 19) study of Al-Muhajiroun, now disbanded, discovered contact with the radical group often required a 'cognitive opening'. This cognitive opening is a gateway to the wholesale transformation of previously held beliefs. According to Wiktorowicz (2005, p. 20), this is often inspired by 'identity crisis', which renders the recipient more susceptible to radical ideology. Thus, early fascination with the radical group often leads to a 'cognitive opening', activating a process of 'religious seeking' (Wiktorowicz 2005, p. 19). The triggers for this opening are multifaceted and greatly hinge on the experiences of the individual, making them vulnerable to the movement.

This view of cognitive change in perception within a group setting has also been referred to as a new shared group norm, and involves members privately and publicly adopting this as their own choice. As a result, individuals are categorised, and placed in an in-group. This membership is then internalised by members as an aspect of their identity. In this respect, the basis for a member's self-definition changes within the group, allowing his or her personal identity to be submerged into a collective identity. Moving from a state of social exclusion to a group setting can drastically diminish one's sense of individuality. Similarly, Newcomb (1943) found that increased interaction with other members prompts individuals to change their attitudes in accordance with the group consensuses. In other words, for the cognitive transformation to take effect the individual must align his viewpoint with HT. As Wiktorowicz (2005, p. 16) explains:

> The movement's schemata must resonate with an individual's own interpretive framework to facilitate participation. The alignment is contingent on fidelity with cultural narratives, symbols, and identities; the reputation of the frame articulator and consistency of the frame; the frame's empirical credibility, and the personal salience of the frame for potential participant. Movements must compete with frames proffered by governments, counter-movements and intra-movement rivals.

In a group setting, members come to understand their social world by way of shared perspectives and representations. According to Snow (1986), cognitive change provides a framework for understanding the external world, by rendering a situation meaningful. At this stage of the HT radicalisation process, an individual aligns their cognitive perspective with that of the group. This alignment acts as a unifying force, moulding the individual's ideas and actions into synchronisation with HT collective identity. This makes the cognitive process an active force in the construction of one's reality. At the heart of this cognitive process is the making sense of the 'other'. A set of processes are undergone through which individuals are reconfigured and various forms of 'us and them' are constructed. Some social theorists believe that this occurs in individuals who have suffered some form of emotional damage, usually at the hands of the 'other', during early life (Knutson, 1973). In theory, the individual then internalises these representations in their actions and responses. Forging a new cognitive essence requires a change in the way an individual thinks and acts, until he or she becomes a walking manifestation of the radical identity.

A good preliminary illustration of this cognitive transformation is Mohammad, a British born Muslim from London.[2] I knew Mohammed for many years and

---

2   Mohammad (actual name changed for privacy) is a 26-year-old HT novice.

spoke to him in an infrequent fashion. There appeared to be one primary social trigger that influenced his newfound cognitive perspective and his resulting radicalisation into HT. Firstly he seemed to develop a greater malevolence towards British society. I recall running into Mohammad several days after a brutal assault had taken place in the local area, in which a gang of white youths had attacked two Asian youths. This rather unsettling episode played a key role in his cognitive transformation. In particular, he ranted about the evil nature of British society and people. In the midst of this discussion, I noticed that he used derogatory terms in describing non-Muslims, something he never did before. Several months after the incident, I bumped into Mohammad outside his local Mosque where he was distributing HT paraphernalia. I was rather surprised by this and asked why he had joined HT. He explained: 'it is *Fard* (duty) to work for Allah's *deen* (religion) on this earth ... and to expose the Kuffar system'. Though a very simplistic illustration, it does exemplify how Mohammad's cognitive perspective had been radically reformatted, internalised and embedded within a new radical HT identity.

Internalisation

Internalisation is a general term for the process of incorporating concepts and behaviours into one's self, and embedding features of the external world into the internal world. This 'internal world' is strongly influenced by group involvement, which actively imposes constraints on behaviour and defines the external world. These representations of the self-exist in relation to other objects, which may be external or internal. In other words, perceptions of 'others' become rooted into one's own behaviour. In regards to the radicalisation process, when a novice enters the group setting in HT, his or her perceptions of others change in accordance with HT's perceptions, allowing him or her to internalise the collective HT identity. This internalisation of ideas and beliefs actively occurs through the culturing process, which completely alters the disposition and creates group loyalty. For instance, a college teacher in London told me, during the 7 July remembrance ceremony, some of his Muslim students made excessive physical gestures throughout the minute of silence. When he asked them what they were doing, they replied no remembrance was afforded those Muslims killed in Iraq. I later discovered young HT members had orchestrated what they described as a 'non-verbal protest', which was sanctioned by the group hierarchy. By adopting a new cognitive perspective, one internalises a new set of beliefs and attitudes, replacing the old perspective. As Wiktorowicz (2005, p. 167) discovered from his respondents, 'the only way to achieve salvation and enter Paradise on Judgment Day is to follow the movement's prescribed strategy'. This transformative phase is integral to HT radicalisation, as it infuses the individual to the group.

New Collective HT Identity and Empowerment

HT is a significant actor in the conditioning of a new cognitive and behavioural disposition, especially as it is the sole interpreter of the radical ideology. Within the group setting, the novice is indoctrinated into thinking in accordance with the group perspective. This is manifested in a new way of viewing the social world, which may contradict established convention. Thus, the first significant aspect of HT radicalisation relates to the establishment of a new cognitive perspective that reflects the group identity. According to Sherif and Sherif (1969, p. 252), the group setting has a powerful influence on individual behaviour, justifying the 'in-group's negative opinions of the out-group'. Similarly, David and Turner (1999) argue that in a group setting people tend to 'depersonalise' and 'stereotype' themselves and other people. Consequently, HT members focus more on the similarities between themselves, which makes it easier to impose differences between them and the 'others'. More importantly, the new cognitive perspective, gained in a group environment, spawns greater self-esteem and empowerment. Empowerment is an essential part of the radicalisation process, increasing the ideological strength of individuals; the empowered develop a greater sense of confidence in their own abilities. In subsequent chapters, I look at the real-world impact of HT radicalisation on identity, as the individual is transformed to incorporate the radical identity. In the context of HT, for example, the member must 'adopt the opinions of the group, its thoughts and its constitution by word and deed' (Anon. 1998, p. 1). This means that anyone who becomes a member of HT has to pledge an oath to adopt everything the group calls for even if he or she is not convinced of some of it (Anon. 1998, p. 2).

Mohammad was not politically orientated, especially during his teenage years, believing instead Muslims should concentrate on spiritual affairs. However, his encounters with HT provided him with a new cognitive perspective that gave him a greater impetus to engage in political activism. However, this radical change should not be confused with politicisation, because the latter pertains to a social, economic or legal issue that has become political in nature, making people become active over that issue, but not making them seek to change the whole social order. In contrast, HT radicalisation is stimulated by a cognitive change at the root of one's identity, which creates a new social perspective. For instance, this newfound outlook inspired powerful emotions in Mohammad, most notably deep frustration in not finding a place within British society. On the other hand, an individual who becomes frustrated could just as well become involved with non-radical politics. To choose to become a HT radical requires sufficient motivation. However motivation is still not enough. The radical would also need the opportunity to join HT, and be accepted. As Wiktorowicz (2005, p. 127) describes, before the group can reformat the viewpoint of the perspective recruit, a 'cognitive opening' must be made in which the recruit is prepared to expose themselves to the ideology of the group. At this stage, HT seek to build a connection between the social problems experienced by the recruit and the solutions group membership will generate for them in their social life (for example, empowerment). This allows the individual to derive their sense of identity, at least in part, from the collective group identity (Knutson, 1973). The group is a powerful force that imposes conformity, which in turn assimilates the novice as a fully functioning member. Taken as a whole, the theory of HT radicalisation will encompass individual and collective life, identifying the shifting patterns of behaviour that take place at the root of a personality.

Agency and Ideology: Differing Modes of Agency in HT

A large part of my fieldwork on HT radicalisation entailed accumulating personal narratives. Many recurring themes emerged from these personal narratives, but one particularly vivid and consistent issue emphasised by most, if not all the respondents, concerned 'agency'. Although, I talk about agency in subsequent chapters, it is worth prompting an introductory discussion about agency here that explains its theoretical framing within the spectre of HT radicalisation. At the heart of the debate about HT radicalisation is whether or not HT activists are free agents in the radicalisation process. According to Sen (1985, p. 204), agency relates to 'what a person is free to do and achieve in pursuit of whatever goals or values he or she regards as important'. In this sense, agency is general, applying to individuals in different social settings. I do not wish to get diverted further by trying to conceptualise agency in more depth, as there is little agreement amongst scholars on this debate, as human 'agency' is a highly complex phenomenon. Instead, I want to examine the interconnection between HT ideology and agency.

Dreze and Sen (1995, p. 104) believe that participation within groups is a direct expression of human agency. The agency for HT activists relates to their capacity to make choices and to implement those choices in reality. In other words, HT activists make their decision to join the group; it is an act of a free agent, who can leave at any point. However, as the case studies in the book will illustrate, structural forces play a key role in influencing HT activist choices. HT recruiters, for example, often argue that joining HT is a religious obligation in which one has no choice but to comply with this religious commandment. In reality, structural strains do not exclusively determine a member's pathway, despite the activist being contained within a system that imposes a worldview onto them, because they control their choices. Therefore, a balance between structure and agency exists. So, a HT activist may be influenced by structural forces, but they are capable of removing themselves from the social structures they are embedded within. In particular, as the narratives in the case studies will show, the recruits took time grappling with their decision to join HT, and in some cases members choose to leave the group.

Within HT, however, joint forms of agency are often constructed, in which a member builds his or her identity in conformity with HT ideology. According to Allport (1924, p. 6), 'there is no psychology of groups which is not essentially and entirely a psychology of individuals'. However, HT is more than the sum of its parts (for example, the members that make it up). For instance, the group, in one sense, is nothing but the members who have joined, but it is also much more than the aggregate of individuals. Through their interactions over time, their social structures, rules, roles and shared understandings are collectively created, and these in turn shape members' responses. This view presents a problem for determining the extent to which the properties of HT membership can be reduced to individual agency. Tajfel (1981) provides some insights into this problem by making a critical distinction between agency and group identities. According to Tajfel (1981), social identity is influenced by a continuum of interaction, which, on one end, is governed by the membership of various groups and, at the other, is directed more by human agency.

In this book, I construct a picture of HT radicalisation, which essentially reduces the phenomenon of HT recruitment to a specific demographic constituency. Even though the evidence I have accumulated clearly shows that HT is predominately represented by middle class Asians, who share a common set of social experiences and problems, there is a need to consider other variables. In theory, ideology should play an important role in attracting individuals to HT. According to Wilkinson (1974, p. 133), Islamic activism cannot be fully grasped unless one accounts for the development of a radical's ideology, belief and life-style. Activists are seen as free agents, as Crenshaw (1981, p. 10) contends, who act on rational choices. However, Crenshaw (1981, p. 10) believes that terrorism is not committed by individuals, but 'by groups who reach collective decisions based on commonly held beliefs'. This analytical approach tends to reduce the rational characteristics of free agents to the group, as group goals are seen through the narrow lenses of collective rationality. This approach ignores the individual, which should be the primary measure of analysis, especially if one seeks to understand why some young Muslims are drawn to HT.

Ideology and agency, if one goes beyond recruitment, should play a role in keeping activists with HT. A salient feature of attachment to HT ideology is the creation of a 'we' versus 'them' dichotomy. From a social context, it is beneficial for people to seek out attachments to groups because groups offer protection in unfamiliar and hostile settings. In this respect, members are drawn to HT to secure specific social needs. Amongst these fundamental needs are recognition, security and identity. During my experience with the group, when the members failed to attain these needs from society, they became frustrated, which in turn caused them to develop a deep psychological need for a sense of belonging. Consequently, within HT, the members swiftly developed a distrust of non-believers and began breeding a hostile identity towards them. According to Dawud (ex-member, 34), 'the members constantly malign the Kufr [non-Muslims], while not understanding that Islam came for the whole of mankind'. By developing an ideology around 'we-ness', a member is made aware that beyond HT is a 'they' that constitutes the dominant culture. This distinction between themselves and the larger society allows HT to shape members' ideologies and identities, which plays a significant role in the very being and functioning of HT. In other words, members adjust their sense of identity – their thoughts and behaviours – to match the collectively defined ideology of HT.

Summary

The issue of how to define radicalisation is subject to much debate, making it impossible to avoid but, beyond the discussion of usage, lies the more difficult question of the nature of the phenomenon itself. However, the two debates, over terminology and analytical understanding, are in many ways inseparable. It is clear radicalisation is a growing problem amongst some young British Muslims, but one cannot attribute the underlying causes of this phenomenon to a single trigger or theory. As explained earlier, radicalisation is a transformative process, taking place at the root of the personality whereby an individual adopts a radical new outlook. Some studies suggest radicalisation incorporates several phases: pre-radicalisation, self-identification, indoctrination and militancy (NYPD 2007, p. 3). After surveying the available literature, it is relatively clear that most scholars agree radicalisation involves three fundamental ingredients: (1) individual change; (2) interaction with social environments and external situations; and (3) contact with radical actors and groups. As Segeman (2007, p. 3) points out, within these transformative phases individuals develop negative associations (for example, discrimination or social deprivation), which distort their reading of the social world, making them susceptible to radical groups. Importantly, it is worth noting these phases are not necessarily sequential or transparent in nature, as they greatly depend on the contextual realities and experiences of the individual. Furthermore, there is general acknowledgement amongst most theorists that identifying generic profiles of radicals is unreliable and problematic (Home Office 2005, p. 31). A cursory look at Islamic radicals reveals their 'normality'.

At first sight, it might be difficult to rationalise why seemingly 'normal' young Muslims in Britain join radical groups, like HT. According to Devji (2005, p. 20), radical behaviour and identities diverge in accordance with the plethora of reasons for joining radical Islamist groups. It is apparent Muslims in this part of the world contend with an array of issues concerning 'identity, the adaptation of religio-cultural norms and values, and issues of everyday citizenship' (Abbas 2007, p. 3). Radicalisation is a multifaceted phenomenon, which in turn, raises questions concerning 'whether Muslims can be or are willing to be integrated into European society and political values' (Modood 2005, p. viii). In particular, two identifiable conditions are commonly cited as catalysts for radicalisation: discrimination and deprivation. Despite the fact these two interrelated conditions have been developed and argued within a specific socio-political and economic frame, they do not deplete the entire range of literature. In other words, radicalisation seemingly appears to flourish amongst those who experience political, social and economic dislocation. In order to unlock the deeper facets of HT radicalisation required carrying out extensive fieldwork. For that reason, as the next two chapters reveal, I examined the social realities and backgrounds of HT activists. This provided insight into the trajectories taken by young HT activists. In Chapter 7, I present findings of the social base of HT and thus attempt to answer why a specific social demographic is disproportionately drawn to HT radicalisation. The fieldwork is critical as it will substantiate a great deal of the early observations I have made.

Chapter 5

Radical Pathways I: Profiles of Male HT Members

When reading the newspapers today it is difficult not to be confronted with examples of Islamic radicalism. One might recall the 2010 European terror plot[1] (The *Washington Post*, 29 September 2010), or that of Roshonara Choudhry, a student from East London, who attempted to murder British MP Stephen Timms in 2010 (The *Guardian*, 2 November 2010). Social scientists do not attribute these disturbing incidents to a single observable cause, except perhaps for their acknowledgment that radicalisation constitutes a distinct and real change in the individual (Crenshaw, 1981; Hoffman, 1998; Roy, 2004). One of the issues I will need to investigate in this chapter, as I think about the causes of radicalisation, is whether the motives and pathways of Islamic radicals can be sketched out. It should be emphasised, however, that my empirical research does not aim to investigate radicalism merely as a psychological process, but to analyse how the radicals' attitudes were affected by the world around them. Without wishing to pre-empt a necessary discussion of these issues, my research in this chapter can be characterised as a case study of male members of HT. Personal accounts of, and reflections on, the radicalisation process are replete with stories of members '*finding themselves*'. Clearly, one could not hope to provide a definitive explanation of radicalisation, but these reflective accounts have the advantage of making the social world of the radical open to investigation.

The Context of the Case Studies

The studies reported in this chapter are set in the national context of Britain, a country struggling with radicalisation. Some political commentators believe the message of HT, for example, 'is attracting more and more young Muslims, and this is worrying Britain's wider Islamic community' (*Newsnight* Report, 27 August 2003). HT tends to operate in a clandestine and murky manner, which makes an investigation into its activities difficult. However, in this book, I will provide detailed analysis of several selected case studies by which, it is hoped, the process of radicalisation may be better understood. Two main case studies are

---

1 The 2010 European terror plot was a plan to launch 'commando-style' attacks in Britain and France ('CIA acts on fear of Al-Qaeda plot to hit in Europe', The *Washington Post*, 29 September 2010).

presented in this chapter, each of which could in itself provide a good starting point for a discussion of the development of radicalisation. Each is like a sketch, from a particular perspective, of a partially glimpsed event. These sketches, or cases, relate and overlap, but they are not reducible to a single view. And, although, when combined, they offer the beginnings of a complete description, my knowledge of the whole is still imperfect. The meaning and significance of these cases will become clearer as each is developed and interpreted. But the cases are not self-contained. Each takes as its focus a different aspect of the same whole process. Each draws upon the same essential phenomenon – the process of radicalisation.

After interviewing and observing 28 respondents, my findings have uncovered some common themes. A recurring theme, which emerged in the accounts from my respondents, is that of identity; and how their current identities seemed greatly dependent on their past and present experiences. Although, I was not surprised that this topic came up so frequently, it was difficult to deal with because identity is crafted from many different sources. Thus, a number of themes and issues must be discussed to reveal the importance of the social settings in which my respondents are embedded. Some respondents, for example, concentrated particularly on race and ethnicity, but other respondents picked up on other features such as religion, home environment and family background, class, and so on. The goal of my research is to map out the 'turning-point moments' in the lives of HT members who have undergone a life-altering experience. Consequently, each of the radicals interviewed exhibits a distinct social world of lived experience. Therefore, the two accounts that have been selected may seem somewhat dramatic, but they offer me a glimpse into the construction of an HT radical in different social settings and from rather different perspectives.

Case Study One – Abdul

Abdul, 27, is a senior software engineer living in London, and is a member of HT. In order to understand why Abdul, at the age of nineteen, joined HT requires dissecting the narratives of his past. This case study explores the impact of change and transition on the subject during specific stages of his life-cycle development. Many social theorists have pointed out the complexities and diversities of youth transitions to adulthood. The paradoxes that young Muslims have to cope with on a day-to-day basis are immense. As Abdul explained: 'integrating into a society, where the culture and viewpoint is different, is impossible'. To some extent, this somewhat bleak view may be traced to Abdul's upbringing in an isolated community that was predominantly white. This makes understanding his early social interaction crucial, because individuals belonging to minority groups may develop multiple pathways to adulthood.

Home Environment: Family Life

Historically, traditional Pakistani families tend to exhibit similar features, which typically consist of several generations living together within the same household (Anwar, 1976). The family is usually patriarchal, with elder males dominating the social affairs of the family. Within any family structure, children are considered as dependents, making them subject to parental control and authority. In other words, the family is a very important social institution, acting as the means by which persons inherit religious and class identity. So what role did Abdul's family life play in shaping his identity? Firstly, as a child Abdul did not experience severe family disruption or upheaval, as he suggested: 'my home life was stable, loving and quite normal'. In dealing with Abdul's family life, it is clear that his parents created a stable and caring home environment in which he received love and encouragement. Secondly, one must understand the patterns of interaction among family members in different generations because this will provide insight into the customs and beliefs transmitted between one generation and another of Abdul's family:

> My parents were not a traditional Pakistani family. Of course, they wanted us [children] to have an appreciation of our cultural heritage, but like most parents they found it difficult to pass on their beliefs. For instance, none of my brothers and I can speak Urdu. Also, my parents were very secular and for them religion was not an important part of life. So, they'd drink at social occasions, we'd celebrate Christmas. And, in relation to Islam, we were not taught how to pray nor did we fast at Ramadan. [Did your parents try to enforce any subcontinent values or customs?] Yes. My parents were quite traditional when it came to having girlfriends, for example, so we had to hide that from them … They'd want us to be connected more to our culture but they couldn't enforce it because there were too many contradictions with their beliefs and our beliefs. (Abdul; Interview 1, 5 November 2004).

To some extent, Abdul and his parents have different cultural standpoints. His parents appear concerned with the continuity of cultural values, which they inherited in Pakistan, while Abdul is attempting to establish independence from his parents' value system. More importantly, his parents appear to construct tradition differently, when compared with other Pakistani parents. The background of his parents may offer an explanation for this perceived difference. Firstly, both his parents are university graduates, albeit from Pakistan, which gave them greater opportunities when they settled in the UK. His mother, for example, is a regional manager for a small UK-based firm and his father is a senior accountant for a large commercial bank in the city. Secondly, because of his parents' secular beliefs they seem more willing to adopt the values of the majority culture, unlike working-class Pakistani parents who often remain more attached to their cultural and religious heritage (Lewis, 2002). Abdul explains, for example, that his mother 'rarely wore traditional Pakistani dress, except for special occasions' (Abdul; Interview 1, 5 November 2004).

Family Lifestyle and Class

Like most children, Abdul's lifestyle was dependent on his parents' income and their decisions about how that income should be spent.

> I received a weekly allowance when I was younger, but that was dependent on good behaviour and keeping my room tidy. I could spend the money on anything I wanted, but most of the time my parents would buy us gifts and stuff we wanted like football shirts and sports equipment etc. ... my father had a tendency to spoil us.

In the context of a labour market, Abdul's class position can be measured in terms of the income and wealth enjoyed by his parents. His parents have gained upward social mobility through education, occupation and property. As Abdul described, 'By the time I was four or five my parents had bought another house so we had a relatively lavish lifestyle'. When his parents entered the social hierarchy, as immigrants, they were positioned near the bottom. They improved their social position mainly through occupation and they 'invested in shares' when the government privatised state industries. As a result of all these factors, Abdul's parents' social status improved throughout the course of his life. Moreover, Abdul thinks of himself as middle class, as he stated: 'I consider myself middle class because of my parent's social standing'.

Social Environment: School

An examination of Abdul's social life will show the differences that exist between the home environment and the social environment. Although, both are interconnected, it is important to isolate the way each impacted his identity. Abdul described with vivid detail his early childhood experiences, as he commented:

> When I was young, everything was ok; I had no Muslim friends, but felt perfectly normal, even though all my friends were white. But everything changed at secondary school; when we moved to a different area, it was a complete shake-up. I'd never been called a Paki in my life, but it soon became a regular occurrence. I remember the first time I experienced racism; being called a Paki at age eleven is a hard thing to deal with. At first I became ashamed of who I was, I wanted to be normal and normal meant being white ... so I felt like an outsider, which made me feel depressed. As time went on I hated myself; then, I hated those kids that abused me, until I started ignoring it, and that's when you get accustomed to it [racism] ... So I kept to myself, making friends with Asians

– we understood each other, because anyone non-white was a victim. (Abdul; Interview 1, 5 November 2004)

Abdul mentioned that he found it easier to mix with white children at primary school, but then found it increasingly difficult at secondary school. This begs the question, what changed? His primary school was located in an affluent area outside of London, but his parents decided to move to London in order to gain access to better resources. As Abdul suggested: 'My parents moved to a large house, but unknowingly enrolled me in a nearby school that was very close to a council estate, full of working class yobs'. Thus, at primary school, Abdul developed a sense of shared identity, an 'us' which contained his early patterns of interaction with other children. As he explained: 'I got on well with them [whites] at primary school' (Abdul; Interview 1, 5 November 2004). In contrast, when he moved to secondary school, he encountered, for the first time, considerable racism. In Abdul's case, racism was perceived as a shared way of behaving, especially amongst his fellow classmates. It is apparent that not all norms are shared, and that people see different norms as requiring different degrees of adherence. Yet, Abdul does not accept this; he believes 'they're all racist … some just hide it better' (Abdul; Interview 1, 5 November 2004).

Abdul was not discriminated against purely because of his racial composition, as he asserted: 'They hated me because I was seen as a rich Paki, which made them hate me even more since they were all poor'. Abdul's exclusion from the dominant social group was a source of conflict and tension for him at school. However, before examining this issue, it is important to understand why his parents seemed unaware of the negative school environment. Abdul reflects on this point, as he stated:

My parents were very naïve about schooling in the west, their education took place in Pakistan and so they were influenced by the Raj mentality … they had no comprehension of the social conditions of the area, they thought that Britain was a magical place where all people sought academic excellence.

To some degree, Abdul places the lack of parental involvement in context, but what he does not mention here is his own lack of communication. He failed to express to his parents the feelings of exclusion and harassment that he was experiencing, as he suggests, because he did not 'want to worry them or involve them' in his problems.

Returning to the issue of exclusion, it is very difficult to address the multitude of problems that Abdul experienced, but it is important to understand the origins of his exclusion and the effects it had on his development. Children began to exclude Abdul on the basis of his race, ethnicity and class. Recent research in the field of developmental psychology has focused on peer rejection and peer victimisation in the context of exclusion from social groups (Graham and Juvonen, 1998). These studies have shown that children, like Abdul, who are rejected from social groups experience 'self-destructive' tendencies (Chansky, 2001). For example, young people who are rejected by social groups are at risk of poor academic achievement, increased depression and delinquency (Chibucos, 2005). Did Abdul experience any of these negative conditions? In Abdul's account, he does not cite any circumstance of poor academic achievement or delinquency. On the contrary, his grades were excellent and he never received any bad reports from school concerning behaviour. This is testimony to his positive home environment, which provided a sense of order and motivation, and which allowed him to achieve high grades.

However, it is clear that Abdul became frustrated when his fellow classmates did not consider him 'normal'. His expectations evaporated, and he forcibly adjusted his personality to cope with his hostile surroundings. He expressed passive anger towards those who were responsible, which was then displaced towards his family members. As he says: 'I don't know why, but I'd take out my frustrations on my parents. They were an easy target and, perhaps, there was a sub-conscious hate there for being Pakistani; I'm not sure' (Abdul; Interview 1, 5 November 2004). This frustration was eventually directed towards those culpable; but it was a passive response, which then became indifference by his acceptance of being an outsider. During early socialisation, racism is extremely destructive, especially for the victim, as it emasculates a person. This was certainly the case for Abdul, who, as the victim, suffered by believing the distortions that were created. This had an adverse effect on his identity development.

Identity, Rejection and Exclusion

A recurring theme in Abdul's childhood was his inability to resolve the question of his identity. At first, he found it very difficult to understand, responding immediately by forming a closer association with his ethnicity. He made friends with Asians and began to distance himself from British culture by supporting the Pakistan cricket team. As he explained:

> The day I realised I wasn't British was the day a few of my friends were set upon by a gang of white youths. Being called a Paki was normal, but being physically attacked, because you're not white, was shocking! That's when I started hating everything British; I stopped supporting England and started supporting Pak-land at cricket. I felt helpless and angry. I just wanted to be around my own people, if you know what I mean, but I was trapped among a population of racist thugs. (Abdul; Interview 1, 5 November 2004)

Throughout Abdul's schooling social groups excluded him, because he did not conform to the expectations of the group, and these expectations reflect criteria regarding group membership, such as race and class. This form of rejection was not a result of his lack of social skills but was an outcome of prejudice and stereotyping. It is important to find out how Abdul evaluates the social events, issues, and transgressions he experienced:

I felt completely alienated and frustrated from British culture, my school, and friends [why your friends?] They were Asian, so they acted like Pakis. They saw me as a coconut, white on the inside and brown on the outside. And to tell you the truth I felt much more alienated from them.

Abdul's reactionary attempts to disassociate himself from British culture were based on localised triggers. From his remarks, one can identify three social contexts; friends, peer group and school. Abdul found it extremely difficult to adjust to these settings. In relation to the peer group that rejected him, he embraced a form of defiance: 'If you don't want me, then I'll go to someone that will' (Abdul; Interview 1, 5 November 2004). Witnessing racial violence in the form of an unprovoked physical attack only accelerated his exclusion, as he suggested: 'After the attack I never felt British again. [Did you want to punish those responsible?] Yeah, but they were much older and I feared the consequences'. Although Abdul did not act on his desire to seek retribution, it is clear that if he could have hurt the culprits without any form of reprisals, then he would have no moral objection to violence. Thus, this would indicate that the effects of adverse socialisation, like exclusion, could lead to increased instances of aggression and violence. Abdul showed a strong desire to punish and hurt those responsible for inflicting suffering, in order to restore the imbalance of his feeling powerless. From a psychological perspective, it appears that Abdul could not express his feelings and emotions after the attack, which may have forced him to cope with the situation by internalising his anger. Thus, a negative identity was created. Negative identity is the perceived notion that an individual develops a covert antagonistic rejection of the roles and rules laid out for them by their family, community and society (Knutson, 1981).

It is clear that Abdul's identity is greatly influenced by his rejection from social groups. He slowly felt alienated; his rejection of British culture was a formal divorce from society. However, after a long family trip to Pakistan he returned even more disconnected and disillusioned, as he described:

I was looking forward to our family trip to Paki-land, but as soon as I got off the plane and onto the runway, I realised that Paki-land was a complete s**thole. Out there, I realised that I hated Pakistan more than England. Everything was foreign: the people, the food, the language. I couldn't fit in and, worse than that, they would call me *Gora* [white person], because I couldn't speak Paki. That drove me over the edge; I felt rejected; what was I? I wasn't English and I wasn't Pakistani; Islam had no role in my life at the time, so I was lost. So, in answer to your question, ethnicity to me is an empty concept; I realised that at age fifteen. (Abdul; Interview 1, 5 November 2004)

His visit had illustrated the complete lack of association with Pakistani culture – he did not speak Urdu, nor could he understand the cultural and traditional differences. The trip to Pakistan made him feel even more isolated and excluded.

Inevitably, Abdul became deeply cynical and hateful, and this only furthered his withdrawal from society, especially with his Asian friends. As he commented:

> When I came back [from Pakistan] I just became unsociable. I only had contact with my friends at school, because I just didn't feel comfortable; they were Asian, and I just was incapable of understanding them. So, I retreated to my home that was my only sanctuary ... [Did you feel alienated?] Of course I did. I wasn't British; I wasn't Pakistani or Asian; so what was I? I didn't have a clue; I couldn't answer that question. (Abdul; Interview 1, 5 November 2004)

A primary function of early socialisation is to integrate the individual into the cultural norms of the society to which he or she resides, which would entail the roles they are to play in life. However, Abdul's passive rejection of these forms resulted in the adoption of an opposing behaviour pattern. Abdul's voluntary rejection of his nationality had excluded him from society, making him susceptible to radicalisation. Socialisation is an essential process of personality formation, and if it is conceived wrongly it will lead to the individual's estrangement from society. Also, it is important to illustrate that Abdul completely rejected his ethnic tradition; this was manifested in a total revolt against the traditional language, feeling disconnected from his Asian friends and, thus, leading to a withdrawal from sub-continent culture. After completing his A-levels, he went to university, and there he encountered Muslims for the first time. This initial encounter enabled Abdul to forge strong relationships, providing him with a perceived sense of belonging.

Encountering HT: The 'Turning Point'

Radicalisation is a highly complex process, for Abdul it involved a major life change. In fact, apart from the changes one undergoes during infancy and adolescence, it is unlikely that Abdul will experience greater changes at any other stage in his life cycle. So, how can we understand such a fundamental shift in his personality development, and make sense of the effects that they have had upon him? In general, there are two distinct methods I can use to account for Abdul's radicalisation. Firstly, I can look to theory to establish the strength of different theoretical notions and approaches to radicalisation. Secondly, I can look at the empirical evidence collected from my interview with Abdul, which provided me with a factual base upon which to make an assessment of his life cycle. However, it should be noted that it is my view that neither approach can provide a complete answer, but they will yield some valuable insight into the process of radicalisation.

University Life – Peer Groups

As Abdul's initial accounts have described, his route towards adulthood was far from straightforward. However, he saw university as an opportunity to start afresh, but his newfound independence was a daunting prospect at first. As he explained:

> I was really looking forward to moving out of my parents' house and going to live on my own at university. My first few weeks, however, were a little unsettled. I'd never lived away from home. So I felt homesick, but that changed when I met the brothers [members of HT].

Many students consider the first year to be one of the hardest, because a lot of adjustments have to be made. In Abdul's case, he was leaving home for the first time and naturally suffered from a bit of homesickness. He suddenly found himself missing the familiarity of home, and did not know quite how to cope with the resulting emotions. This is entirely normal, especially in the first few weeks, and often students long for the secure and the familiar. However, during this period of uncertainty, it is quite significant that Abdul encounters HT:

> I was headed towards the canteen, when I saw a mass of students gathered around outside. To my surprise a few Muslims had a *dawah* (preaching) stall outside and they were debating issues that were totally foreign to me. I didn't know they were members nor did I know about Hizb ut-Tahrir ... I was really impressed by them. After the stall I met with a couple of members, we went to their halls and had some food. I remember we had a long discussion about my purpose in life, and to tell you the truth I'd never really thought about it ... I started to meet with the brothers regularly after that, we became very close. The brothers helped me a lot; for instance, they taught me how to pray. It was a real turning point in my life, so I am very grateful to Allah [God] for guiding me to the truth.

A couple of key points emerge from the above account: first, the creation of a peer group, and second the transition towards greater religiosity. In Abdul's biography, it is important to consider his university friendships, because on the surface these ties appear to be freely chosen. How he forms his friendships, what activities he engages in, who his friends are, all seem to be extremely relevant to the radicalisation process. Firstly, Abdul is able to form successful relationships with his university peers, spending an ever-increasing amount of time with his friends. As he recalls, 'I know it sounds bad, but I hardly went back home to visit my family ... I'd do everything with the brothers from cooking to washing my clothes'. The role played by peers during this period of Abdul's life is very critical. To some degree, the peer group replaces parental influence, allowing for a transfer in closeness from parents to peers. As Howe (2010) points out, teenagers spend twice as much of their time with peers as with parents. He suggests that the influence of peer groups becomes stronger when family relationships are not supportive, turning young people to a peer group for emotional comfort.

As the amount of time spent with peers' increases, so does the influence and support they provide. So, why is Abdul attracted to the peer group? Peer groups provide a sense of identity and belonging. On the surface, Abdul's peer group opted to associate with each other based on a common identification with Islam. Young people tend to be friends with those who are most like them, which explains Abdul's attraction to the members. Indeed, recent research has shown that socio-demographic characteristics are key components in peer group formation (Way and Hamm, 2005). Thus, what is the composition of Abdul's peer group? According to Abdul:

> The brothers' backgrounds were very similar to mine … they came from all across the country … I'm fairly sure they were all middle-class because their parents were doctors, accountants or teachers. I had this very superficial worldview growing up that Pakistanis were all poor and unemployed, and that my family was the only well-off family. But the brothers were just like me … we even had similar experiences growing-up [Racial harassment?] Yes. So the brothers, like me, suffered from racism. If I'm honest, I think some had it far worse than me.

It is quite apparent that the peer group attracted the same types of individuals. These individuals emerged from similar social, cultural and economic backgrounds. More broadly, living away from home at university enabled Abdul to develop greater autonomy, which enabled him to see situations from another person's point of view. Therefore, as Abdul's account shows, class and ethnicity were important features in patterning his friendships, but perhaps the most crucial structural feature was religion.

The Role of Religion

There is a long history in Abdul's account of things not being quite what they first seemed. His biographical insight of the radicalisation process is jam-packed with 'turning points'. In its simplest form, this term can be understood as a pivotal moment that shapes one's life. In trying to uncover the various turning points Abdul experiences in his life, I realised that more attention needed to be paid to the role of religion. As his early biography indicated, although he emerged from a very non-religious household, he had the potential for religiosity. As he commented, 'I grew up knowing nothing about Islam, which is sad. But I do remember, as a child, having a strong craving to learn more about my religion'. However, Abdul experiences an abrupt intensification of religiosity after just four weeks of attending university. The intensity and tempo of the religious awakening, from a non-religious state, in Abdul's personal life becomes quickly visible; increased attention to religious practices, greater emphasis on Islamic dress and custom. So what triggered this seemingly spontaneous intensification of religiosity?

Religious Change

One thing that emerges strongly from Abdul's account is a sense of acceptance which he received from his peers. However, does this properly explain his heightened state of religiosity? Abdul firmly believes that his religious enlightenment took shape within an intellectual framework. As he described:

> In Islam, a Muslim cannot arrive at faith through imitation. In contrast, to other religions, the Islamic *Aqeedah* (doctrine) is *attasdiq al-jazim* (decisive belief). So, in regards to myself, I became convinced through rational proofs. I was pushed to think about existence for the first time, so I started to think about what came before this life and what will come after it ... As soon as I realised Islam was the truth, I knew that I had to live my life according to it, so this realisation was reached through rational thinking.

As you can see, there is a richness and complexity to Abdul's account, forcing me to concentrate on some key themes. Firstly, many religious experiences invoke the feelings of being 'called' or 'chosen' by a higher power. In spite of this, Abdul never refers to himself as someone who has been appointed. His experiences are more closely related to the phenomenon of conversion, because he seemingly undergoes a sudden transformation.

However, Abdul's instance that his religious transformation was firmly embedded within the intellectual greatly undervalues the eschatological influences of HT rhetoric and ideology. From an eschatological perspective, HT seeks to connect individual behaviour and actions to the afterlife, or more significantly the '*Qiyamah*' (Day of Judgment). This connection to the afterlife is critical, because it allows HT to apply fear of punishment in the afterlife as a way to influence actions in the present. Therefore, if a recruit wishes to gain salvation in the next life, then he or she must work for HT. The fear of punishment in the afterlife has mixed responses, as one member suggested: 'if the shab (novice) has a religious basis then you can link their actions to jannah (Heaven) and Jahannam (Hell) ... but if there not religious then you need to convince them through social ills'. This would indicate that some novices are coerced by the fear of punishment. Therefore, Abdul, who had a religious awaking through the HT peer group, was influenced by the fear of the afterlife and joining HT was connected to the eschatological.

Secondly, Abdul reduces this process to the cognitive aspect, leaving the impression that his religious experience was distinctly private and individualistic. In reality, his religious experience takes root through the interaction of the public and private spheres. In particular, the transformation is experienced in the context of the peer group. Abdul stresses how he was part of a group, in which the brothers would 'hang out' and talk to each other about Islam. Therefore, even though Abdul spent a considerable amount of his time mulling over his existence, this was not without its social dimension. In other words, a social encounter occurs in which Abdul, the religious seeker, meets and interacts with HT members who seemingly have already found the answers to the questions being asked. Thirdly, as the religious transformation progressed, Abdul was encouraged to engage in further study of the party culture and to cut off his contact with non-Muslims who might deplete his new-found beliefs.[2] As Abdul makes clear: 'my behaviour completely changed when I became practising ... for instance, my classmates found it strange when I stopped mixing with them'. The 'turning away' from one's past life and behaviour could indicate that Abdul finally became 'converted' or 'practising'.

Radicalisation

In this section, I want to look at radicalisation from a group perspective. This will help me to understand why HT affected Abdul so strongly. It is very difficult to establish when Abdul developed into a radical, because radicalisation might be conceived as a continuing process. As he explained:

> I think after seven or eight weeks I joined the party. I was invited after some discussion to *Halaqah*. At this point, everything was new. In many ways, I was a blank canvas ... and that's why it took me a few months to carry *Dawah*, because I wanted to be fully convinced. [Convinced of Islam or HT?] Both.

A brief glimpse into Abdul's early university life revealed that he was not fully radicalised until he joined HT. For the moment, I want to consider what happened to Abdul's identity when he started to attend *Halaqah*. Abdul described the *Halaqah* as a 'deep and profound culturing experience', giving him a totally new cognitive perspective with which to view the social world. This would indicate that, first of all, the *Halaqah* was the basis for the creation of Abdul's new cognitive perspective, as his personal identity gives way to the group identity. Abdul explained that the *Halaqah* would be used, as the fundamental process to ensure that both the '*Aqlya*' (mentality) and the '*Nafsyya*' (disposition) of the novices were radically transformed.

The *Halaqah* was used to indoctrinate Abdul with a new belief system, awakening in him a host of feelings and ideas entirely different from those to which he was accustomed. As he explained:

---

2   This attempt to control the social environment of a recruit is very similar to the indoctrination tactics used by cults. Singer (1995) points out that 'cults have used tactics of coercive mind control to negatively impact victims'. It has been argued that cults often use behaviour modification techniques on recruits. For instance, Hassan (2001) suggests that 'thought-stopping tactics' and installing an 'us-versus-them' mindset help to coerce the person into joining the group.

> When I started to study the culture [HT] it immediately had an impact. My parents quickly noticed a difference in my behaviour and personality. [What was their reaction to you joining HT?] It was very negative. I had a big clash with my father, our viewpoints were totally at odds, and so it caused problems.

The short-term effects of the indoctrination programme could be seen once Abdul returned home. The conflicts at home pushed Abdul to isolate himself from his family, alienating him from his previous group memberships. As Abdul's case has shown, given the intensive challenges he received to his newfound beliefs, it was not surprising that he emerged stronger and unchanged. This shows the strong interplay between individuals and groups, which enabled HT to permanently change Abdul's identity.

Case Study Two – Tariq

Tariq, 26, is a successful computer analyst living in Berkshire, and is an active member of HT. The purpose of this case study is to provide a personalised explanation of how he joined HT. A biographical study of HT members is fascinating not only because it has the potential to tell us so much about the processes of radicalisation, but because it can also tell us so much about the early social life of members. Like all life histories, Tariq's account is actively woven together to tell a story from his life experiences. This type of approach has been necessary in order to draw out more clearly some of the differences and commonalities that exist between HT members. Having identified the focus for the case study, the next step will be to develop a precise understanding of how Tariq came to construct his identity and how this, in turn, made him susceptible to radicalisation.

Home Environment: Family Life, Class and Upbringing

Tariq, a British-born Muslim of mixed-race, found it very difficult to come to terms with his own ethnicity. He talked, for example, about the way his identity had to be formed from fragmented sources. As he described:

> My dad is Pakistani and my mum is [a non-Muslim] English [white]. So I felt out of place in family situations as a kid. I'd be conscious of my fair skin when I was with my dad's family. My parents never understood … I couldn't explain it to them. I was different from them. I wasn't fully Pakistani or English. (Tariq; Interview 2, 7 November 2004)

This brief glimpse into Tariq's early experiences reveals how difficult it was for him to integrate contradictory parts of his identity into a coherent whole. We see, in this extract, neither his mother nor father were capable of empathic understanding, because they are not mixed-race. His parents failed to provide

Tariq with all the cultural knowledge necessary to construct his identity as mixed-race. As several social theorists have noted, unless a unified perception of the child is maintained, ethnicity can become a constant worry (Wetherell, 1987; Jenkins, 2004). Research on parents in an Asian-white marriage has focused on the need to foster a multi-cultural behavioural range in order to guarantee their multi-racial children's survival (Piscacek and Golub, 1973). The awareness of being different in physical complexion from the rest of the family reinforced Tariq's feelings of 'not belonging'. In adult life, ethnicity is still a salient feature of his identity. He told me, even though he has both Pakistani and English heritage, he never found complete acceptance in either community. As Wilson (1987) points out, mixed-race children find it difficult to balance between majority values and minority culture.

Family Conflict – Religious Identity

The years from about the ages of six to twelve were very important in the development of Tariq's identity. During these years, he became aware of the religious and cultural differences between his parents. As Tariq explained:

> My parents always fought about how to raise us [Tariq and two younger siblings]. I'd be forced to take sides … Eventually, I became closer to my dad, so I started to go to the Mosque with him, which upset my mum. Ironically, back then my father was not that religious – he was influenced by Paki pride. [What do you mean?] His sons couldn't be Christians, that'd bring shame on the family.

By not being able to involve Tariq in both sides of their religious heritage – such as celebrating religious events – his parents made him feel marginalised. This feeling of exclusion experienced within the family setting greatly impeded his relationship with his mother. As Tariq explained, '… my mother was distant. All day she'd go on about how much she had to suffer from my dad and his family, so she'd take it out on us [Tariq and his siblings]'. According to Knowles and Cole (1990, p. 161), if a mother's efforts are rejected it can lead to a vicious cycle in which the mother feels emotionally wounded. Some social theorists argue that conflict and frustration is natural in the mother-son dynamic because mothers misunderstand what their sons need (Smith, 1997). In other words, when adolescent boys conceal their vulnerability, mothers can mistake this emotional posturing for masculinity.

In family gatherings, the religious beliefs of Tariq's mother were often degraded and stigmatised. This unsettled environment made forming a coherent religious identity for Tariq more challenging than for those adolescents in non-mixed religious households. As a result, he experienced a period of confusion and exploration before accepting a religion. As he explained,

> I really started to ask myself what religion I should belong to, but I had no help from my parents … they just wanted me to follow them blindly. So, I really felt lost and confused.

It is very important to help children of mixed religious heritage to understand that they are part of both groups, allowing them to ask questions about their identity. In Tariq's case, when family conflict arose, his parents expected him to categorise himself into one specific religion, not accepting that he could belong to two. This prejudice was reinforced in family gatherings, for example, spending time with his father's relatives helped skew his view of Christianity. Tariq was greatly inspired by hearing his uncles' and grandparent's accounts about Islam, but this overlooked his mother's religious and cultural heritage.

Living between two religious traditions had shaped some of Tariq's values and beliefs. However, family conflict over religion pushed him away from religion as he grew up. As he mentioned:

> My dad just wanted me to be Muslim, so I accepted that. But I was not religious. I never prayed, fasted or cared about Islam. I saw religion as something bad; it caused so many problems at home … So, I considered myself Muslim in name only.

To some extent, this period marked a time of exploration of different ways of looking at his religious and racial identity. Raised Muslim, Tariq appeared very fair, and felt that he was an outsider. According to Marcia (1993, p. 146), the balance between identity and confusion lies in making a 'commitment to an identity'. Although, Tariq was actively involved in exploring different identities, he did not make a real commitment to a religious identity. Some social theorists believe that those young people who make a strong commitment to an identity tend to be happier than those who do not (Marcia, 1993).

Family Structure

Recent research has shown that the quality of family interactions has important associations with the formation of a child's identity (Kellaghan, 1993). This makes it essential to examine the ways in which Tariq's family members interacted. So far we have observed that Tariq's parents were unable to offer a balanced religious perspective. Within the family setting, Tariq's parents failed to provide a unified set of experiences for their children. Unlike most families, his household was fragmented by religious and cultural differences. It was on this muddled foundation that Tariq set out to find and shape his own identity. As he explained, 'I grew up very confused about my religion... So it [religion] was not a defining feature of my childhood'. Alongside the parental conflicts there were major shifts in his family's structure and the relationships within the family were clearly disrupted. As he commented: 'Religion became the focal point of conflict and I remember that my father left for a while. When he returned, my mother was less confrontational. She pretty much gave in to his demands'. In fact, his parents tried to re-negotiate the balance of power within their relationship. His mother surrendered to her husband's religious demands, after a short separation. Estrangement can become an opportunity for growth or decline; it can serve as an incentive to modify the boundaries of relationships. Accompanying this hierarchal change was a revision of his mother's role and boundaries within the family, which prevented her from influencing the children's religious upbringing.

In the family, all decisions inevitably became dominated by Tariq's father. As he explained, '[after the separation] my dad really started interfering in my personal life... he'd wanna know about everything, especially the conversations I'd had between my mum and brothers'. A somewhat common problem in fragmented families is a weak boundary between sub-systems. As Minuchin (1974) points out, for a family to function correctly it must have cohesion among the parental sub-system. Unsurprisingly, the shifting role of Tariq's father can be attributed to the conflict over child rearing. In particular, his father tried to become more involved with Tariq's religious upbringing. As Tariq explained, 'When my dad came back home, he really pushed us to pray, but I knew it was a fake gesture ... because after a while he couldn't be bothered'. Both parents were competing for the parental sub-system role in order to exact their authority over the children. However, after the short separation, the rules that regulated the interactions between parent and child became distorted. His mother, for example, assumed the responsibility for nurturing and his father took greater control of family decision-making.

Class

Over the past three decades, class has played a greater role in Tariq's life and upbringing. The movement of his family up and down the economic ladder has made him very sensitive to class cleavages. When his father immigrated to the United Kingdom from Pakistan in the early-1970s, he struggled to support himself despite having a master's degree in electronic engineering. As he commented:

> My dad worked in a factory for years when he came over from Pakistan. He was highly educated, he was an engineer. So, I remember life being very hard for my family in the early days. We lived in a small flat, and both my parents worked. [Is your mother educated?] Yes, she has a degree in English ... she is a primary school teacher ... So, we were a working class family, in a financial sense, during the 70s. But my parents came from middle class backgrounds.

Whilst migration forced downward economic mobility for his family, his migrant father still held onto his middle-class values and aspirations. However, the changing political and economic landscape of the 1980s radically altered his family's economic fortunes. In fact, after the privatisation of British Aerospace, Tariq's father was employed as an engineer. The family saw their standard of living dramatically improve. Soon, his father took a position as a senior engineer. His parents bought a large house outside London, where they raised their family. Tariq's family have gained considerable economic independence since the early 1980s. However, economic self-sufficiency is not the sole determinant of an individual's position in the class hierarchy. In general, social theorists believe that a variety of social factors need to be considered in order to identify class – such as education, employment status and grade, home ownership and lifestyle (Goldthorpe et al., 1987).

At this point, I wanted to understand how Tariq conceptualised class, and thus I asked him to which class grouping he felt he belonged:

> I think I'm middle class, because my parents are both educated professionals, they own several freehold properties and the home I grew up in … and I went to university. So, I think that makes me middle class.

What strikes me about this extract is Tariq's need to be recognised as middle class. This can be problematic since individuals tend to distort or exaggerate their social aspirations. According to objective standards, Tariq and his family should be considered middle class (Goldthorpe et al., 1987). However, in the United Kingdom, social lifestyle and status are also considered important indicators for determining class – such as accent, manners, place of education, heritage and acquaintances (Cooper, 1979). Some of these issues are important because when I first met Tariq, he did not strike me as being middle class. He seemed to retain the mannerisms of his original social group. He talked about this briefly:

> I never went to private school, for some reason my parents wanted me to go to a good state school. I really regret not having the benefit of private schooling … my friends come from mixed backgrounds but most of them were working class, which was hard because I had to hide things from them. [Can you give any examples?] My parents enrolled me into a private tennis club.

My interview with Tariq showed that he is very aware of class issues. He talked, for example, about articulating a middle-class identity, within a set context, in order to fit in with his middle-class friends. However, with his working-class friends, he would hide aspects of his social lifestyle and status.

Finding Identity – Friendship, Schooling and Racism

In the preceding discussion, I looked at the central most important interactions and relationships in Tariq's family life. As Laursen (1993) notes, the diverse function of friendship is fundamentally different to a parent–child relationship. Like most people, Tariq has formed strong ties and relationships that have evolved, developed and changed over time. As a result, I need to look at what these relationships mean to Tariq and what he has gained from them.

When it comes to understanding Tariq's friendships, one must appreciate the situational factors that seem to influence his friendship selections. By this, I mean that his friendships cannot be viewed simply as a 'private and voluntary act' (Bell and Coleman, 1999). Rather, friendship is constituted within the constraints of class, age, ethnicity, gender and proximity. This is very important because in one setting, the tennis club, Tariq would describe his friends as close, but not in other settings. This places substantial doubt upon the notion that friendship is based on voluntary selection. As Tariq points out:

> My school friends and I weren't close, they were just school friends. And that's the same for my mates at the [tennis] club … At school my friends came from poorer backgrounds, and my recreational interests never quite matched-up.

If, as Tariq suggested, he did not share in his friends' interests then, apart from geography, why did he associate with his working-class friends? The relationships he formed with his working-class friends at school were simply based upon utility. This explains why these friendships eroded when he went to college, utility changes according to need and circumstances. As Tariq explained he was pursuing his own advantage:

> School was divided by race [and] in order to survive I made friends with ethnic kids. It was benefit. That's why I never hanged out after school … I never even liked'em.

Recent research has found that young people who lack friends can suffer from psychological problems later in life (Howe, 2010). It seems clear that the type of relationships Tariq is able to form in different social settings is based on practical necessity, rather than choice. Thus, by and large, Tariq's friends remain bounded by the initial setting for interaction, such as school or the tennis club.

School and College

Recent research into student transition has revealed that children need to feel socially connected to their school (Newcomb and Feldman, 1994). In other words, they want to be socially accepted by their peers and teachers. This is important because those students who feel disconnected display greater behavioural problems. In Tariq's case, he experienced significant difficulties adjusting to his secondary school, which had a negative effect on his attitudes about British society. In particular, his school experiences are littered with frustrations based on the inability to fit into a racially-divided community. As Tariq explained:

On my first day of school a white kid came up to me and asked if I was a Paki
... I reacted [to racism] with hate; I hated white people [and] being called a Paki
every day made me feel different ... Race became a big issue for me because the
school was divided by skin colour. The whites kept to themselves, which was
fine, because I despised them. So, school was us against them, whites versus.
ethnics, which would always erupt in a fight, and it was clear which side I was
on ... So all this talk about integration is complete rubbish; white people will
never accept a Paki. I realised that at school, you can't integrate with white
people, or be their friends. I was only comfortable hanging around my own kind
... I felt safe with Asians and Blacks [Afro-Caribbean and Somali] ... Also, the
teachers would always favour the white kids; they were all racist [teachers].
(Tariq; Interview 2, 7 November 2004)

This highly revealing extract shows us that racism is a very destructive
phenomenon. It distorts Tariq's image of white people, leaving him emotionally and
mentally discounted. The racial interplay between the multi-ethnic communities
manifested itself in an excessive divide that had a significant impact on Tariq's
social development. He was exposed to severe racial discrimination during his
childhood, finding it extremely difficult to adjust. He experienced all forms of
racial prejudice as a child; ridicule, abuse, physical assault and harassment. Tariq
found it easier to cope with these direct forms of racism, becoming acclimatised
to them because they were overt acts. In contrast, the perception of covert racism
seemed to agitate Tariq more intensely than the overt type, because gradually he
developed a means of protection against direct racism by associating with Asian
and Black gangs. Vigil (2002) argues that problems of identity among minority
groups are most often concentrated in larger, inner-city schools that are breeding
grounds for gangs. However, a gang cannot provide an individual with protection
from covert racism, perceived in an institutional from, that is, teachers and police
officers. As Sanchez-Hucles (1998, p. 74) notes: 'The trauma and emotional
abusiveness of racism is as likely to be due to chronic systemic, and individual
assaults on the personhoods of ethnic minorities as a single catastrophic event'.
Thus, a social distrust was aroused, especially concerning institutions, which
became more pronounced as Tariq grew older.

The racial discrimination that Tariq experienced had a number of parallels with
Abdul's case; it adversely affected his personality in the same way. However, unlike
Abdul, Tariq did not adopt a solitary lifestyle; rather, he sought shelter in groups.
This had a major influence on his entire outlook; he felt a sense of confidence
within the gang environment. As he explained: 'there was power in numbers, and
I knew my friends had my back' (Tariq; Interview 2, 7 November 2004). Tariq's
socialisation should be viewed within the context of the sub-culture from which
he emerges. The gang environment offered him, and other members, a form of
protection and belonging, which originated in response to a common problem felt
by all gang members. The gang brought together young Asian and Black children
from similar circumstances and backgrounds for mutual support, as they found

themselves isolated and neglected within mainstream society. Within the gang, Tariq adopted the sub-culture of violence in a passive manner, which accepts violence in certain social situations. As he described:

> When you're in a gang, as I was, there's always instances of violence; for instance a white kid insulted me at school once; soon after we [the gang] reacted by giving him a beating. (Tariq; Interview 2, 7 November 2004)

The approval of violence, as a norm, affected Tariq's daily behaviour, because it was in conflict with conventional society. However, the experience of a sub-culture environment did not establish a permanent connection between Tariq and the behavioural patterns of the gang. Rather, once he was at college, Tariq was able to adjust to a more stable environment. As he described:

> I suppose I was alienated in the social sense. I had minimal contact with whites, though things changed as I matured. I started reading the works of Trotsky and that really helped ... I found myself drifting to the labour movement. At college, I found the Socialist Workers; they offered an outlet. I thought I'd found a group of individuals that I could integrate with, although I had my own views on issues. (Tariq; Interview 2, 7 November 2004)

The experiences at college reinforced the implicit need Tariq displayed to be part of a group; also, on finding the Socialist Workers, he instantly formed a bond with them. They restructured his sub-culture ideals according to the ideology of socialism, reshaping his mind-set and providing him with a renewed feeling of belonging. However, this did not erode his frustrations, as he had been raised a Muslim and felt that this was under-represented in his disposition. As he explained:

> I remember getting vexed with some SWP [Socialist Workers Party] member's in the canteen, they insulted Muslims and Islam badly. And I ignored it, which burned me deep. From that day I realised that the socialists were fools, but this incident really sparked my interest to learn about the *deen* [Islam].

From a social perspective, Tariq was not able to establish close ties, because he was still overwhelmed by identity issues.

University: Finding Islam

Like many students, Tariq found moving to university a huge transition. Going to university meant moving away from home for the first time, which he found daunting and unsettling. As he explained:

> University was a big step. I always relied on my mum for everything … so I
> had to take responsibility for myself, which was really hard at first. I never liked
> my halls [of residence], it was constant *jahiliyah*.[3] This made me miss home,
> I felt detached from these people [non-Muslims]. So I went clubbing with my
> neighbours a few times. But I realised this was wrong.

Most university students enjoy the transition from home life to complete freedom.
It gives them the opportunity to find new friends and enjoy an adult social life.
However, for Tariq, living among non-Muslims greatly unsettled him. He felt
alienated by his initial experiences, and there was no help and support when he
needed it. However, he soon found the support and love he needed. In the morning,
after a night of clubbing, he awoke feeling very guilty. He decided to go to Friday
prayer, for the first time at university. As he mentioned:

> You need to understand that for the first few months I was trying to integrate,
> I went clubbing two or three times a week and I never bothered about Islam
> during that time. But I couldn't remove the guilt … I knew what I was doing was
> wrong. So, *alhumdullah* [praise be to God], I went to *Jummah* [Friday prayer]
> and that changed my life. I met the brothers [members of HT] there for the first
> time. In fact, one of the brothers was giving the *Khutbah* [service/speech] on the
> topic of raving – he destroyed the issue of split personality – living like a *kaffir*
> [non-Muslim] and Muslim. It was so true; I'd been living that life. So, after the
> *Khutbah*, I went and met the brothers [and] they invited me to have some food
> with them.

After an unpleasant few months at university, Tariq was thrilled to discover that
the university setting provided him with an opportunity to meet peers whose
backgrounds and lifestyles were similar to his own. This interpersonal experience,
taking place in an environment that encouraged intellectual inquiry, seemed to
foster profound personal growth.

Finding Brotherhood: The Peer Group

Tariq's interview, and that of other HT members in my sample, has revealed an
important link to peer group relations. As Asher (1990, p. 3) makes clear, peer
relationships are important sources of companionship, providing 'stability in
times of stress and transition'. If as suggested, Tariq experienced great difficulty
in adjusting to university life, feeling alone and disconnected, then it makes sense
given his penchant for collectivity. Tariq's peer relationships developed strongly

---

3   *Jahiliyah* literally means ignorance. However, it is commonly used to refer to
corrupt and ignorant practices, for example, like fornication and drinking alcohol (as based
upon Islamic scripture).

because he felt the group could facilitate his goal of becoming Islamic, which he believed would influence him in a positive way. As he explained:

> I realised after meeting the brothers they'd teach me about the *Deen* [Islam]. So I spent time with them, attending events, which introduced me to the party [HT] culture ... I'd never heard of Hizb ut-Tahrir before university. I never knew about political Islam: that Islam offered an alternative ideology. So, in a nutshell, I joined the party in my first year and, yes, I did feel like I belonged to something real, because everyone had the same collective goal; we were working [carrying the party mission], learning and living like brothers. (Tariq; Interview 2, 7 November 2004)

This extract gives us some insight into Tariq's emotional need to belong. He seeks out support from his peers, which in this instance is facilitated by HT. In effect, this provides him with a collective identity and purpose.

Tariq's description of his relationship with the peer group raises some intriguing questions about what attracted him to this group of young Muslims. As Newcomb and Feldman (1994) points out, commonality among peers based on attributes such as attitudes, interests, and beliefs facilitates social attraction.[4] Recent research has shown that individuals are less likely to accept, or will avoid communicating with, those who are different (Howe, 2010). Unsurprisingly, Tariq is attracted to the cultural homogeneity of the peer group. As he explained: 'The brothers were just like me, we'd grown up in this cesspit [Britain] and faced the same problems [and] troubles ... we were Asians from good backgrounds, but that did not unite us, it was Islam that brought us together'. Islam might have been the overt symbol of the peer group, but it was similarity in attitudes, age, ethnicity and class that attracted Tariq to the group. Individuals make a greater effort to seek out homogeneity in their social relations. Recent research has indicated that students are more likely to form friendship ties based on commonality of race and ethnicity (Mollica, Gray, and Trevino, 2003).

Beginning the Indoctrination Process: Contact

The goal of this section is to show how indoctrination is used in HT. In order to do this, I have used Tariq's account because it provides an overview of indoctrination at three key stages; contact, novice and member. As Singer and Lalich (1995) note, indoctrination is the systematic application of psychological and social influence techniques. The primary aim is to fabricate behavioural changes within a closed and structured setting. As briefly described earlier, Tariq felt excessively isolated

---

4 Newcomb's research is very important as he conducted his study on university students (Newcomb and Feldman, 1994). He discovered that the vast majority of student friendships were constituted by common attitudes.

and lonely. These negative feelings soon went away once he became friends with HT recruiters at university. This stage is critical because Tariq became emotionally and intellectually connected to the peer group. Speaking retrospectively, Tariq candidly talked about his experiences as a HT 'contact'[5]:

> I never knew that I was a contact or that the brothers had an agenda other than friendship. I was completely innocent at the time, but now I know what they were up to [recruitment], because I use the same methods. They first sought to develop a relationship with me. This allowed them to get to know me: My thoughts, concepts and personality. For example, I mentioned that I went clubbing the night before, which gave the brothers insight into what thoughts I was clearly lacking … Developing a relationship also means living with the contact, as the brothers did with me, in a natural way. This allowed them to guide my *aqlya* [mentality] and *nafsyya* [disposition].

This extract has given me considerable insight into the beginning of Tariq's indoctrination. Firstly, the peer group sought to form a 'physical relationship' with him in order to understand, and then exploit, his personality. According to Lifton (1989, p. 5), indoctrination consists of two key elements: 'confession' and 're-education'. In Tariq's case, the members encouraged him to confess and renounce his sins in order to begin the process of individual change. Secondly, unprepared for their indoctrination techniques, Tariq concluded that only the members could re-educate him, providing absolute certainty and conviction in Islam. He was unaware that the members sought to 'remake' him in HT image (Lifton, 1989, p. 5).

Intermediate Stage: Becoming a Novice

Tariq spent considerable time with his new peers, interacting in the same social space. More significantly, he started to view the world in a similar fashion, transforming his behaviour to gain 'peer acceptance'. Tariq talked, for example, about modelling his behaviour around the members. He changed his style of dress and use of language in an effort to consolidate his group membership. More significantly, the peer group conditioned Tariq to internalise HT ideology, reshaping his thoughts and behaviour. As he commented: 'I started maturing in the [HT] culture, and I really pushed the guys for more … so eventually they asked me to join the *Halaqah*'.

As an observer, I am struck by the way in which Tariq so willingly surrendered his individuality for the group experience. Moving from a state of isolation to a group context can reduce one's sense of individuality. In *Halaqah*, Tariq adjusted his thoughts and personality to match the collectively defined ideology of HT. The

---

5   Potential recruits are often referred to as 'contacts' by HT insiders.

perspective of Tariq, a member of HT, is surprisingly open and frank on the issue of the *Halaqah*. As he commented:

> The *Halaqah* is designed to culture the *daris* [novice], building them with the correct thoughts and ideas about Islam. So, we begin each *Halaqah* with *Nidham al-Islam* [System of Islam, book]. This is the best party book, in my opinion, because it builds the Islamic foundation. For example, the first chapter talks about change: in order to create change [individual and society] one must change the thoughts because thoughts lead to action. This is a fundamental concept; it allowed me to appreciate how to create change in myself and society. So, take a simple example, a Muslim drinks alcohol, this is a corrupt action. So, if you want to change that action then you need to address the corrupt thoughts that motivate that action, like freedom ... I want to make it clear that the Halaqah does not brainwash, I became convinced by the intellectual arguments of Hizb ut-Tahrir, and if you do not accept that then you are distorting the reality of the culturing process of the party.

This observation underscores some of the limitations of the interview method. Tariq, for example, is not aware of all the contextual factors that are influencing his behaviour and personality. Consequently, he cannot identify or understand the types of indoctrination techniques being employed against him.

Lifton (1989), a prominent psychiatrist, observed three psychological techniques used by the Chinese government to indoctrinate young students. As Lifton (1989, p. 7) points out, these techniques 'represent the successive psychological climates to which the student is exposed as he is guided along the path of his symbolic death and rebirth; the great togetherness, the closing of the milieu, and submission and rebirth'. During the intermediate stage of indoctrination Tariq became a novice and joined a six-person *Halaqah* in which he received culturing on HT ideology and aim. Then, after three months, a noticeable change took place – there was a large shift in emphasis from the intellectual and ideological to the behavioural. Tariq casually acknowledged this shift, as he commented: 'The first three chapters of *Nidham* [System of Islam] focus on *aqlya* [mentality] – the correct way of thinking – and chapter four really targets *naffsyya* [behaviour] because the concepts need life'. Tariq began to realise that his views came under intense scrutiny and his *Mushrif* (*Halaqah* teacher) started to exert considerable pressure on him to adopt HT ideology in totality. 'Milieu control' was a powerful technique used to control Tariq's environment. According to Tariq: 'the party [HT] is the only group today that understands the Islamic ideology [and] the *Halaqah* maintains this purity and knowledge'. The concepts he studied in *Halaqah* were strictly controlled, and thus no alternative sources could be used, as this would distort the new world view being crafted.

Final Stage: Membership and Ideology

When Tariq began conveying the thoughts of HT effectively, as if they were
his own, then he was considered for membership. This was not a free choice;
significant coercion was used in order to manipulate him into joining the
organisation. Although, there was no physical pressure, the coercion was clear.
During the weekly *Halaqah*, intellectual pressure was applied, which forced
Tariq to bend towards group expectation. The novice is seen as intellectually
inferior, especially if he or she displays independent thinking. According to
Fahim (senior member), 'most *shab* join the Hizb knowing very little ... they
are like empty pieces of clay, making it the *Mushrif*'s job to mould them into
members'. However, Tariq showed desire for membership by imposing himself
on the organisation, which served as the first indicator of his readiness. He talked
openly about his membership:

> I recall being summoned, without any explanation, by a senior member. I
> arrived at the location to find several members already present, among them
> was the *Naqib* [committee head] and *Masool* [area leader]. To my surprise, they
> offered me membership into the party, which I accepted. The *Naqib* at the time
> explained that the party stipulated that in order to become a member, I must take
> *al-Qasm* [the Oath].

The first condition of the oath demands that a member must be 'a faithful
guardian of Islam'. To be a guardian of Islam entailed that Tariq propagate the
Islamic message, as interpreted by HT, in a political fashion to the wider society.
Secondly, anyone who becomes a member of the organisation has to adopt the
party ideology. In this respect, the member must be a walking manifestation
of the ideology, acting in full accordance with it, even if he disagrees with
some aspect of it. According to Lifton (1989, p. 430), another characteristic
of indoctrination is 'the subordination of human experience to the claims of
doctrine'. In other words, Tariq's personal experiences were subordinated to the
ideology because HT doctrine is more important than the individual is. The third
condition relates to confidence and trust in the leadership, which is imperative.
The fourth requirement stipulates that once the oath has been taken a member
must execute every decision made by the party, regardless of his own view, 'as
decisions are made for implementation'. The fifth condition demands that as a
member you commit to carry the party ideology with all your effort and energy.
Finally, the oath ends with a self-declaration to uphold all the aforementioned
conditions, confirming this oath with God as the witness. This is very important,
as violation of this oath would be considered a contravention against God's law.

Becoming a Radical: Common Trends

Although I looked at nearly 30 case studies, this chapter has documented the radicalisation of just two young Muslims. The extracts have provided a powerful source of information, and now I need to make sense of them. There are many characteristics that I can identify, and diverse kinds of category that I could use to conceptualise these accounts; but any type of analysis will be selective in the features it focuses on and the categories used to classify them. So what features should I use? Although each respondent is unique, common patterns of experience can be singled out. However, as I will show, these are not conclusive. They constitute issues to be discussed, rather than clear-cut features of radicalisation. My analysis has drawn out three key commonalities; socialisation, peer group formation and collective identity.

Socialisation

The collection of case material clearly indicates that the respondents did not operate independently from society. Instead, I discovered that the respondents were embedded in a complex set of relationships with other social forces and settings outside of the family, such as school and peer group contexts. Abdul, for example, tailored his identity at home in relation to his ethnic culture, but beyond the home he struggled to develop relationships with the white majority. In spite of this recognition, a great deal remains to be examined in regards to the ways in which these social influences affected the respondents.

To be a radical, or, more precisely, to be susceptible to becoming one, involves subjective experiences. Each case history provided important insights into the cognitive ways in which the respondents processed and made sense of their adverse experiences. Each of the respondents experienced the world through their own particular frame of recognition, actively trying to understand, predict and explain their own perspective. Much of Abdul's awareness, for example, is made up of racial discrimination, which deeply affected his perception of the 'other'. The very way Tariq presented himself emphasised the fragmentation of his ethnic identity. Leading psychologists suggest that the ways in which children cope with adverse experiences is dependent on the individual's early emotional history and the unconscious motivations that this history produces (Storr, 2005). This can provide a way of coping with the world, and of maintaining some sense of control.

It is noticeable that in both cases the respondents' childhood experiences became a trigger for radicalisation. Storr (2005) believes the anger provoked by a sense of powerlessness in childhood is likely to be twisted into hate in adulthood. Many of the respondents became disaffected and marginalised through their experiences; for instance, Abdul and Tariq never fully recovered from racial victimisation. Those young people that suffer an abusive socialisation are more likely to develop a dysfunctional identity. According to Adler (2002), feelings of helplessness that originate in childhood precipitate an inferiority complex, and can encourage a child to compensate for these feelings in adulthood.

Socialisation assumes the individual is constituted by their inherited culture, but, in the case of the respondents, the substance of this was disjointed, which left then feeling deprived. In this respect, the respondents struggled through their life cycle, trying to adjust their identity; but the changing social environments they encountered triggered a host of frustrations that they were unable to resolve. Tariq, for example, could not alter his identity to fit into a distinct social grouping. If socialisation is not developed properly then it can foster negative feelings in adulthood. However, a prerequisite of radicalisation is not necessarily a violent childhood, because many children are exposed to violent acts, but this does not always turn them to a violent path in life. For this reason, not all instances of adverse socialisation will result in radicalisation; rather, I contend that a turbulent socialisation may increase the potential for radicalisation in later life.

Effects of Racism

According to Abdul, 'racism was not a black and white thing ... kids were picked on because of their religious beliefs; refugee kids were always singled out because they looked different and couldn't speak English' (Abdul; Interview 1, 5 November 2004). It is clear racism, in the form of violent physical attack and harassment, had a deep emotional effect on the respondents. As Miles and Brown (2003) point out, at the heart of racism is a process of making sense of the 'other', which distorts the social perspective into various forms of 'us' and 'them'. The distorted representation of others can validate discrimination, but how did the respondents perceive and interpret their social world? In general, the challenge for me lies in explaining how racism affected the respondents, and whether it provided some motivation for embracing a radical identity. During initial interviews with Omar Bakri (the former leader of HT, Britain), he explained how the experiences of young Muslims of being racially attacked, in the cases he observed, caused them to be 'distrustful of [the] *Kuffar* [non-Muslims]' (Omar Bakri Muhammad, Interview 26 March 2004). Consequently, these and other adverse social experiences were exploited by HT to cultivate a group of young Muslims who had been marginalised through racism. According to FAnon. (1968), racism has a significant effect on an individual's psychology and raises issues of self-alienation.

The case histories presented indicate that radicals were greatly affected by their interpersonal interactions with others, providing me with extensive insight into the causes of their eventual radicalisation. Clearly, radicalisation requires some form of emotional trauma in the recruit's life cycle, principally during early socialisation, which would make them more prone to radicalisation in adulthood. This is perpetuated by the inability to balance racial prejudice with one's own cultural distinctiveness. To some extent, this appears to be generally true of many of the respondents, as their external perception of others changed based on their negative interactions. Synder and Tilly (1974) asserted that individuals recall information about 'others' based on their stereotypes, which allows them to selectively interpret and draw upon subjective experiences. Consequently, the respondents perceived situations and processed information that was dependent on their prior stereotypic experiences. These events have radically altered their cognitive outlook; many have internalised their feelings and developed a 'negative identity'.

Social Alienation

At the heart of the respondents' radicalisation lay a catalogue of grievances that had traceable markers to alienation. This would suggest alienation had a destructive effect on all the respondents. Keniston's (1967) framing of the term, which he used to study the psychology of alienated students, is of crucial importance to my study. As Keniston (1967, pp. 189-90) notes, alienation means 'an explicit rejection of what are seen as the dominant values of the surrounding society'.

It follows from the above definition of alienation that not all young Muslims are equally alienated from their society. Why did my respondents feel alienated, while other young Muslims do not? Clearly, the socio-psychological features of alienation are different for each alienated Muslim, and no composite account can deduce a single profile of an alienated young Muslim. According to Sageman (2005), Muslims who live abroad tend to become more isolated from their cultural origin, which makes them, feel 'more royal than the king'. He found that second-generation immigrant's experienced similar feelings of disaffection from their cultural origins. My respondents experienced similar emotions, especially since they felt culturally separated from the dominant values and cultures around them. Abdul, for example, could not associate with his migrant culture, nor did he feel British. This clash of cultures had a destructive effect on Abdul, as he was not able to find a sense of identification with people of his own ethnicity, nor with the white majority, making him feel socially excluded. By viewing alienation in accordance with other social factors, I can account for the causes of alienation among the respondents.

Radicalisation in Context: Why Abdul and Tariq Chose HT?

The radicalisation of both Abdul and Tariq into HT was explored from an environmental perspective, namely the social milieu in which they emerged from. This to some degree may undervalue other potential variables. For example, the innate connection an activist may have to HT ideology. Therefore, it is important to contextualise both men's radicalisation in a way that explores their social context and intellectual motivation for joining HT. Firstly, Abdul joined HT in 1999, while Tariq joined in 1998. This is somewhat symbolic from the perspective that their radicalisation pre-dates the terror attacks of 9/11. This would suggest the international context had little impact on their respective decision to join HT, as Abdul asserts: 'global events didn't influence me (joining the Hizb) ... it was solely based on conviction'. This telling statement raises one significant question, does context matter?

The trajectory of Abdul and Tariq prior to joining HT revealed a deep social need for belonging, which made them seek out like-mined people at university. In fact, the vast majority of HT activists are recruited within the same social setting, namely amongst university peer groups. This would suggest that HT radicalisation is context-specific. In other words, HT activists emerge from similar social realities and backgrounds, making ideological motivation less salient. Hoffer (2002), utilising a social psychology approach to study why and how mass movements form, concluded that mass movements, irrespective of their religious or political disposition, attract similar personality types. However, if this is true, then why do similar types of Muslims select HT? Well, according to Hoffer (2002), groups like HT proliferate amongst certain social demographics because they promise fulfilment of particular deficit-needs, which the activist has been lacking in society. Therefore, whatever the motivation, whether political or religious, HT appeals to a specific group of frustrated young Muslims who struggle to identify with society and community. In other words, HT offer young middle class Muslims, who are seeking to escape a feeling of social exclusion, a way to gain a real sense of belonging. Therefore, the process of joining HT has very little to do with ideology. In actuality, acquiring social acceptance within a homogenous social peer group is a key feature of joining HT. This is why events like 9/11 were not significant in the narratives of HT activists; instead the peer group offered the novices a sense of social belonging.[6] Therefore, leaving HT is considered extremely difficult, as members become institutionalised within the social group and leaving would essentially mean returning to a state of social isolation.

However, the above does not totally explain why Abdul and Tariq opted for HT over other Islamic groups, like Young Muslims or JIMAS? There are a number of issues that provide an answer to this issue. Firstly, in respect to recruitment strategy, HT operates in an evangelical style at university, looking to actively recruit from a closed pool of Muslims predisposed to HT radicalism. In contrast, rival groups do not actively recruit members, as they are not structured as a religious-political organisation. As Abu Yusuf, a member from London commented:

---

6   The data I have accumulated clearly shows that the vast majority of recruits were not influenced by global events, such as 9/11 or 7/7. In particular, out of the 28 male members interviewed, 17 were recruited pre-2001 while 10 were recruited after the 2001 terror attacks. The narratives of the 10 members recruited after 9/11 talked little about such global events, and instead focused on the national context of their upbringing. In actuality, none of the respondents cited 9/11 as a precipitating trigger to joining HT.

> We [HT] were rampant at university, literally unstoppable, the other groups
> couldn't compete ... they had no organisation and were not politically active.
> We [HT] literally took over campuses and groups like YMO watched on from
> the side lines to afraid to challenge us.

The free reign HT seemingly possesses at university enables them to be the first
point of contact for young Muslims arriving at university for the first time. This
was supported by the evidence collected from my fieldwork, which indicated that
the first Muslims most members encountered at university were HT recruiters,
who they befriended and within the peer group became radicalised. Secondly,
rival Islamic groups struggle to relate to those young Muslims predisposed to HT,
namely middle class Asians, because they are mainly populated with working
class activists. Respondent I, who prior to joining HT was associated with YMO,
suggested that he struggled to connect with YMO members, because they emerged
from totally different social worlds. As he mentions:

> they [YMO] were full of uneducated idiots ... I just couldn't relate to a bunch
> of labourers and gang members ... I grew up a million miles away from those
> people and what they felt were social problems were a million miles away from
> my reality and problems.

This would further support my contention that personal contact and relationships
underpin the joining process. In other words, social need may have predisposed
Abdul and Tariq to HT, but social connection to likeminded individuals pulled
them to the movement. After the initial pull factor, Abdul and Tariq were able
to fulfil secondary interests within HT. Abdul, for example, displayed more
affinity to religiosity and thus devoted significant attention to religious learning.
While Tariq remained solely interested in HT political activism, spending the
majority of his time and energy immersed in reading the news and discussing
HT politics.

On the surface, it may appear that Abdul and Tariq were drawn to HT by
different motivations. For instance, Tariq seemed more inclined to the political
aspect of HT activism, while Abdul was more orientated towards religious
activism. In fact, the religious and political motivation of the men evolved after
encountering HT recruiters. As Abdul and Tariq explain:

> ...before the Hizb [HT] I knew nothing about the *Deen* [Islam], I never cared
> about the political situation and I had a passing interest in religious matters...only
> after joining the Hizb did I realise the importance of the *Deen* [Islam], which as
> you know brother combines politics and religion...and that is the power of the
> Hizb, it brings politics and religion together making the *Deen* [Islam] come alive
> ... so in answering your question, the *Deen* is both political and spiritual ... so
> praying, fasting or pursuing the news are all acts of worship (Abdul).

> I was never religious growing up, I actually learnt to pray properly after I encountered the Hizb at university ... Islam had no practical meaning before that. When I joined the Hizb I was amazed by its culture, after reading political concepts [HT book], my political world view changed, I never knew how the world ticked until I joined the party...I learnt about all aspects of the *Deen* [Islam], its spiritual parts and its political parts... (In particular) I started to develop a deep interest in the political culture and intellectual ideas of the Hizb (Tariq).

From the above two statements, it may be argued that ideology is somewhat marginal at the joining phase, but it begins to take shape after radicalisation. Once the old worldview of the novice is dismantled, and as radicalisation deepens, it gives an opening for a new worldview. In other words, exposure to HT ideology takes place within the *Halaqah* (culturing stage), which means the primary prerequisite for joining HT is social need and peer group socialisation. In addition, HT recruitment is context specific. This means specific personality-types, such as those matching the homogenous disposition of the HT fraternity, are sort out at university. Therefore, the social need to join HT predisposed Abdul and Tariq towards HT, irrespective of their political and religious orientations.

Relationships and Interactions: Peer Group Formation

The process of becoming a radical is strongly dependent on the social settings in which the person lives. In this respect, understanding how the respondents reacted to 'others', often on the basis of stereotyped views, is of great significance. The accounts of my respondents showed me how they were adversely affected by other people's perceptions and responses to them. As a result, many of the respondents experienced substantial difficulties in forging durable relationships during their early experiences, leading them to manifest a host of confusions concerning their race, ethnicity, culture, religion and class. All the respondents emerged from a distinct minority culture; because of this, they struggled to contend with rejection. This directly affected their identity development, creating an 'attachment disorder', and provoking a greater propensity towards disaffection and alienation. As a consequence, they felt that they did not belong to a specific social classification or group, leading to their withdrawal from mainstream society. Tariq, for instance, emerged through multiple sub-cultures; first, the teenage gang, then, the Socialist Workers, until these are permanently replaced by HT. The respondents lacked a deep sense of attachment, which meant they could not establish a proper place in society. All individuals, especially adolescent children, must feel loved and feel that they can belong to a social group in order to feel comfortable within their surroundings. When the respondents were denied security and belonging, they withdrew from those situations to seek safety and love elsewhere.

A common feature in all 28 case studies was the university peer group, which had a considerable influence. In particular, the respondent's self-identity was refashioned in accordance with their exposure to the value system of the peer group. Upon entering the peer group the respondents became conscious of alternatives to their own cultural and social voices, they began to question old ideals (for example, family/minority traditions). Both Tariq and Abdul found the new worldview extremely persuasive. These new-found concepts became entwined with feelings of belonging, as group participation brought positive rewards. As mentioned earlier, one of the difficulties encountered by the respondents during their childhood involved establishing relationships with others. A stable relationship requires the interrelation of two distinct social worlds. According to Laursen (1993), individuals display greater happiness when engaged in active relationships. Individuals are most happy when they are with friends, followed by being with family, and they are least happy when alone (Argyle, 1992). Besides the peer group offering protection from alienation, it introduced the respondents to a group of individuals that had the same interests and goals.

Empowerment: Collective Identity

I am greatly interested in what happened to the respondents' identity and motivation when they became members of HT. Let us first explore this issue through the words of my respondents, which will allow me to gain a sense of collective identity from their perspective. According to Abdul: 'the [party] culture is a liberating force ... it gives you supreme confidence and total conviction, because it's the truth'. Similarly, Tariq, on entering HT, described his experience as an 'overpowering feeling of absolute confidence, as you know you've found the truth'. These views are only a small glimpse from much longer discussions, but they can be used to make some important points about the nature of radical identities. Most importantly, the respondents' cognitive processes were radically transformed in HT. In other words, the basis for the respondents' self-definition changed in the group setting. The respondents' personal identity gave way to the '*Hizbi*' (collective) identity. Moreover, because they adopted the characteristics of the group, their perceptions of themselves changed.

I need to look at why HT affected the respondents so strongly and how the radical identity was formed. In order to examine these issues, one must consider the minimal group studies of Tajfel and Turner (1979), because they identified three key components that transform identity in a group setting; 'categorisation, identification and comparison' (Tajfel, 1981). Within the radical group, the novice will adjust their sense of identity, their ideas and their dispositions to harmonise with the collectively defined attributes of their group. In effect, the novice will take on the group characteristics, making them their own, which conditions the novice towards group conformity. Also, the novice's self-esteem becomes firmly attached to the fortunes of the group, seeking to achieve positive and negative value connotations, so as to differentiate their in-group from a comparison out-group (Tajfel, 1981). This search for 'positive distinctiveness' shapes the individual's sense of identity. In the case of HT, this positive distinction also applies to other Muslims, who become less relevant sources, as they represent the out-group members – those who do not belong to HT. Turner (1991) links this to self-stereotyping, which involves radicals stereotyping themselves when they identify with their group. I witnessed a good example of this in practice, while visiting a respondent at his home. As I arrived, his neighbour had just returned an item that he had borrowed and they appeared to have a pleasant conversation; but, as soon as he had left, to my shock, The respondent furiously berated him: 'dirty *Kuffar* [disbeliever], I should burn this [foot pump]'. He continued for much of the conversation with this theme; he later suggested that his other neighbour, a Muslim, would always return a borrowed item immediately. This situation demonstrates the process of 'self-stereotyping', in which a person may have very different responses to people at different times. For instance, the respondent responded to his neighbour in terms of his personal identity, but in my presence he switched to his collective identity.

The group appears to be a recurring feature in the radicalisation process, as it provides a sense of belonging, a feeling of self-importance, and a new cognitive system that fashions a fresh identity. The social setting within HT, for example, is strongly governed by the '*Hizbi*' (collective) identity, which allows the member to adopt the characteristics of HT. The transition from personal identity to a '*Hizbi*' (collective) identity is achieved, firstly, by building the '*aqliyah*' (mentality) on a specific idea that serves as the bond linking the individuals in the group together. Secondly, the '*nafsiyah*' (disposition) must be changed in accordance with the work of the group: 'This requires that the *shab* [novice] engage himself in studying the *Hizbi* [group/collective] culture, adopting it as his viewpoint in life, and interacting with it in such a manner that it shapes his course of actions as a Muslim' (Anon., 1994, p. 1). The '*Hizbi*' identity must acquire full domination over the individualistic aspect (ibid.). Once the members have attained this shared sense of collective identity, it becomes the basis for their wider identification. According to HT (Anon., 1994), for the novice to be considered part of the group, he or she must adopt all processes related to the group:

> This means that he must forsake some of the individualistic aspects in order for him to be part of the Hizb ... Even if the *shab* [novice] is a *Mujtahid Mutlaq* [highest grade of scholar], he is to abandon his opinion for the opinion of the Hizb (Anon. 1994, p. 1).

The radical identity that emerges from the group dynamic often gives rise to a deep feeling of empowerment, increasing a radical's sense of confidence and self-worth. On entering HT, for example, individuals are assimilated into the cultural norms of the group. Most importantly, the group exploits the need to belong within the novice, providing him or her with a feeling of self-importance by conveying a new belief structure that defines the individual identity. As the radicalisation process deepens, the novice is gradually conditioned to accept the moral supremacy of the group identity. Shaw (1986) makes a similar assessment of membership in a terrorist organisation, as the group often offers an answer to the pressing personal needs that is not achieved in the wider society. This provides the individual with a new identity and a role in society, albeit a negative one, which, in a passive sense, imposes conformity. Post (1990, p. 159) goes further, as he suggests that radicals 'whose only sense of significance comes from being terrorists cannot be forced to give up terrorism, for to do so would be to lose their very reason for being'. This is equally true for members of HT, as they cannot envisage life outside of the group. The group provides a way to enhance social status, a quality greatly under-represented in a recruit's social life. For instance, a loner at school or work becomes a high-ranking figure, gratifying their ego.

Summary

When I started writing this book, I found the prospect of constructing a radical's pathway based on their biographical experiences somewhat daunting. However, the task in practice was not as difficult as I first assumed, since HT members' identity processes have coherence even when dysfunction appears to be the norm. If I accept that a HT member's identity is structured in some manner, then the task is to ascertain the key features of that structure. One thing that emerged strongly in the accounts from Abdul and Tariq, for example, is a sense of continually evolving identity. In other words, the process of being made and remade, as we saw, heavily depended on their past experiences. In Abdul's case, his radicalisation can be tracked back to several stirring events. Firstly, racism and class left him alienated from his classmates, making it difficult to develop close relationships. Although these features were beyond his control, it still indicates that society has a lasting effect which cannot be easily washed away. Yet, on the other hand, it would be simplistic to suggest that society determined his pathway towards radicalism. Therefore, it depends upon how social experiences, either negative or positive, become translated into everyday life. For example, Abdul argued that one thing which had a strong impact on him joining HT was university, as he affirmed: 'If I never went to university, I probably would've never met the *Hizb*, and my life would've been totally different if I hadn't'. Abdul acknowledges that university was a pivotal event. For example, he becomes religious, develops close relationships for the first time and joins HT, directly affecting the kind of person he becomes.

Chapter 6
Radical Pathways II: Profiles of Female HT Members

The British media often depict Muslim women as victims of cultural and religious fundamentalism, in desperate need of western emancipation. I must confess, before starting this book, I had a very narrow and distorted image of Muslim women as relatively powerless. This image has been somewhat changed by my encounters with HT female activists. These women appeared very active and eager to enter the political landscape, albeit in a radical fashion. On the surface, however, HT seems to be a predominantly male-dominated space. What is less clear is how far HT makes room for female activists. If Muslim women are drawn to HT, then it is equally unclear what roles they take on within it. These issues caught my attention because there are considerable misunderstandings and ambiguities about the role of women in HT. As I tried to examine these broad topics, I discovered that most of the female activists I encountered had strong commonalities – in terms of age, education, ethnicity, socioeconomic status and background. This chapter therefore seeks to understand the paths taken by a group of Muslim women into HT radicalism. Painting a picture of this largely unknown subject requires insight into the influences within home, school and wider society.

Family Environment

Past research on the migrant communities in England has revealed that they are overwhelmingly kinship-orientated (Joly, 1995; Lewis, 2002). I therefore expected to encounter examples of extended family networks and traditional family life. While I found that the idea of kinship remained relatively strong, the results from the focus group indicate, however, that it is a less significant feature. Moreover, many of the women challenged such assumptions, one member commented:

> Our parents came over here [UK] from the subcontinent, bringing with them a host of corrupt traditions that were not compatible with the west and for that matter with Islam. They had a link to their ancestry, but we don't ... I personally struggled to accept their ways and traditions.

The movement from one social world to another can be extremely problematic. As the above comment reveals, migration can expose a gap between the generations, as two distinct social and cultural worlds collide. Pearce and King (1987) describe this process as 'poly-cultural', since the features from both the native and host country become fused into a new identity. More significantly, it seems that the women chose to reject their parents' cultural indices in order to accommodate integration into the dominant culture. Given the women's membership of two diverse worlds, it seems necessary first to explore their family life and upbringing before investigating the above issues.

Family Life and Upbringing

A number of studies on family life have highlighted the importance this social setting has on child development (Lareau, 2003). This makes it vital to paint a clear picture of the women's upbringing because a variety of influences within the home can affect identity formation. As Amina suggested: 'my parents tried to bring us up in a traditional way but my mum was very western and liberal ... this meant I could pretty much do as I pleased'. Amina's family dynamic allowed her to develop a fairly independent and open world view. This is somewhat unusual since most Muslim families impose rigid controls on their children's behaviour. Nina's upbringing, for example, was stricter. As she explained; 'My parents are very traditional. I couldn't go out with my school friends and my movement was restricted ... I lived a dual life though; at home I was a traditional Pakistani girl but at school I was western'. One of the most surprising aspects of the women's family life seems to be their constant endeavour to acquire freedom from parental authority. Although they could not fully achieve this in the home, their parents had no control over them beyond the family environment. As a result, the women clearly developed a dual identity, facing conflict at home and freedom in school.

A cursory survey of the literature on family processes indicates subtle differences are to be expected in culture and ethnic background (Chibucos, 2005). Although family processes can be expected to vary, I observed several common features among the women's family structure. First, during their youth, the rules that governed the interaction between the girls and the outside world appeared imbalanced. In particular, it seems stricter boundaries were enforced because of their gender. As Nina commented: 'My brothers were given total freedom, they'd be able to visit their friends and go out till late, but I had really strict and unfair curfews'. The majority of the women cited similar experiences, which resulted in acts of deception and rebellion. Deception, in the case of the girls, was needed in order to live within two conflicting social settings. This can have a considerable psychological effect on children, because they are constantly forced to act out different social roles. Second, as I see it, the girls underwent socialisation in their own South Asian culture as well as within the majority culture. As Nina explained:

> My mum wanted me to be traditional. She wanted me to learn to cook, look after my brothers and get married ... I was never forced by my parents. This gave me freedom to go against Pakistani tradition, for example, I wore western clothes

and I was able to pursue academia ... I attribute this to my parent's openness because they were not from some village in Pakistan, they were educated, and they wanted the absolute best for me. So sometimes they'd try to pass off their cultural stuff on me, but if I refused, that was the end of it.

Despite this freedom, the girls' identities were continually challenged both from within and without. As Nadia observed: '... When my grandma visited us from Pakistan, she had a go at my mum for allowing us to become western. While she was here I had to wear Pakistani clothes, which I hated, but it kept my family happy'. If one scrutinises the narratives of family life, as told by the women, then it is clear a number of confusions and contradictions exist. On the surface, for instance, the women all seem at odds with the ethno-religious traditions of their parents, yet there are instances when the girls conformed to the traditional value systems. As Nadia suggested: 'of course we had limits ... I never had a boyfriend in school because it was deemed something strictly taboo in our culture'. Although it is not a salient issue here, the idea of *Izzet* [family honour] may have had an underlying role in the above extract. The majority of the women suggested, however, that such a concept had greatly diminished, owing to social changes and modernity. As Amina said: 'On the surface, my parents were traditional, but they knew the reality of living in Britain. We [the family] had to adapt to England and become integrated. That was their view twenty-odd years ago ... and that's my parents' mentality today, unfortunately'.

Social Class and Lifestyle

The women's families migrated to England during the 1960s and 1970s, in search of greater socioeconomic prosperity and stability (Lewis, 1988). The pull factors are the economic forces – such as greater job opportunities and higher living standards – that motivate migration (Jackson and Hudman, 1986). As I observed from the discussion, the phenomenon of migration had a significant impact on the development of the girl's socioeconomic situation. In particular, after the families had established themselves permanently, they struggled to gain upward social mobility (Tajfel, 1978). It is not surprising to find that social status and class were seen as important social categories for the girls when they were growing up. As Nadia commented: 'My parents started at the bottom [after migration], and it took them a while to settle down, but after that our situation changed. My dad was a qualified doctor and he quickly started a practice'. The socioeconomic changes to the women's families were very similar: for example, their fathers are all well educated professionals.

In most South Asian households, it is common for women to assume the role of homemaker and child carer, while husbands perform the function of economic provider (Joly, 1995). In contrast with this norm, the women's mothers entered the labour force and developed careers for themselves, while maintaining their household duties. As Sara explained: 'My mum was a biochemistry researcher for over thirty years ... and even though she did most of the chores, like cleaning and cooking, my dad did a lot to ease the burden of housework'. This attitudinal shift reflects a somewhat modern approach to family structure and life, especially among South Asian families (Robinson, 1988). I mentioned earlier that the parents of the respondents seemed eager to raise their children in a traditional fashion, which seems at odds with their mothers' active career pursuits. Nadia provided greater insight on this issue, as she explained:

> Our [focus group] parents, I think, wanted us to be traditional, because they didn't want to abandon all their Pakistani traditions. So they tried to pass on these concepts to us, not by force, but by guidance or stories. But my mother, for example, is a consultant ... she dresses in a western way because it is expected ... it would be contradictory for her to tell me how to dress, even though she does. My parents started to lose their cultural identity when they started to work so how could they pass it on to us ... this is a by-product of integration [loss of identity].

The cultural influences on the families appear to be underpinned by socioeconomic status. In particular, the families seem prepared to discard parts of their cultural identity for upward social mobility.

Ethnicity and Religion

Ethnicity is a highly complex component of identity, because individuals are assigned and identified by labels, which they may not agree with. Nadia, for example, did not like any type of racial or ethnic identifiers: 'I thought of myself as British, everything else was just not relevant...I hated being referred to as Pakistani because I was born and raised here [UK]'. As Modood (1997) points out, ethnic labelling is an imposed identity created by the colonialist. An ethnic marker can be wrongly applied and stick, causing immense frustration for individuals who are trying to meld into the dominant culture (Sanchez-Hucles, 1998). As Sara explained: 'Growing up here [England] can be difficult, because you have to live two lives... At school I was British but in family gatherings I was Pakistani'. The women would have preferred to use the label British, it seems, but social forces pushed them to emphasise their ethnic and racial identity. This artificial sense of identity is not healthy. Many social theorists have argued that a stable concept of self needs to be constructed both in terms of personal and group identity (Wetherell, 1987). The inability to replicate a sense of ethnic identity contributes to the feeling of 'becoming like them [white people]'. In some respects, it could be argued that the parents of the girls were slightly responsible for not establishing an ethnic identity, which might have reflected cultural and religious distinctiveness (Modood, 1997). Although the respondents largely rejected ethnicity, they were unable to select a free and independent identity from the dominant culture, which continued to perceive them as Asian.

It became clear through the discussions about the girls' upbringing that their attachment to ethnicity became attenuated. Trying to explore the factors undermining the importance of affiliation to ethnicity was not an easy task, as there were several possible causes. First, the distinctive attributes of ethnicity – such as cultural values, customs and traditions – were not properly transmitted to the girls. As Nadia said: '… I was given mixed messages about Islam, for example, not having a boyfriend. But my parents never cared about practising Islam, they were totally secular. It was pointless to use Islam because none of us practised'. A superficial glance at the girl's family life may lead one to believe religion was relatively insignificant. Nevertheless, I think the lack of religious identification helps explain why the women felt disconnected from their ethnic identity. Islam is often seen as a key identity marker for the Muslim South Asian community in Britain (Gardner and Shuker, 1994). Islam is also often connected to and reinforced by ethnicity (McLoughlin, 2002). Nonetheless, the discussion with the girls supported the view that they seldom felt like they belonged to a religious community: for example, they never attended the local Mosque or participated in communal gatherings. Their families showed a lack of commitment to religion, which in effect perpetuated a sense of not belonging (Stark et al., 1980). Second, ethnic affiliations became weakened by migration and economic burdens, which directly undermined cultural values. More importantly, status became associated with socioeconomic achievement, giving the girls access to alternative cultures at school. As Sara explained: 'I never thought about religion or ethnicity growing up, because I felt totally integrated'. Clearly, individuals can perceive themselves as more 'ethnic' in certain social settings, drawing upon their own cultural identity at varying levels.

Gender

When I first talked to the women, I was somewhat taken aback by their active interest in ideological and religious perspectives regarding gender. It was therefore not surprising to find them participating in the political struggle to make their theological beliefs work for them and the wider society. At this stage, however, I wanted to understand the role of gender in relation to the girls' upbringing. As discussed earlier, the women felt freer in the school environment and enjoyed less freedom than their male siblings. Although the girls had limited independence, it seems that their boundaries were broadened after they reached the age of fifteen or so. As Nina said: 'My parents were less protective of me when I started my GCSEs, I visited my friends unaccompanied … and when I started driving I had pretty much the same freedom as my brother'. Similarly, the other girls talked about a more relaxed curfew at around this age.

More importantly, the identities the girls created are clearly marked by gender influences at many varying levels. Within the family setting, broad power relations between father and mother have an impact. Nina described her mother as very 'authoritative and controlling' within the home environment. The other women perceived their mothers to be equally powerful within the domestic sphere, providing a positive gender archetype. This gave the girls the opportunity to craft an identity more in keeping with secular western tradition. As Sara acknowledged:

> When I was little my mum wanted me to wear shalvar-kameez [traditional Pakistani clothing], even though she'd wear western clothing for work ... I hated it and told my mum I wasn't going to wear shalvar-kameez because it made me stand out. [What about your father?] He never cared. I think my mum felt she was betraying her culture [and] so she'd try and overcompensate with me.

This is a rather interesting extract as it reveals to a certain extent that identities depend heavily on ideological beliefs, cultural and religious values, and social position. Owing to the lack of cultural influences, the girls' adolescent identity is formed through a more open perspective, which has a significant effect on their ascribed gender roles. Notwithstanding their views on some gender inequality, the girls were prepared for productive work in adult life, in the same fashion as their brothers, and not as homemakers. As I will explore later, however, after radicalisation, this view was totally overturned. The women, for example, adopted a domesticated role, seeing this as the natural responsibility of women as constituted by their newfound HT ideology.

Internal Agency: Breaking Out of Tradition

In the previous chapter I suggested that socialisation played a critical role in the radicalisation process. In the case of female activists, they were brought up within a predefined set of values and traditions, which became instilled into them during their early upbringing within the home environment. At school age, for example, the effects of this socialisation meant the women were aware of the ethno-cultural distinctions between themselves and their white classmates. Therefore, the more parents treat their children in ethnically differentiated ways, for instance over emphasising ethno-cultural norms, the more it is believed that a child will reflect such stereotypes. Through this process the women became 'socialised' into culturally structured gender roles. This begs the question did the women join HT to break away from the traditional path mapped out for them?

The answer to this question is rather complicated, as it hinges on whether or not the women joined HT freely. In earlier chapters, I mentioned that participation within HT is a direct expression of human agency, albeit with structural influences. In the context of joining HT, agency was exercised by free choice, which counteracted the stereotypical characteristics of South Asian cultural expectations. As Sara explained:

> Islam is a liberating ideology, it sweeps away the falsehood and guides people to the right path … growing up in an Asian family meant we [Sara and her family] adopted many corrupt practices and I never want[ed] to live a traditional lifestyle – were community defines the way you live – Islam is the reference point and with Allah's guidance I found a way out.

From this statement, there are several conclusions that can be forged. Firstly, despite the internalisation of Asian culture during childhood, the women sought to actively break away from the cultural mores of their parents. In this respect, HT was an important mechanism for making sense of the world, especially as they facilitated the creation of a new ideological viewpoint. For the women, as Sen (1985) notes, internal agency represents the ability to act on behalf of goals that matter to them. In this respect, the women were actively involved in determining their own fate, and thus escaped becoming submissive heirs to their parent's traditions. Secondly, for the women, agency was expressed as a form of resistance to social and cultural norms perceived as backward and overbearing. Research has shown that immigrant families seek to transmit from one generation to the next a series of ethno-religious cultural markers (Lareau, 2003). The passing of traditional values and norms to offspring is seen as a way to reproduce and continue a connection with the land of origin. However, as the life-stories drawn from both male and female HT members have shown, activists struggled to reconcile the diverse nature of the two opposing cultural worlds they inhabited. As a result, consciously or unconsciously, the women's choice to join HT was influenced by their deep desire to resist the traditional patriarchy of their home upbringing. Thirdly, from an outsider perspective, it would seem that the women replaced one form of subordination for another, as HT ideology is equally rooted in patriarchy. In actuality, as the women intimated endlessly, the choice to join HT was an expression of self-agency, while the cultural values and norms of their parents were enforced upon them. According to Mahmood (2005, p. 172), women often gain a sense of 'self-empowerment through the cultivation of self-esteem'. In other words, joining HT enabled the women to pursue 'self-directed choices and actions', giving them an opportunity to break away from traditional Asian constraints (Mahmood 2005, p. 172). In fact, the women felt voiceless and powerless within the constraints of Asian culture, and thus joining HT gave them a feeling of empowerment. So, even though the women's agency is subsumed and side-lined in HT, it is still voluntarily discharged, and thus can be reclaimed at any juncture during their membership. In this respect, the women are free agents because they appear to construct their own desires, values and goals.

Intersections between Ethnicity, Class and Gender

According to Crenshaw (1992, p. 1467), women from minority backgrounds are trapped between 'the rocks and the hard places of racism and sexism'. In other words, minority women are subject to dual forms of social vulnerability, which intersect in their lives to form experiences that are often unique to them (Crenshaw, 1992, p. 1467). Through the concept of intersectionality, I will hopefully be able to put the distinctive experiences of HT female activists into focus by looking at the intersection of class, ethnicity and gender. In particular, the women experienced discrimination in a totally different manner than white women. Firstly, they all experienced discrimination based on their membership of a particular ethnic group. As Nina mentions, 'by virtue of skin-colour I was stereotyped as Asian ... which meant I was seen as culturally backward and uneducated by English people'. This reflects how the women often experienced unique forms of stereotyping, placing social barriers upon them in relation to ethnicity and gender. As Kane (1992, p. 311) points out, 'the intersection of racial and gender inequalities creates unique structural positions for black women, black men, white women, and white men'. Secondly, the women grew up within a middle class household, which left them disconnected from working class Muslim women. At university the women struggled to relate to Asian Muslims from working class backgrounds. As Sara explained, 'they (working class Muslim women) had to fight to go to university while education was encouraged for us'. As the women reflected, being a member of the South Asian ethnic group and being female created unique experiences for them, which may ultimately have influenced their pathway into radical Islam? Therefore, it is clear from an intersectional perspective that HT women experienced multiple and overlapping forms of discrimination, and thus they collectively felt socially excluded on the basis of race, ethnicity and gender.

Social Environment

The process of immigration places natural demands on the host country, as it involves working with diverse cultures and preparing the local labour market to welcome a new source of supply. Unsurprisingly, this can be a highly complex and challenging process because it places considerable demands upon the migrants. In most cases, immigrants are expected to modify their behaviour to conform to the dominant culture, which devalues their sense of cultural identity (Hutnik, 1985). As I discovered in the previous section, the girls and their families had to make their own choices about which aspects of their native identity they wanted to preserve and which to discard. Through this process, the girls developed their own social and cultural milieu, which in turn enabled them to feel integrated into society. Consequently, the girls' identities were not constructed in a vacuum but within a variety of social settings, making it essential to examine these social domains.

Schooling and Friendship

Some social theorists have argued that the family setting provides a powerful seed-bed for young people's educational success and professional ambition (Kellaghan, 1993). As Amina commented: 'My parents had university degrees and so I was expected to go to university ... my parents wanted the best for me so I had extra tuition after school'. Although the girls acknowledge that their families assigned considerable importance to education, it is difficult to ascertain which family influences were the most significant. According to Lareau (2003), social status and family background provide children with greater access to educational resources, giving middle- and upper-class families a distinct advantage. Through social mobility, the girl's parents expressed high aspirations, providing motivation to pursue higher education. As Sara explained; '... they [parents] were involved in my education right up to university'. Thus, the motivation of the girls was strongly influenced by the social class to which they belonged and their family environment.

This helps explain some of the family influences on academic ambitions, but I want to explore the different social contexts that triggered the girls to think, feel and act on the basis of their social identities (Turner et al., 1987). As discussed earlier, the girls felt that the Asian and Pakistani identity labels were imposed upon them by family networks and the dominant culture. Despite their dislike of labelling, most of the women insisted that they liked almost everything else pertaining to British culture and society. Hogg and Vaughan (2002) believe social identity is the individual's self-concept, which is extracted from perceived membership of social groups. I found it very interesting to hear about the social groups the girls belonged to when they attended secondary school. Amina, for example, attended a private girls' school and she talked about some of her experiences:

> I hated my first year of school because I was having silly squabbles with some girls who were gossiping about me – I think because I was the only Asian girl in the class – but things changed. I became really good friends with those girls and we stayed friends until university.

The friendships between young girls can be very unstable (Bell and Coleman, 1999). Most of the girls described similar experiences of disruption of friendships, but after changing their allegiances they developed very strong bonds. Nina observed: 'It's nice to fit in, I hung out with my friends, who were all English [white]'.

In general, school friends tend to share the same interests and children tend to reject other children with dissimilar interests. This is very important, as Nadia explained:

> My friends were English as well ... We had the same tastes in clothes, music and other stuff. My thoughts and concepts were very corrupt and westernised,

so I was accepted by my friends. But there was an Indian girl in my class who
was always bullied. She'd recently come over [from India] – so her dress and
language really made her stand out – everyone would pick on her … when I was
younger I thought she deserved it [bullying] because she never tried to integrate.

Being part of a social group helped the girls to feel close to others. They might
have moved in and out of different groups, but that is natural as children drift
apart and make different friends. More importantly, the girls felt accepted in their
social groups at school. The above extract, however, shows the darker side of
exclusion, as social groups establish group norms and rules for self-categorisation
in ways that favour the group members at the expense of the out-group (Turner and
Tajfel, 1986). As soon as the girls started identifying themselves as belonging to a
group, they took up an identity in their own eyes and in the eyes of others. However,
this social pressure was embedded within an undercurrent of racial inferiority.
As Amina explained: 'in retrospect I was forced to hide my culture amongst my
friends because it was seen as odd, and maybe even backward, because I was seen
as different even though I fitted in'. This is a salient point, as it appears the girls
social acceptance came with a subtle precondition. In order to integrate within
the white peer-group the girls were forced to hide aspects of their home identity,
which facilitated the creation of a dual identity. Moreover, it underscores their
deep feelings of being seen as socially 'different' from the white majority.

After-school Activity

A common feature of the girls' narrative is their after-school activity, which
indicated a very free and unrestricted social life. They talked, for example, about
being allowed to visit friends without a chaperon. Moreover, their accounts often
depict their social lives as being active and spent in public areas: 'We'd [friends]
go to the cinema, spend hours in shopping centres and just hang around' (Nina).
This is surprisingly different from the perceived and often well-documented
notion that Muslim girls are restricted to the home (Modood, 1992). Close friends
often see each other during the school day and in after-school activity, spending
considerable amounts of time together. This interaction can have a powerful effect,
exerting considerable influence on a child. As Sara explained: 'I'd hide parts of
my life so I'd fit in … I never really let my friends come over to my place because
I didn't want them to see my Pakistani side – like food and stuff'. Despite having
minimal presence, the girls chose actively to shun their ethnicity and cultural
heritage. This perceived rejection of ethnicity was essential, as Nadia suggested:
'Even though I am Asian, I was accepted by my white friends because I integrated.
Integration literally means adopting their [Western] viewpoint. If you don't, then
you'll get singled out, and that happened to a lot of Asian children at my school'. It
would appear that the girls failed properly to experience dual socialisation, which

allows two cultures to overlap. The failure to retain an ethnic identity is in many ways, however, a natural response to the realities of being Asian in a white society.

Racism

In the previous chapter, the male members described how racism was used to marginalise and exclude them on the basis of their skin colour and ethnicity. The physical manifestation of racism was more visible among the male members, and so was more readily understandable, whereas covert means were preferred by girls, making the behaviour of girls more difficult to predict and understand (Miles and Brown, 2003). Although the girls were not victims of any racially-motivated violence or intimidation, there was an undercurrent of racism which some of the girls experienced. Amina observed:

> My friends were all white ... we'd occasionally pick on other girls. On one occasion, two Asian girls were singled out and racially insulted for the way they acted and looked. I bumped into them on the bus later. They couldn't understand why I hung around with racists ... they referred to me as a coconut – brown on the outside and white on the inside ... I hated Asian culture. But I never felt British either.

This highly complex extract reveals several unsettling components of racism. First, a negative judgement was made of those seen as different, containing a positive valuation for those imposing it. Living in a social environment in which prejudice is reinforced towards a minority group has been shown to have deep psychological impact on the development of young people (Sanchez-Hucles, 1998). Second, as it was described to me by the women, racism emerged from within a social context, rather than the belief or ideology of having innate superiority. As Nadia said: 'I suppose they [friends] were a little racist, but they were my friends ... I tolerated it because I wanted to be a part of the clique'. This reveals some important issues; feeling socially accepted required hiding their ethno-religious culture in order to fit in. However, racism evoked deep confusions about identity, as it reinforced their sense of difference from the wider society. Third, the women questioned the validity of applying generalisations about social groups. They strongly believed that ethnicity could not provide knowledge about them as distinct individuals, especially since despite some contradictions they saw themselves as British. In other words, the girls did not want to be placed into, or represented by, a particular social group. As Nina commented: 'Growing-up, I thought of myself as British, so I hated it when people would ask me where I was really from, implying that I'm not really British ... that's why I grew up confused about my identity, I felt British but I was not seen as British ... it left me feeling like an alien'.

Radicalisation

The radicalisation of Muslim women receives considerable attention in the literature but it is still difficult to understand why growing numbers of women appear to be attracted to a wide range of activities within a radical, and sometimes violent, setting. The radicalisation of women, unlike men, is often thought to be stimulated by different social realities. These gender-based assumptions assert that female activists are less influenced by political involvement or ideology. Galvin (1983) tries to argue that family networks, namely husband and brother relationships, play a significant role in the recruitment of female activists. Similarly, MacDonald (1992) noted a large percentage of boyfriends recruited their girlfriends into Euskadi Ta Askatasuna (ETA). I am not disputing these claims, but it is unwise to apply male-derived assumptions regarding female behaviour. The notion women are less likely to become radicalised because they are inherently more passive has been widely discredited (Skocpol and Campbell, 1995). Helene Deutsch, a psychologist, argues that female passivity in work or politics is greatly misunderstood, because 'the ego can be active in both men and women'. She believes political passivity does not translate into 'inactivity, emptiness or immobility' (*Times Magazine*, 20 March 1972). My goal is therefore to examine why the women in my focus group became radicalised.

University

Ruth Kelly, the then Secretary of State for Education and Skills, in the aftermath of the London bombings on 7 July 2005, addressed a conference of university heads, in which she declared: 'I believe that higher education institutions need to identify and confront unacceptable behaviour on their premises and within their communities' (*Times Higher Education*, 16 September 2005). It is apparent from these remarks that the authorities recognise radicalisation as a real and dangerous threat to university students. University can be a very unsettling experience, as young people grapple with a sense of purpose, beliefs and future direction (Erikson, 1968). There is extensive literature on the general nature of the university experience and its impact on student behaviour, but this research tells us very little of the actual processes by which Muslim women adapt in different ways to their university environments (Newcomb and Feldman, 1994). I needed to identify how the four women became radicalised at university. The *how* was crucial because without knowing the processes of radicalisation, one cannot counter it.

Transition to a New Social Environment

The girls had very similar social backgrounds, emerging from, and belonging to, a homogeneous social group during their early upbringing. Most of the women were optimistic about moving away to university, as it would allow them to gain autonomy from their parents. As Nina said: 'I wanted to live on campus because

I felt sheltered at home. Moving to university gave me the opportunity to become independent and meet new people ... so I was excited'. The reality of the first few months, however, brought many unforeseen complications, proving to be very disruptive to the girls' adjustment. Research into student transition indicates that many find the early alteration to a new social milieu very difficult and challenging (Newcomb and Feldman, 1994). As Sara described it: 'University was different ... I'd never seen so many Asians in my life [and] I found it hard to develop friends, because my interests were western'. Amina experienced the reverse: 'I hated it [university]. Everyone was white, but really stuck-up, and I felt excluded because I was Asian'.[1] Overall, each of the women struggled to integrate into the social environment of university life. As Levitz and Noel (1989, p. 66) acknowledge, the 'first two to six weeks' are a critical period for adjustment and integration. Although many students find the social aspect of university life enjoyable, the respondents found it difficult to establish meaningful relations with their university peers (Paul and Kelleher, 1995).

The women appeared quite deflated by their initial experiences, as summed up by Nina: 'It [Student life] was like being surrounded by children: you'd have loud music playing all night, food was constantly stolen, [and] I even started to miss my parents' nagging after a while'. This disconcerting introduction to student life made some of the women question the very purpose of university. As Amina explained:

> It was hard leaving home. I'd never lived away from my parents for such a long period. My first term was really difficult. I felt out of place; it [university] was a daunting experience...I was going to transfer after the first year to a university near to my home, because I really felt alone and I missed my family.

Most of the women cited similar problems in adjusting to the university setting which involved a degree of social isolation and loneliness. Whenever an individual experiences a shift in behaviour – moving away from home to university – they can become unsettled. More significantly, a few of the women cited peer rejection as a salient cause for their loneliness, which is supported in the literature on student transition (Asher and Coie, 1990). They seemed deeply affected by their inability to find acceptance within a peer group, resulting in heightened anxiety when membership was denied to them.

Overall, I identified two distinct problem areas which the women encountered in making the transition to university life: forming peer relations and disconnection from family. First, the introduction to university life was blighted by feelings of loneliness brought about by peer rejection. These emotions varied in intensity. For Nadia, university 'lacked warmth', while Nina felt it was an 'intimidating environment'. The feeling of isolation in the midst of dense collective activity

---

1   Amina talked about her experiences among upper-class white people – she felt her accent, clothing and interests made her unable to integrate with her university peers.

– student union events – had a negative effect on their identity and self-esteem. When the women had trouble forming peer relations they felt lonely because they had no emotional support or companionship. An underlying factor in the women's peer rejection can be attributed to a failure to integrate because of class and ethnicity. For Sara, ethnic divisions became difficult to bridge: 'I never wanted to be bound by my race and culture … so I felt like an outcast because I rejected my people' [South Asian]. Second, the women struggled to adjust to being away from home, missing their family's support and love. Although home-based students find it difficult to forge new peer relations, they benefit from continued family and friendship ties (Komarovsky, 2004).

Peer Group

I intend in this section to focus predominantly on the role of the peer group, and on the nature and impact of relationships between my respondents and female HT members, within a university context. In selecting themes that have direct relevance to the radicalisation process, I have chosen the development of religiosity and peer socialisation, since out of the many available themes these appeared to me to be two key issues. In a general sense, a peer group often attracts a collection of people, roughly of the same social background and age, to a shared sense of values (Hartup, 1983). Even in my brief glimpses into the personal experience afforded by the women, I saw the part played by peer groups.

Encountering the Peer Group   As I was writing this chapter, there were several stories which consistently featured in the media – Muslim women wearing the *Niqab* (face cover) and female suicide bombers in Iraq. These issues are reminders that the boundaries of the individual and the social context cannot easily be separated from each other. If social processes influence the formation of identities, then I needed to make sense of how the women's social life changed after encountering the peer group. According to Howe (2010), peer groups have a psychology that overwhelms the individual. If this assumption is true of my respondents, then it is important to hear these experiences from the women's perspective first. Nadia described her earliest encounter with HT peer group:

> I was given a flyer outside the canteen, inviting Muslim students to the freshers' dinner … so I decided to go along. I found the talks really interesting, because I thought Islam was just a religion. The talks presented Islam as a complete way of life and they exposed the fallacy of the western civilisation … the dinner gave me a chance to meet some of the sisters [HT recruiters] and we had a long discussion. After the dinner, the sisters would visit me at my halls regularly and we became friends. Initially, we'd chat about the fundamental question and I really started to think about my life and my purpose … I became interested in the *Deen* [Islam] and I spent a lot of time with the sisters. We became very close

friends … they helped me to practise Islam. Without them I would not have discovered Islam, so I'm grateful to Allah. [How long did this process take?] Well, I started university in September and by the end of that semester I would say I was practising, so about four months.

The extent to which Nadia felt negatively about herself influenced the social realities of her university experience and interactions. In previous extracts Nadia mentioned she struggled to form stable relationships within the social space of university. In many ways, her need for peer recognition might have been a defensive construction to provide a sense of continuity and belonging. First, throughout her life she had developed the belief that Islam was just another religion, as a result of her family interactions. The HT gathering challenged this self-definition of Islam, at a time when she was experiencing low self-esteem and isolation. More significantly, after several personal visits her identity was gradually replaced. Religion became the focal point for change, as it provided answers to the meaning of life. As Shupe and Hadden (1988, p. 133) assert, religion is the pursuit of ultimate truth and values. The religious aspect acted as a catalyst for the substantial change in Nadia's intellectual and behavioural outlook, resulting in a reassessment of her role in this life. This spiritual dimension was extremely powerful and important in the radicalisation process, so I intend to expand upon increased religiosity in the next section.

What strikes me about her experience is the rapid speed with which significant behavioural changes take place, especially those within a peer group context. From Nadia's perspective, encountering the peer group had a positive impact. For instance, Nadia talked about how her relationship with the 'sisters' changed from just friendship to 'close friends' when she became a member of the peer group. The need for acceptance and the desire to avoid peer rejection were important to Nadia. This is not surprising, because within a group setting individual identity often gives way to the collective identity (Tajfel, 1981).

What follows is the account given by Sara of how she encountered and developed relationships with HT female activists.

I came across the sisters during *Ramadan*. I tried to fast and pray for the first time. I just wanted to know about Islam, so I went to the prayer room. There I met two sisters; they were living in my halls but I'd never really seen them … we started to hang out. I really liked them and we became close. They helped me a lot, they introduced me to the culture and it had a big impact on me … like the other sisters [focus group], I started to think about this life and the next. For me, accepting the *Deen* was an intellectual process, because you have to change concepts to change behaviour.

Although her personal experiences are different from Nadia's, this short extract contains some common themes – such as peer group relations and religious transformation. In theory, peer relations may not be as vital to human survival as attachment relations, but they clearly provide social and developmental advantages. After her encounter with the peer group, Sara grew dependent upon the supportive social relationships. She had to secure peer acceptance first, however, which she described as intellectual and behavioural change. In other words, she was expected to conform to the religious culture of the peer group; for example, she had to start practising Islam. According to Marcia (1993), this type of behavioural transformation is marked by two distinct processes: exploration and commitment. Sara, for example, attended gatherings and encountered the peer group with an open mind, which allowed her to explore various identity alternatives. After a brief period of association with the peer group, she pledged commitment to their values and beliefs by adopting the identity offered by her HT female peers, to which she remained stubbornly faithful.

Amina's account exemplifies a more interpersonal relationship, which served as the foundation for her identity change. She talked about how her friendship triggered a turning-point:

> In the second semester I opted to take a sociology module. There was a sister in my class who would wear the *hijaab* and *Khmer*. I thought badly of her, at first; perhaps she was oppressed or unintelligent. I had never seen anyone wear *hijaab* in my area, so I couldn't quite understand why someone living here [the west] would wear it. But she impressed me – she'd make these brilliant comments that challenged the lecturer on intellectual issues … so I became friends with her. We were the only Asians around. I never thought that I'd become practising or that I'd wear the *hijaab* … but that is the power of the truth. We became inseparable; we'd hang out, cook together and discuss the *Deen* [Islam]. A major turning-point for me was the conversion of a classmate to Islam. She was English, and when the sister gave her *dawah*, I'd be there and it affected me, especially when she converted. After that the sister would teach us both about the *Deen* [Islam] from the beginning. Eventually, she started giving us formal *Halaqahs* when we joined the party.

Amina's account exemplifies a more interpersonal relationship that served as the foundation for her identity change. She describes the shift from an old identity structure, seemingly built upon western ideology, to her new Islamic identity. Mead (1934), the architect of social psychology, might view Amina's identity transformation as a reflection of her social experiences. More significantly, her identity is formed and contained within the relationships and the cultural context of the peer group. Clearly, the development of close ties with the female activist was central to Amina's radicalisation. From the earliest interactions between them, joint or shared activity was evident. A large part of Amina's time at university was spent doing things with the peer group – such as studying, engaging in recreation and learning about Islam. All these involved the development of joint activities wherein the peer group had established shared patterns of action, shared understandings and feelings. In other words, by embracing these patterns of joint activity Amina acquired a sense of shared identity, which emerged from continued interactions and conversations with the peer group.

The final account is given by Nina. Her encounter with HT is more contingent upon social circumstances. As she explained:

> I signed up to the Islamic society at the freshers' fair. After about a few weeks two sisters visited me and I got to know them. I was struggling to fit in at university. I was living next to some loud and annoying students ... I moved in with the sisters, they had a house near to campus. It was excellent living with the sisters and we became close friends. The house was *dawah* central; we'd bring contacts over and have talks. I became convinced so quickly, literally a week after moving in I was practising, it was a great atmosphere ... it was a turning-point for me.

In documenting the various paths the women took in joining the HT peer group, it is clear that they were harbouring deep feelings of isolation and loneliness. To overcome this, Nina turned to the peer group who were very sympathetic to her needs, and in due course Nina revealed her unpleasant experiences of university life to them. According to Bean (1985, p. 35), university students actively chose favoured 'agents of socialisation'. He argued peer group influence can be an overriding factor in changing student behaviour (Bean, 1985). After Nina became acquainted with the peer group, she found they had similar backgrounds and interests. Not long after their friendship began Nina discovered that the women, whom she came to depend upon to lighten her despondency, were in fact members of HT. More significantly, she seemed unaware that the peer group had an agenda other than friendship, and were in the process of recruiting her into HT. Van Gennep (1960, p. 11) summed up this type of student transformation in three stages: 'separation, transition, and incorporation'. This albeit simplistic representation rather accurately depicts the stages Nina, and the other women, went through in their encounter with the HT peer group.

Religious Transformation within the Peer Group   It seemed fairly apparent HT targeted emotional weaknesses in their recruitment of the women. From the impression given by the respondents the peer groups were seen as spiritually complete, the female members appearing unaffected by the disappointments that plagued the daily lives of the respondents. In particular, religion was used to help make sense of their social circumstances, giving them the vital inspiration and energy to overcome their perceived problems. As Hood et al., (2009, p. 24) point out, religion focuses on two basic human needs: unlocking mysteries and circumstances. This understanding offers an overview of the women's sudden religious change. First, all the women cited the need to answer the fundamental mysteries of existence. This was achieved, they all insisted, through Islam, which provided them with the correct answers to the fundamental questions regarding their existence. Islam, it was argued, addressed the issue of their purpose in life and integrated it into the grand scheme of existence, i.e. 'what came before this life and what will come after it' (Nadia). Second, the women found themselves socially and culturally isolated at university. This situation gave rise to feelings of frustration, since their previous beliefs left them feeling unfulfilled. Consequently, these feelings made them susceptible to the peer group, which prompted them to become religious seekers.

In many ways, it is important to contain the religious transformation experienced by the women within the context of the peer group. Their religious experience never took place in a vacuum: rather it was directed, if not initiated, by the peer group. Some of the women suggested this was a rapid transformation, but breaking from one's previous beliefs is not a sudden process as it takes time to integrate a system of beliefs. As Sara suggested: 'Practising the *Deen* [Islam] is an on-going struggle ... I had to overcome many contributions from my corrupt secular viewpoint, like wearing the *hijaab*, which was a huge step'. This statement puts the religious experience into some sort of perspective, as comprehensive identity reformation takes effect gradually. I have refrained from using the term 'conversion' to describe the women's experiences, because it is somewhat ambiguous and it does not quite match the realities of the women's circumstances. Peel (1977), for example, defines conversion as a shift in primary religious affiliation. The women were born into the Islamic faith, however, and thus never transferred their religious allegiance. Their experiences can consequently be described as a process of turning away from old lives towards not a new but rather a revitalised or idealised version of Islam. In some respects, this experience is analogous to feelings of being 'born-again', which in a Christian context refers to a spiritual rebirth and salvation. However, the term is firmly embedded within the Christian theological tradition and its usage would be confusing as a result.

My discussions have revealed that the women's religious involvement was based in the first instance on friendship, and then on belief. I am not, however, trying to play down the role of belief, which is critical. The religious revitalisation was only completed when the women transcended beyond social relationships and fully accepted the beliefs of HT. This was quite apparent during my discussions with the women, as I found them very passionate, even arrogant, about their beliefs. The women encountered many challenges after their revitalisation: for example, they all cited family disputes. As Nina recalled:

> When I returned home from university for the winter break my parents were in absolute shock. I was dressed in *hijaab* and *jilbaab*. They were really upset and concerned that I'd been brainwashed or something ... I've slowly turned my mum around, but my dad still has a problem with it [Islamic dress].

This raises the issue of what behaviour or rituals had to be enacted by the women to be deemed as practising by the peer group. According to Nadia:

> After I accepted Islam as my viewpoint in life, the sisters taught me the things
> that were *Fard* [duty] and the things that were *Haram* [forbidden] in Islam ... so
> I learnt how to pray and I started wearing the *Jilbaab* and so on, really.

When the women became religiously revitalised, the way in which they interpreted life was transformed. They adopted a 'holistic' viewpoint, which gave them guidelines and systems that applied to every aspect of their daily life. As Durkheim (1984) points out, the function of religion is to make us act and to aid us to live. In other words, revitalisation changed the women's self-awareness, as their new religious beliefs took centre stage in their lives. Religious revitalisation is an on-going process, however, a struggle to refrain from sin and regression to past beliefs (Eliade, 1987). In sum, the women found themselves disconnected in a new social world, which made the peer fellowship very appealing. The peer group provided religious meaning and purpose to the women, and thus a strong bond was forged between them.

Indoctrination

The issue of indoctrination proved a difficult topic, as the women refused to acknowledge the term. They felt it had a negative connotation and it implied that they had been forced to join HT. From the women's accounts, it is difficult to assert Singer's (1995) view that all religious change involves mind control. Their transformations did not include any form of physical confinement, coercive persuasion or bodily threat. Can I therefore still use the term indoctrination to describe the women's experiences with HT? After consulting the literature, I discovered a more suitable definition. Some theorists have described indoctrination as 'milieu control' (Lifton, 1989). This entails the enforcement of 'unethical practices' to control intellectual thoughts within the group setting, manufacturing a deep sense of separation from society (Snook, 1972, p. 12). This definition needs more clarification. Unethical practices may refer to the inculcation of concepts and beliefs into an individual in a closed environment, like the *Halaqah*. There is a noticeable problem with this definition: it is too general. According to this definition, teaching children in a classroom environment could be classified as a form of indoctrination. Using the term in this way ignores the content of teaching, which determines whether or not teaching is indoctrination. As Flew (1972, p. 11) stated: 'No doctrine, no indoctrination'. By using the above definition (Snook, 1972), I will be in a position to see how the women became indoctrinated. It is important to divide indoctrination into two distinct stages: primary (the *Halaqah*) and secondary (peer group).

Primary Indoctrination: The Halaqah

The content of the *Halaqah* was deliberately engineered and delivered in such a way as to generate collective indoctrination. As Sara explained:

> Before I joined [*Halaqah*], the sisters would discuss concepts, but it wasn't structured and I never felt connected to the party. But when I started H [*Halaqah*] things became clearer; I could understand the concepts and culture better … it really helped. I became connected; before I felt like an individual or an outsider.

Unlike peer discussions, the *Halaqah* leader would convey the ideas in an authoritarian manner and the content was continually drilled into the women's psyche. As Nadia said: '*Halaqah* is a building process … corrupt concepts are destroyed and the correct concepts built'. Clearly, the outcome of the *Halaqah* is an 'indoctrinated person'. It is important, however, to emphasise that the women objected to my use of the term indoctrination, as they collectively felt it implied a lack of rationality. Some social theorists have assumed that indoctrination is arrived at through 'non-rational methods' (Wilson, 1972, p. 19). In the context of the *Halaqah*, the discussions are controlled and restricted, which determines the outcome of the discourse. This means that rationality is contrived, making the *Halaqah* an ideal setting for indoctrination. As I concluded in the previous chapter, the aim of the *Halaqah* was to create a quite different world view. Unfortunately, the women were reluctant to enter into any detailed discussion regarding their experiences and development within the *Halaqah* system. As Nina explained: 'The *Halaqah* is an administrative issue, and as members of Hizb ut-Tahrir we're not at liberty to discuss these matters'. In spite of this, I know about the *Halaqah* from a variety of sources – such as my own personal experiences as a *Mushrif* (teacher) and other biographical accounts.

Secondary Indoctrination: the Peer Group

From the women's accounts, it was quite evident that indoctrination occurred within the peer group setting. Although I believe that the women's lives were greatly affected by their encounters with the peer group, it is not easy to describe these processes. First, it is clear that the peer group exerted significant influence over the women. As Nina said: '… practising was hard early on because you'd be told what to do and how to do it'. This interaction appears to be very one-sided, allowing the peer group to stimulate deliberate behavioural and mental changes. Second, the peer group developed close relationships with the women, making indoctrination easier. As Sara explained: 'I really trusted the sisters; we became close and I revealed a lot to them about myself'. Close ties within peer groups enable weaker or newer members to be socialised into the group (Howe, 2010). Peer socialisation was an important developmental stage in the radicalisation process, as it gave the women definitions of acceptable ways to handle the social world. The women became submerged within the peer group, which developed an unquestioned attachment to the 'sisters', including automatic obedience and willingness to sacrifice for the group. As Amina observed: 'I'd miss a lot of lectures because I'd be busy with the sisters carrying the *dawah* [Islamic message]'. As with all group dynamics, the peer group indoctrinated a deep sense of group identification among the women. In sum, the women sought identification with the peer group for the following reasons: (1) membership provided benefit; (2) it offered distinctiveness from other social groups (for example, dress); (3) there was a sense of common experience. These influences were undoubtedly present within the women's accounts, and thus indoctrination played an important role in preparing the women to join HT.

Effects of Indoctrination on Identity

When the women joined HT, they acquired a new outlook, which from their perspective empowered them. I want to look at this issue by exploring the women's aspirations prior to joining the peer group, as this may reveal insight into the effects of indoctrination. Rather surprisingly, most of the women entered university not anticipating professional careers. As Sara explained, 'After graduation I expected to get married and have children'. Upon radicalisation, however, some of the respondents began to shift from a traditional women's role to a more career-orientated outlook. As Amina suggested, 'The culture [HT] gave me confidence ... my interests began to grow in [the] social sciences and I ended up following that path after graduating'. This newfound career expectation was not just restricted to the social sciences. For example, after her degree in mathematics, Nina pursued a teaching career. Nadia, however, after graduating got married and settled into a traditional homemaker role. At this point, the discussion became slightly confrontational, as Nadia insisted that Islam does not advocate symmetrical role allocation in marriage. According to her, 'Women are responsible for child rearing and looking after the husband'. The female respondents all acknowledged that God sanctifies their role as different from that of men, owing to the biological differences between the sexes. According to the Quran (verse 4:34): 'Men are responsible for women because God has given the one more than the other, and because they support them from their means'. This states woman alone can give birth and nurture, so men are required to provide material support. The women agreed unanimously, however, that this verse does not restrict women from providing material support. After some lengthy discussion, they concluded that a career combined with family life is the truest portrait of a Muslim woman.

This revealing discussion shows that indoctrination changed the women's social roles and perspectives. As Marcia (1993) acknowledges, social roles are highly important in understanding adult behaviour and development. In university, for instance, the women adopted new social roles that expanded their perceived opportunities for self-expression, giving structure to their identity. According to Parsons (1960), social roles connect individuals to social environments. If this is true, then the indoctrination process took place within a set environment, namely university. I want to find out, however, what happened to the women's identity once they returned to their family homes. As expected, the women maintained their newfound identities, even though their beliefs were not supported by family members. This would indicate that the women's old values and beliefs had been effectively altered by indoctrination. More significantly, after encountering HT, the women physically changed their outward appearances in accordance with their newfound ideals. As Amina confirmed:

> *Alhamdulillah* [Thank God] I found the sisters, who brought me to Islam ... I started praying, and then I adopted Islamic dress. Wearing the *hijaab* and *jilbaab* was the biggest step...Naturally, my classmates and lecturers were shocked, but I was totally content, because I was pleasing my Rubb [God].

Apart from physical changes, the women's behaviour was reshaped in harmony with their new identity. For example, the peer group enforced segregation from the male student population within a social context. This behaviour came as a shock to some of the women's classmates, as Nadia explained: 'When I stopped mixing freely, I experienced some negative reactions – one *Kuffar* student called me a nun'. The women's new identity was tested by a variety of social interactions, but they remained committed to their remodelled identity. From a social psychology perspective, they successfully resolved previous identity conflicts and developed an identity capable of moving on to other adult challenges like work and marriage.[2]

Inside HT – A Female Perspective

On the surface, HT appears to be largely male-dominated, making the role of female activists unclear. Some feminist commentators have suggested that if the social landscape becomes widely dominated by men, then women become suppressed and passive (Komarovsky, 2004). Before embarking on the study, I suspected that this gender imbalance would be visible in HT, but nothing could be further from the truth. The women I met – through their educational, political and social activism – appear to be setting their own agendas. To demonstrate this more effectively, I will look at the women's ideological beliefs and party activities.

Motivation and Ideology

On the question of ideology, I was not surprised by the women's responses. The party *Mabda'a* (ideology) came to the forefront of the discussion, because it is

---

2   *Identity conflict* refers to issues that affected the women's student life and interpersonal relationships, which seemed to bring on a crisis that forced them to redefine themselves (Jenkins, 2004).

viewed as a 'comprehensive way of life that organises every aspect of society' (Amina). Similarly, Nina stated: 'the ideology is the foundation of the party ... it is the soul of its existence and without it the party would die'. Their idealistic rhetoric made it difficult to delve into deeper issues and motivations concerning ideology. Instead, my questions only seemed to gain a combative response and they did not elicit any credible information. I decided to gather more insight into the ideological mindset of the women. By asking questions about living in the west, I was able to understand their ideological commitment rather better. In particular, we discussed the proposed ban of the *niqab* (face veil). They questioned why a liberal state was interfering in the freedoms of its citizens, and the subsequent erosion of personal liberty. The women were agreed that the establishment of the *Khilafah* (Islamic society) would resolve this imbalance and other problems, because the Islamic State alone can reflect ideology through social relationships. These women believe in their adopted ideology and embrace its ideals in practice throughout their lives.

I have extrapolated a few key inferences concerning the women's perception of their adopted ideology. First, they believe their attachment to the ideology was inspired by intellectual enlightenment. As Nina observed, 'the Islamic ideology is built on the correct basis [divinity], which is established through rational thought'. Second, the women believe they have freed themselves from all social, political and moral forms of western ideology, completing their presumed emancipation from secular convention. Third, the women appear to be more vigorous than men in their adherence to ideology. Amina suggested: 'I think some of the brothers are more affected by secularism ... we [women] have to wear the *hijaab*, which makes us much stronger'.

MacDonald (1992) also considered female activists to be stronger and more dedicated to extremist ideology. Although there is no clear way to determine the levels of ideological commitment between men and women, I have tried to look at ideological motivation. Galvin (1983) asserted that women appeared more idealistic than men. He also suggested that women join radical groups with different motivations (Galvin, 1983). My data has struggled to produce clear answers to these issues, but I did find that male members seemed more drawn to the power of group membership. In contrast, the focus group discussion indicated that the women were attracted by promises of a better life. My research, however, has continually shown that an individual's personality, background and experiences are equally, if not more, important.

Structure and Activism

Patriarchy is commonly defined as a male-dominated system in which women are subordinate to men. According to the women, patriarchy does not exist in HT, because men and women operate in separate spheres. The administrative rules of HT are not gender-biased in their configuration, and thus women are invited to perform party activity. As Nadia explained, 'the women's structure has its own *Mutamad* [national leader], its own committees ... we carry the *dawah* in the same way as the brothers'. Historically, women were not governed according to the party structure, but as their participation grew, so did demands for equal representation. By the mid-1990s considerable effort had been made to encourage women to become autonomous. According to Nina:

> Before I joined the party, the sisters' structure was organised by the brothers, which was disastrous. There was little communication and the sisters became disconnected ... afterwards the party addressed this issue. We [sisters] were given control of women's *dawah*.

Female members had become a separate entity within HT, which allowed them to set up their own structural hierarchy. The equal participation of women must be understood in terms of the positions which they hold; they are the same as those of the men, but operate in two separate HT systems. So, for example, both Sara and Amina are *Mushrifs* (teachers); they perform these roles in exactly the same fashion as their male counterparts.

Gender Equality

In terms of activism, female HT members secured their own political space. However, to what extent, if any, has HT empowered its female populace? I wanted to know, from the perspective of the women, whether HT ideology is a response to the patriarchal interpretation of divine text that is dominant among Muslim societies. According to one female activist: 'Islam is the truth, it has been revealed to humankind by Allah and therefore it is the most just system ... it ensures true equality between the sexes unlike capitalism which exploits women'. According to this, Islam and for that matter HT ideology derives its understanding and mandate from the Quran and Sunnah. In theory, this guarantees rights and justice for women, and for men, in the entirety of their life.

HT would claim that it has enabled its female members, through enlightenment, to acquire the ability to interpret the divine rights bestowed to her. This process has resulted in a complete rejection of ethnic cultural-tradition, which has subjected women to gender discrimination within many ethnic communities. Yet, I struggled to be convinced by these rather formulaic responses to my questions, so I sought to challenge the women's idealistic notion of equality.

Firstly, I asked about the concept and practice of '*Qiwama*'.[3] There was a lengthy discussion about the precise meaning of the term, Amina, for instance, suggested that it meant 'men having responsibility over women'. While, Nina explained that it just relates to men providing for women in a financial capacity. The

---

3   *Qiwama*, as mentioned in the Quran, is a highly controversial notion. Taken literally it implies that God has given men guardianship over women because 'Allah has given one more than the other because they support them from their means' (4:34).

women gave me the impression that they were all in agreement concerning gender equality in Islam, despite the fact that 'men and women have differing roles and responsibilities' (Nina). The concept of superiority was hotly contested in relation to *Qiwama*, and it was clear the women were resolutely adamant about men having no everlasting superiority over them. This unified stance quickly dissolved when the discussion moved to the issue of 'beating'. In the same Quranic verse as *Qiwama*, God grants men the right to 'banish them to their couches, and beat them' (Quran, 4:34). Surprisingly, the women seemed to be firmly split over this controversial piece of text. One group believed literally men have been granted legal mandate to control and police women, even to the extent of beating them. While the other group argued that this text has been misunderstood and misinterpreted. In other words, men do not have the right to beat women. This skewed division between the women goes somewhat deeper. In particular, the women who disagree with the text also argue that Islamic scholarship is excessively masculine, which enables men to define the role of women as subservient. Dwyer's (2000) study of Muslim women discovered a strong connection with men monopolising religious space and discourse in order to validate their influence.

The women collectively attributed the cause of gender inequality to ethno-cultural practices and traditions. In essence, they all drew a clear division between religion and culture. In this regard, as Sara surmised: 'our place is not the home … men and women are equal in Islam'. However, this rather programmed response underscores confusion between religious belief and practice. In theory, the women believe Islam grants them gender equality, but they manifest male prescribed practices (for example, asking permission before leaving the home, wearing Islamic dress and child nurturing). Somewhat surprisingly the respondents fervently argued that they were more liberated then western women, because they had accepted to live within the moral boundaries established by God. Therefore, their Islamic identity provided them a means to repel the dominant non-Islamic culture (for example, both Western and Eastern). Dwyer (2000) found similar responses amongst Muslim women, as they used Islam to assert rights and freedoms that are often denied to them by ethno-cultural practices. However, as Malik (The *Guardian*, 25 October 2006) suggests, religious and cultural practices are in a constant state of flux, because 'they have a mixed and changing social meaning'. Therefore, HT female activists are equally equipped with male members, in terms of education and career opportunities, but they seem less forceful to interpret religious principles.

Summary

Two key thoughts inspired my focus in this chapter. First, I sought to understand the experiences of four HT female members. Second, I wanted to find out what impact these experiences had on the women and whether they made a difference to their radicalisation. As my discussions have shown, the women emerged from very similar social backgrounds. During their early upbringing, namely at secondary school, the women did a lot of things to gain acceptance amongst their white peers. Importantly, in order to belong to the peer group, the women consciously concealed their ethno-religious identity, which allowed them to fit in. This caused deep identity confusion. The women evolved through their youth with an incomplete and fragmented sense of identity, as they constantly had to negotiate between conflicting social worlds and value systems. As Nadia explained: 'I could never hide my Asian side totally, for example, my friends had boyfriends but I never did ... this always made me feel like an outsider'. In many ways, these confusions in identity and sense-making reflect the intolerance of the majority culture. Therefore, the women were fearful of showing fragments of their ethno-religious identity because they were essentially seen as backward and inferior. So, clearly at this stage of the women's trajectory they were struggling to find themselves in a society that on some levels rejected their presence, making them feel socially vulnerable.

In relation to social vulnerability, when the women went to university they encountered more complex problems and realities, which made them susceptible to radicalisation. To start with, living away from home increased feelings of loneliness, which made the peer group an attractive prospect. An obvious issue to consider at this point is how and why the respondents were drawn to HT activists at university? Based on the research accumulated during my fieldwork, it appears clear that both male and female HT respondents became radicalised within the closed boundaries of a peer group. It appears the young women gravitated towards relations with people that were alike to them, based on similar social experiences. In essence, the women sought refuge in the 'familiar', seeking out women with the same ethno-religious and social class backgrounds. According to Burleson (1994), adult friendships are rooted in similarity, as this facilitates the sharing of beliefs, allowing for spiritual self-exploration. More interestingly, Murstein (1977) grounded friendship within a proximity paradigm, which he termed 'closed-field friendships'. In other words, the pathways to friendship are governed by closed social settings. The respondents at university, for example, were thrown into an unsettling social environment in which they found safety in the closed relations with HT activists.

The exposure to HT rhetoric which takes place in this setting has a powerful influence on the formation of a new cognitive perspective. Within this tightly-knit context, respondents fashion a radical identity by demarcating themselves in accordance to HT collective identity and membership. This creates a symbiotic connection with HT, as one female activist eerily put it: 'the Hizb (HT) does not need us, we need the Hizb'. The effects of this collective identity were more visibly seen when the respondents talked about non-Muslims. In particular, the respondents saw their own collective HT identity in opposition to 'others', which in turn, enabled them to dehumanise non-Muslims as the enemy. This in essence merges the group with the individual, producing a powerful sense of belonging. It is clear HT radicalisation takes place within a peer group setting, and this is supported by other scholarly work. Della Porta (2006, p. 167) makes a similar conclusion, when she asserts that the choice to join a radical movement involves 'cliques of friends'. This was further reinforced by Bakker's (2006) research on radical Islamist movements in Europe. He discovered that peer group associations were a key variable in the radicalisation process: 'a picture emerges of networks including friends or relatives … that radicalise with little outside interference' (Bakker 2006, p. 56).

In the context of HT, the discovery of like-minded women who shared the same economic and ethno-religious backgrounds made it easier to offset the negative effects of social isolation felt during early university life. Given the identity confusions surrounding their early socialisation, it is no surprise the women emerged from multiple social worlds, which reinforced feelings of social difference. At university within the HT peer group, the women formed and maintained a new identity construct that challenged Western and Eastern value systems.

Chapter 7

Radicalisation: 'It's in the demographics'

The study of radicalisation has become an important research topic. Many articles and reports have been published, largely as a response to acts of terror. One such report, commissioned by the New York Police Department (NYPD) intelligence division, stated that the majority of Islamic radicals lived 'unremarkable lives' and had 'unremarkable jobs' (Silber and Bhatt, 2007). I regularly come across imprecise observations that tend to generalise radicalisation, ignoring the fact it is a highly complex and diverse phenomenon. In the previous chapters, I attempted to study the process of radicalisation by observing individual experiences, which allowed me to arrive at several important conclusions based on this examination. Now I need to determine whether these findings hold outside of my investigative sample. A great deal of what I know about HT, such as its social composition, the social status of its membership, the education and ethnicity of its members, has been obtained through surveys. Correlating this data would, in theory, allow me to determine whether a specific demographic is more susceptible to HT radicalisation. Of particular interest is whether HT members in Britain share sociological characteristics. This might be useful in profiling Islamic radicals, if profiling is at all feasible, and in understanding somewhat better the motivations of Muslims who become radicalised.

Background

I have been interested in the phenomenon of radicalisation for several years, trying to understand it, and determine its possible causes. The group interviews I carried out explored radicalisation in some depth, providing a relaxed environment in which the respondents openly expressed their views and experiences. Nonetheless, the views that the women conveyed, for example, may not be representative of the wider HT population. Despite the meaningful data I collected from my interviews with male and female members, I realised the need to conduct surveys. These surveys allow me to extend my knowledge of the radical condition within HT, beyond the individual members. In particular, my research has indicated that the current identities of members strongly depend on their past and present social experiences and backgrounds.

Before determining the key sociological characteristics of HT radicalisation, it is useful to briefly summarise some of the key findings of Russell and Miller (1977). They conducted a sociological study that involved investigating the likely settings of radicalisation amongst militant German groups. The distinctiveness of their work has been lasting primarily because it identifies a number of features of radical groups, and, subsequently, this has gone on to inform my own standpoint. They concluded that radical groups exhibit common sociological characteristics, such as age, social background, race and gender. More significantly, Russell and Miller (1977, pp. 17-25) identify universities as the major recruiting ground for radical-terrorist organisations. This was certainly the case for HT members I interviewed, but while this sample was very revealing it is not sufficient in itself. This is because, unlike Russell and Miller, I am not trying to develop a generic profile of radical behaviour; instead my goal is to sketch out a common profile of HT membership. With this goal in mind, I needed to concentrate on class, age, gender, ethnicity and race, but other sociological features of organised social life, such as religion and peer groups, might also need to be examined.

Youth Radicalism: Age

After each survey, I would briefly reflect on the information given by members in order to pick out possible themes for further investigation. One very noticeable theme that emerged from my survey was the disproportionate number of young people involved within the group. For instance, 85 per cent of the members were below the age of 30 and 96.3 per cent were recruited before the age of 25 (see Table 7.1 and 7.2). Therefore, age should not be taken for granted, because it has a powerful effect on the way members see themselves and others. Just as religion and ethnicity shaped member's identities, so does age.

The radicalisation of the youth is not a new phenomenon; rather it has been the youth that have formed the foundation of countless popular movements. Iran, for example, experienced a significant 'youth bulge' that fostered the conditions for its revolution in 1979. So, why do young people appear more inclined towards HT in Britain? Some social theorists believe that identity is an unstable collection of perceptions in which age grapples with other social imperatives like ethnicity

Table 7.1   Age of HT Members

Age (Current)	Male Members	Female Members	Members	Average (%)
Under 20	9	6	15	8
20-25	35	37	72	39
25-30	32	39	71	38
30-35	14	8	22	11.8
35-40	5	1	6	3.2
Over 40	0	0	0	0
Total	**95**	**91**	**186**	**100**

Table 7.2   Age of Recruitment

Age of recruitment	Male Members	Female Members	Members	Average (%)
Under 20	53	51	104	56
20-25	35	40	75	40.3
25-30	7	0	7	3.7
30-35	0	0	0	0
35-40	0	0	0	0
Over 40	0	0	0	0
Total	**95**	**91**	**186**	**100**

and class (James and James, 2004). In some respects, a member's age is tied to their identity, which shifts over time. Trying to understand this process is extremely difficult. Cote (1996) formulated a theory, which ties identity shifts to historical cultural markers. Another more influential model was proposed by Van Gennep (1960). He identified three key stages of social development: 'separation, transition and incorporation' (Van Gennep, 1960, p. 3). This process provides a way of looking at how the social transition to new age identities takes place. In the following sections, I seek to describe and explain how these stages help answer the question of youth involvement in HT.

Separation

Van Gennep (1960), a noted French ethnographer, developed his theory of rites of passage, which he suggested define a period when an individual reaches a new and significant change in his or her life. More importantly, these rites of passage are designed to help people to understand their new roles in society. In the separation stage, members experience a feeling of detachment from the family environment, entering into a new role and social setting. This rite was mainly felt when members left the safety of the family home for university. In particular, the members I interviewed looked forward to their university experience, as they felt it would give them independence from their parents. Hutnik (1985) found that identities are often crafted to maintain distance from others. In the case of HT members, this is not surprising, as the older generation have found it difficult to impart the traditions of the subcontinent to the newer generation. From my discussions it was clear that members sought not to be represented by their parent's identities. This somewhat negative identity formation pointed to a more confused identity ambivalence, which was usually directed to their parents' culture and ethnicity. Although, the cause of radicalisation cannot be exclusively defined within the context of a generation gap, this has undoubtedly contributed to conflict with and separation from families.

The most notable difference between the two generations relates to mindset. The first generation arrived in the early 1950s to fill the labour shortage in Britain. As a result, they never envisaged permanent settlement, instead they believed in returning home. This belief allowed the first generation to transfer the values of the homeland, which legitimised a separation from British culture. Therefore, this generation has been strongly influenced by a transitory or migrant mindset. As the prospect of returning home diminished, the first generation sought to establish a religious base that would transport their morals and values in opposition to those of the receiving culture. However, this mindset could not be passed on to the newer generation, as they have found it difficult to adopt the beliefs and lifestyles of their parents. The second generation are born and educated here, giving them direct access to the majority culture. This has enabled them to experience two distinct social worlds, which have inspired some to challenge the conservative values of their parents; attitudes and behaviours that have been transplanted from the subcontinent. In particular, the rejection of these religious and cultural mores is evidence of a different mindset. The younger generation have adopted a different way of living in Britain, reflecting a symbolic separation from their parents, who were economic migrants.

Transition

When young people are in the transitional stage, they are in a state of interruption, separated from their previous roles and not yet incorporated into the new one. The transition to new social settings can be extremely unsettling, especially for minorities who are more vulnerable to rejection. The transitional stage can be usefully applied to the experiences of HT members at varying points in their life cycle. Young people often struggle during adolescence, because this stage of development is perhaps the most disruptive. During this stage, young people are greatly concerned with the perception of others. In the previous chapter, many of the respondents failed to understand how they 'fitted-in', which resulted in them developing a 'dysfunctional' identity. As a result many of the respondents suffered from role confusion, meaning they were uncertain about their position in the social world. The transition stage is a period when members ought to learn the appropriate behaviour for the new stage they are entering. However, identity problems are very common during adolescence, as young people naturally struggle to contend with the changes that take place. Therefore, the most important transition for members appears to be to university. Some social scientists believe that young people are more inclined towards getting involved with movements concerned with protest and rejection at university (Russell and Miller, 1977). This is because university is seen as a natural social space for young people to actively learn and grow, and prepare them to become independent actors. Newcomb and Feldman (1994) conducted research into identity shifts during life transitions, focusing on students going to university. They concluded that young people become unsettled by leaving home and struggle to form new identities, which can often lead them to discover alternative identities.

Incorporation

The ways in which members move between social locations are often age-related, for example, leaving home to go to university. This is a key rite of passage for young people, as it allows them to discover themselves. In the previous chapters, I discovered that members often emerge from childhood as incomplete social actors, which contributes to their perceived separation. This makes young people the most sensitive age group in society, especially when their aspirations and needs are not satisfied. Therefore, the final stage of incorporation takes place when the members are formally admitted into the new role. Joining HT is the most visible example, as the member adopts a new and different identity, which has been stimulated by earlier transition and separation rites. Although, the rites of passages are important, there are more practical issues that relate to age. The British Muslim community, for example, has the youngest age profile of any other religious group (The Muslim Weekly, 15 October 2004). Therefore, radicalisation tends to be a condition associated with youth. Therefore, HT's fraternity is almost exclusively comprised of young people, making age a very important component.

Social Background: Social Class

Age has been suggested as a very important variable, but the rapid radicalisation of HT youth must be seen from a wider social perspective that includes social background. According to Warner (1949), social class should be isolated within a socio-economic framework that relates to fixed properties, such as income, education and wealth. In line with this analytical approach, the 2001 census, and a separate Labour Force Survey conducted in 2004, has indicated that British Muslims are one of the most deprived social groups in the UK (The Muslim Weekly, 15 October 2004). Huntington (1996) believes that large-scale unemployment among young people provides a likely source for radicalisation. However, in the context of HT, it was found that the majority of the population occupied a higher than average social status. For instance, 97.3 per cent of the sample classified themselves as middle class.

Are HT Members Middle Class?

Most HT members claimed middle-class status, even though they seemed somewhat unaware of its precise meaning and application. This has made it very difficult to pin down how much members overestimate their socio-economic

Table 7.3   Social Class of HT Members

Class[1]	Male Members	Female Members	Members	Average (%)
Upper class	2	0	2	1
Upper middle	29	19	48	25.8
Lower middle	64	67	131	70.5
Working class	2	3	5	2.7
Lower class	0	0	0	0
Total	**95**	**91**	**186**	**100**

Note: [1] Taken from the five-class model developed by Thompson and Hickey (2005).

status, making it unsuitable to let members assess themselves as middle class. Furthermore, individuals do not always evaluate themselves in exactly the same manner. I needed to find a way of classifying the socio-economic position of HT members, before trying to understand the role of class. After consulting the extensive literature on social class, I defined middle class using four key criteria: occupation, income, property and education (Davis and Moore, 1970; Parkin, 1979). Most social theorists tend to study class stratification through these distinct variables, which allowed me to fairly assess the class demographic of HT.

Firstly, questions related to occupation revealed a large grouping of highly qualified professionals who occupy relatively privileged positions (see Table 7.4). There is a particularly strong focus on non-manual occupations among the members, giving them a natural advantage in the labour market. Nonetheless, some social theorists would argue that this mobility is artificial and short-ranged, due to a social and cultural 'buffer zone' between the middle and working classes (Parkin, 1979, p. 56). This view assumes that movement from manual to non-manual occupations occurs superficially, and thus workers are employed at the lower levels of the work hierarchy (Goldthorpe et al., 1987). However, HT members do not occupy such positions; rather they have moved into professional posts, providing them with long-range mobility. Indeed, as Davis and Moore (1970) have suggested, Britain appears to have become a meritocracy, which means that emphasis is placed on achievement and this determines the position in the occupational hierarchy.

The occupation of female members falls into three key groupings. The most common is that of intermediate, but the proportion of female professionals is considerably lower than that of male members. The second largest categorisation is that of homemaker, which was indicated by 34 per cent of female respondents. In relation to some of these gender inequalities, it is worth noting that many female

Table 7.4   Occupational Activities of HT Members

Occupation	Male Members	Female Members	Members	Average (%)
Professional	47	15	62	33.3
Intermediate	38	33	71	38.2
Skilled (non-Manual)	2	0	2	1
Manual Partly Skilled	0	0	0	0
Unskilled	0	0	0	0
Unemployed	0	0	0	0
Homemaker	0	31	31	16.7
Student	8	12	20	10.8
Total	**95**	**91**	**186**	**100**

Note: Adapted from Reid (1977, p. 32).

members suggested that they wanted to have children, and thus maintaining a professional career alongside this goal seemed far too challenging.

Secondly, a member's household income tends to be higher than the national average.[1] Private firms employ most members, which has widened their economic capital. This income differential between occupations is somewhat apparent between those employed in the public sector, compared with the members in the private field. The income distribution among the members shows that over 60 per cent are located in the highest income categories. Thirdly, I was somewhat surprised by the relatively large number of members who privately own property (see Table 7.5). This is because many of the members are quite young, and thus I would have assumed were just entering the property ladder. This indicates that members have shown a strong tendency to acquire property assets as a means of social mobility. As Parkin (1968) acknowledges, property ownership provides access to economic power, and thus is a key feature of the division of labour. Moreover, from my discussions with members, I realised that their parents had placed significant importance on creating a successful property portfolio. This gave them a significant financial advantage when house prices surged in the late 1980s. According to Cannadine (1999), middle-class families have greater financial resources, placing them in a better position to assist their children in purchasing a home or passing on their property. Thus, inherited property accounted for 27.4 per cent of the sample. Furthermore, with the recent introduction of Islamic mortgages, many members have used this as a means to acquire larger properties and gain greater economic independence.

---

1   It was estimated that in 2007 the top fifth of households in the UK was £72,900 (after tax £52,400). Refer to www.statistics.gov.uk.

Table 7.5   Property Ownership

Property Ownership	Male Members	Female Members	Members	Average (%)
Free Hold	41	43	84	45.2
Inherited	29	22	51	27.4
Islamic Mortgage	19	23	42	22.6
Renting	6	3	9	4.8
Council	0	0	0	0
Total	**95**	**91**	**186**	**100**

Fourthly, higher education is clearly important for HT members, as it relates to their desire to gain employment advancement. As Cooper (1979) has discovered, most professionals are graduates, thereby allowing them to move into higher income categories. For example, evidence from the sample revealed that 87.6 per cent of members graduated from a higher education institution (see Table 7.6).

Table 7.6   Education Levels of HT Members

Education Level	Male Members	Female Members	Total Members	Average (%)
Postgraduate	13	8	21	11.3
Graduate	73	69	142	76.3
College	1	2	3	1.6
School (GCSE)	0	0	0	0
No qualifications	0	0	0	0
Current Student	8	12	20	10.8
Total	**95**	**91**	**186**	**100**

This is not surprising since members' parents have similar academic backgrounds, which helps to duplicate class status across generations (see Table 7.7).

Relatively few members had limited education, indicating the propensity to acquire university admission and gain professional qualifications. More significantly, HT members have very little obstacles in going to university, as they have substantial financial support from their parents. Therefore, education is certainly a defining feature of HT's middle class disposition, which allows it to maintain itself as a class. It is worth noting, however, that social theorists have struggled to agree upon a precise and coherent understanding of the middle class. For example, some theorists believe that culture is a defining feature of the middle class (Cooper, 1979). Then again, as Roberts et al. (1977, p. 107) has

Table 7.7   Parents' Education Level

Education Level	Father's Education	Mother's Education	Total	Average (%)
Postgraduate	8	11	19	10.3
Graduate	85	79	164	88.2
College	2	0	2	1
School (GCSE)	0	0	0	0
No qualifications	0	1	1	0.5
Current Student	0	0	0	0
Total	**95**	**91**	**186**	**100**

insisted, it is no longer possible to define a core middle class culture because within the white-collar strata no coherent set of values exists. If one assumes, like Goldthorpe et al. (1987), that social classes are groups characterised by shared income, lifestyles and cultures, then HT members certainly comprise a homogenous grouping. Clearly, the data gathered from the sample indicate that social mobility has been achieved or maintained through occupation, education and wealth (property and income).

Throughout this book, I have used the generic term 'middle class' to define the social composition of HT. However, it is not entirely precise, as Parkin (1968, p. 175) points out, 'it lacks the analytical precision necessary for considering issues which cannot be posed in terms of class polarisation'. Parkin (1968, p. 176) is referring here to comparisons made between 'white-collar groups'. In relation to HT, I noticed very early on that activists seemed to be drawn from specific occupational fields (see Table 7.8).

Although the above data does not conclusively support my initial observations, it does illustrate that HT membership is drawn from the ranks of the educated middle class. This identification is important as research has shown that the educated, namely university graduates, are more inclined to 'left-wing politics than those of similar social status but less educated' (Parkin, 1968, p. 178). More interestingly, I found that disproportionately large numbers of HT members were drawn from non-social science fields. In terms of radical behaviour, this is significant, as it is largely believed that radicalism is usually equated to specific occupational categories (Glazer, 1961). Firstly, it is not surprising to see a high percentage of teachers and doctors in radical organisations, as these professions are constantly confronted with bleak social problems (Parsons, 1960). Indeed, very few HT members have experience of social disadvantage, and thus when confronted with these social realities may trigger inclination towards radical or right-wing politics. Secondly, their occupations are grounded within more technical or professionalised subjects, namely computing and science. This trend is harder to understand. When I started to give this greater thought, I remembered from my discussions that most HT members appear greatly fascinated by political concepts,

Table 7.8   The Occupational Fields of HT Members

Education Level	Male Members	Female Members	Total Members	Average (%)
Medical/Sciences	13	11	24	12.9
Engineering	8	1	9	4.8
Computing	38	10	48	25.8
Finance	14	8	22	11.8
Law	0	0	0	0
Arts	0	1	1	0.5
Social Sciences	1	2	3	1.5
Academia/teaching	12	15	27	14.6
Student	8	12	20	10.8
Other	1	312[1]	32	17.3
Total	**95**	**91**	**186**	**100**

Note: [1] This table represents female members that are homemakers.

like ideology. In fact, non-social science related students seemed unaware that HT appropriated these concepts from the Western political tradition, which is easily noticeable to those with a social science background.

The Role of Class

There appears to be a disproportionate number of middle-class recruits in HT, but this is not reflective of wider socio-economic trends among the Muslim community in Britain. In fact, the Labour Force Survey (2004) found that British Muslims were most likely to be economically inactive and 31 per cent of Muslims in work had no formal qualifications (Labour Force Survey, 2004). These rather bleak figures are all the more surprising when compared to the socio-economic success of HT members. In order to understand this disparity, one must look more closely at the social position of HT members. In particular, why is the middle-class drawn towards HT? To start with, HT young people are the progeny of largely middle class immigrants, originating predominantly from South Asia. According to Parkin (1968), family plays a key role in positioning individuals at certain stages in the class structure. Moreover, HT members' families sought to ensure that their children gained considerable advantage through education. Their parents relied on their academic qualifications to gain upward mobility, which motivated them to impart to their offspring a similar ambition. In contrast, most working class families have a tendency to assign greater value to employment (Lareau, 2003). Thus, the members inherited a strong middle class ethic that required the completion of higher education. This academic tradition provided members with greater options and access to better employment opportunities.

More significantly, two very different sets of value orientations exist among the middle and working classes. HT members have secured a stable economic lifestyle through their class position, enabling them to become more concerned with non-welfare related politics. In contrast, the working class place greater emphasis on material security. Thompson's (1988) study of working class Asians in Coventry indicated that children begin to contribute to family income at a very early age due to economic need. Therefore, the young Muslims who join HT tend to differ from other young Muslims. In fact, they seem to have emerged from very different social conditions. The vast majority of young Muslims in Britain live under very poor social conditions, which is often a reflection of their social class and limited education. Conversely, most members of HT can be characterised as middle class. Despite these socio-economic differences, the experience of being socially marginalised is very real for both groups. So, why has HT been largely unsuccessful in recruiting working class Muslims? There are several possible explanations for this failure.

Firstly, it could be argued that a difference in 'post-materialist values' has skewed recruitment. This theory places individuals within a continuum of needs, with economic survival being a primary need while the pursuits of religious and political ideals are considered secondary in nature. Thus, as Lewis (1994) noted, South Asian Muslims constituted the underclass of the male working class.[2] The Labour Force Survey (2004), for instance, has estimated that South Asians have the highest rates of unemployment among any minority group. Therefore, it is fair to assume that the values placed on economic security are proportional to one's class position. Working class Muslims, for example, are more likely to suffer from economic deprivation. This has a tendency to influence their political activism, which is more geared towards material and economic gain. On the contrary, HT members are not driven by economic need, nor do they seek exclusive rewards for their specific subgroup, unlike the working class. These two sets of value orientations provide both groups with divergent economic and cultural strategies, making it difficult for HT to recruit working class Muslims.

Secondly, one of the key traits of working class men is their dependence on local territory and their local community for a sense of identity (Thompson, 1978). It might seem to be too simple to say that the social position of working class Muslims limits their recruitment within HT, but the sociological data indicates a class divide. Let me explain this in a bit more detail. HT has failed to capture the support of the large Pakistani communities in the north of England. These dispersed communities are configured into introverted working class colonies. The Pakistani community is an amalgamation of different ethnic groupings, yet in the North of England Mirpuris form the majority. Mirpuris arrived as working class migrants, settling down in the

---

2   The underclass, as defined by Mann (1992, p. 2), describes a 'section of society that is seen to exist within and yet at the base of the working class'.

industrialised North, and their children assumed the same patterns of stratification as their parents. This sub-ethnic group appears to be less responsive to HT, due to their inability to transcend their ethnic and class positions.

It is somewhat obvious that HT has failed to recruit across class boundaries, but I wanted to know what members thought about this issue. After surveying members' views, it was clear that no consensus existed. Most members denied a failure to recruit working class Muslims, but once the data was presented to them they were often unable to provide an explanation. Some members argued that Muslims are solely motivated by the pursuit of money, because they come from the most deprived regions of the world, at the expense of Islam. Another popular suggestion focused on the Asian working class tendency to follow the economic and cultural norms of their community, making it impossible for HT to break into these closed and isolated colonies. There is some truth to this argument, as Asian working class communities encourage their children to follow similar employment patterns, assigning greater emphasis to work. Consequently, those young Muslims inherit a working class tradition from their migrant parents, making them less likely to enter into higher education. Access to university gave middle class members the opportunity to interact with people of a similar social background; it was within this setting that radicalisation took place. As I have shown in previous chapters, new identities emerged during university. Such changes, therefore, clearly impacted the members' lives, leading to a new outlook, which was a significant transitional moment in their development. Although, I will address these points in more detail in the sections related to university and peer groups, it is important to note here that the members found belonging amongst their middle class peers. Characteristically, as the data shows, it is the middle classes who show greater inclination towards recruitment within HT.

In order to understand why the South Asian working classes show little propensity to join HT, I decided to talk to some working class activists in the East End of London. The respondents, including some who consider themselves on the radical right of the Islamist spectrum, generally felt HT lack any appreciation, even downplaying, working class lives and backgrounds. As Trigg stated, 'HT don't exist here (East London) because this is a working class area – the struggles of our community involve poverty, housing, drugs and so on – HT members live sheltered lives away from real problems … so they (HT) can't relate'. Clearly, HT activists have emerged from different social worlds, making it difficult for them to identify with the struggles and histories of working class Muslims in Britain. The inability to empathise with the economic realities of working class Muslims has meant low support for HT ideology, which was viewed as idealistic and abstract. As Imran explained, 'their (HT) politics is about Khilafah … how is that going to solve the problems we (Muslims) are facing in Britain'. These issues reveal that class has shaped two distinct mindsets. The working class, for example, tend to have large families, which makes work an immediate priority. In contrast, the stability and resources of a middle class household provides greater support for education, intellectual reflection and other leisure pursuits.

Ethnicity

Ethnicity provides a powerful source of attachment and solidarity, as it stems from a deep sense of 'people-hood' (Stack, 1986). More importantly, ethnicity offers an individual perspective, which differentiates members of the social group from non-members. In this respect, ethnicity is a key sociological attribute, especially within HT, because it provides a common source of identity. Not surprisingly, South Asians constitute the largest ethnic cluster, forming 98 per cent of the party body in the UK. Although this recruitment trend might appear disproportionate, it does correspond to the wider demographics of the Muslim community, since South Asians are the single largest ethnic group (Ansari, 2004).

Table 7.9   Ethnicity of HT Members

Ethnicity	Male Members	Female Members	Members	Average (%)
Pakistani	67	59	126	67.7
Bangladeshi	18	19	37	19.8
Indian	9	10	19	10.5
Arab	1	0	1	0.5
African	0	1	1	0.5
Other	0	2	2	1
Total	**95**	**91**	**186**	**100%**

While I was conducting the sample, several members insisted that, for them, ethnicity retains no significance, especially in terms of their identity. Yet, as shown in the above table, HT is ethnically homogenous. This does raise an important question: how does ethnicity affect a member's self-image and, perhaps more importantly, what role does it play in their lives? Before I can properly address this question, it is worth briefly reappraising our definition of ethnic identity. Tajfel (1981) frames ethnic identity within the confines of group membership. This assumes an individual draws their self-image – which encompasses thinking, feelings and behaviour – from their membership of a particular ethnic group. Thus, individuals naturally seek to form a unified conception of themselves (Wetherell, 1987). For ethnic minorities the task of identity construction is far more complex, as they struggle to integrate diverse and conflicting social positions. Some members suggested that they had little control over their identity choices, particularly ethnicity, within the home environment. On the other hand, some members drew greater significance to skin colour and race, which they believed singled them out as different. The life histories of Abdul and Tariq, for example, showed how their ethnicity often emerged when they tried to reassert themselves in different social situations. When they felt victimised, for instance, they tried to renew their ethnic bounds. This would indicate that ethnicity is partly adopted by choice, as Banks (1996) asserts.

Beyond the restrictive measures of my survey, through ethnography, I was able to observe how ethnicity came to dominate members' self-perceptions in certain social environments. I witnessed members switching on these identities in family and religious gatherings, for example, in response to majority group expectation. In other words, members tend to modify their behaviour when faced with different ethnic identity options. For example, I observed some members who seemed to adopt and identify with the national culture, while others seemed to revert to their ethnic culture. In most cases, I witnessed a hybrid identity, which integrated facets of both cultures. Thus, it seemed apparent that members selected multiple identities, which allowed them to navigate through society. For example, members in their work environment clearly identified themselves as British – in terms of their language, dress and behaviour – while in community settings their ethnicity became more vocalised.

In spite of this, it was quite obvious that when I talked to members they seemed reluctant to accept that their ethnicity was a part of their overall identity make-up. Some social theorists think this is natural, since ethnic identity is endogenous, especially among second and third generation immigrants (Hutnik, 1985; Samad, 2004). This approach assumes that ethnicity develops from within, but after several discussions with members, I realised that a more complex picture of ethnicity was emerging. Firstly, it seemed their image of ethnicity had been distorted by the wider society. In particular, adverse experiences twisted the members' views of their surroundings, reinforcing a feeling of difference. I discovered that most members actively sought integration during their childhood, to the extent that the only visible difference would be skin colour. However, when this goal became disrupted, many members reverted to their cultural roots – in an effort to develop identification and meaning. Yet, most found it extremely difficult to derive meaning from their heritage, since they were also estranged from their culture. As one member aptly pointed out, 'I lived in the community [Pakistani], but I never felt part of it'. Secondly, within a family context, members did not develop an understanding of their ethnic identity. As one member commented, 'I never knew much about my culture growing up'. In general, a child's perception of ethnicity is usually stimulated within a family setting, which is dependent upon the connection a child has to their parents. Rosenthal and Feldman (1992) discovered that parents' participation in the community openly influenced their children's ethnic self-identification. Thus, most members never visited there local mosque or had any involvement in an ethnic community, which left them feeling detached.

In sum, though the vast majority of members preferred to identify themselves as Muslim, I would treat this self-imaging with a degree of caution. For a start, I have often seen members reasserting their ethnic identity in accordance with family custom. For instance, members tend to marry from within their own ethnic groupings. More importantly, it seems that ethnicity often emerges, and is identified with, during times of social difficulty and estrangement. For example, most members join HT at university, forming close ties with people of the same ethnicity and background.

Ethnicity across the Fraternity

Before conducting the survey, I was fully aware that South Asians formed the vast majority of the fraternity, but offering an explanation for this phenomenon is very difficult. HT has had little success in recruiting Somali, Arab, Turkish, Algerian and Moroccan Muslims. There are several possible reasons why HT has struggled to gain a foothold in these communities. Firstly, many of these are newly established communities, comprising working class immigrants. Somali Muslims, for example, have recently arrived in the UK as refugees and asylum seekers. They have sought low-paid manual work, as they have little education, which makes them less susceptible to encountering HT. Secondly, these communities are very introverted, having little contact with the values of the indigenous culture that occurs through the medium of education. These ethnic communities wish to retain a sense of their cultural heritage, maintaining a firm link to their language, religious beliefs and traditions.

On the other hand, the Yemeni community is one of the oldest migrant communities in Britain, so why are they not attracted to HT? I asked this question to some HT members, and I found their explanations quite insightful. One member suggested Yemeni's rarely formed ties with non-Arabs, especially at university, making it hard to develop a relationship with them. Similarly, another member argued Arabs in general have a tendency to look down upon non-Arabs, especially related to Islam because 'they believe Islam was revealed to them [Arabs]'. In spite of this, most of the members I spoke to were adamant that they rarely saw Arabs on university campuses, let alone Yemenis. There is some truth to this sentiment since the Yemeni community is very small, never exceeding fifteen thousand (1991; 2001, National Census). This is why Halliday (1996) describes them as the invisible Arabs. It is perhaps understandable that, given their extremely small population size, the Yemeni community is not widely represented within HT. Nonetheless, I do not think attraction to, or support for, HT can be reduced to just population size. For empirically, it has been shown that ethnicity seems to be an integral part of the overall scheme of radicalisation. In particular, as the above comments reveal, there are ethnic boundaries at work that inhibit relationships between Muslims of differing ethnicities. As Barth (1982) asserted, these boundaries dichotomise individuals into culturally separate groups. According to one member, segregation among ethnic groups is the norm at university. He suggested that students are drawn to their own ethnic heritage – of language, culture, food, music and so on.

Given the fiercely demarcated divisions between social worlds, it is not surprising to see a lack of representation among Yemeni Muslims within HT. As already mentioned, recruitment into HT tends to hinge upon ethnicity. In fact, the social base of membership for HT is drawn from South Asians who have very similar social backgrounds. In short, it is not ethnicity itself that is of major concern so much as the issues it helps to shed light on. For example, working class South Asians are not widely represented, making class and family status equally important. Thus, a better profile of those involved with HT would suggest that they are middle class South Asians.

Language and Culture

In the previous chapters, my respondents seemed very disconnected from their cultural roots, making it crucial to explore this issue in the survey. The process of migration makes it very difficult to maintain a sense of cultural identity. In particular, many cultural traits and customs are often lost in order to gain acceptance in the new social setting. According to Waters (1995), language usually fades away, as it becomes harder to transfer over the generations. In Britain, most working class Asian families teach their language of origin to their offspring, because it is considered a primary means of transmitting culture from one generation to another (Geaves, 1996, p. 68). Mosques often reinforce vernacular languages, creating a link between religion and ethnic origins. Thus, it is very common to find young people being taught Urdu or Bengali in local mosques. However, the sample data indicates that the vast majority of HT members failed to receive knowledge of their ethnic language.

Table 7.10   Language Fluency

Language	Male Members	Female Members	Members	Average (%)
Urdu	3	3	6	3.2
Hindi	1	2	3	1.6
Bengali	5	7	12	6.6
Arabic	1	0	1	0.5
Other	0	1	1	0.5
Mixed	23	20	43	23.1
None	62	58	120	64.5
Total	**95**	**91**	**186**	**100**

In general, the inability to speak one's native tongue is often perceived by the first generation as a symbolic rejection of their social group and culture. The sample indicated that 64.5 per cent of the members claimed no understanding or ability to speak a vernacular language. This was not surprising since I discovered, through my fieldwork observations and interviews, that members seemed completely disconnected from their ethnic culture. The loss of culture was somewhat inevitable, as the members were not taught about their culture during childhood. After I spoke to some of the parents of HT members, I gained a clearer picture. Some parents felt when they arrived in the United Kingdom they had no duty to maintain a foreign language and culture, because they came here with the goal to become British, which meant adopting the values of the dominant culture. In contrast, working class immigrants believed in the myth of return, and thus viewed their culture as a symbol of their social identity. The parents of members left their inner city dwellings in search for middle class status. Although, this departure was economically motivated, it did indicate a rejection of the ethnic community. Thus, most HT members grew up with little or no ties with, or experience of, ethnic communities.

It should be somewhat clearer from all this, then, that culture is viewed slightly differently by the middle classes. One possible reason for this steady erosion of cultural values among the members relates to family socialisation. In general, culture and language are formed at a relatively early age, through childhood exposure to parental influences. It is assumed that these processes shape an individual's cultural outlook throughout his or her life cycle. Among working class immigrants, for example, there was greater desire to re-establish their cultural identities in the receiving country. As Anwar (1976) notes, working class Pakistanis have used the institution of *Biradri* (kinship ties) to maintain traditional and cultural structures. Consequently, working class Muslims seem more successful in transmitting cultural values to their children. In comparison, my findings have shown that none of the HT members sampled were sent to Islamic schools or mosques to learn about religious or cultural matters during their upbringing. From this, it is noticeable that members' parents were less inclined towards transferring cultural mores to their offspring, which may have contributed to a steady erosion of cultural values among HT members.

Religiosity

Trying to better understand HT members is a very challenging endeavour. One aspect of their lives that remains difficult to document is their religious and spiritual lives. The survey indicated that members' religious beliefs and practices are important components in their daily lives, providing them with guidance and tranquillity. For the purposes of my study, I needed to find out when members became involved, or committed, to their religion. Before I present my findings, it is imperative to first explain the meaning of 'religious commitment' (Roof, 1979, p. 17). As Stark and Glock (1968) have pointed out, this can be very difficult because religiosity has a plurality of meanings. In other words, individuals perceive religion in different and conflicting ways. Despite this plurality, Stark and Glock (1968, p. 62) developed a five dimensional approach to understand religious commitment.[3] There classification principally relates to religious seekers, and not to wider sociological aspects of religion (Furseth and Repstad, 2006).

In the context of HT members, the belief dimension would entail 'Iman [belief] in Allah, his angels, his books, his messengers, the last day and al-Qada wal Qadar [divine fate]', which must be built on 'attasdiq al-jazim [decisive assent]'. Second, the ritualistic dimension involves performing and adhering to a set of structured religious practices (for example, five daily prayers). Thirdly, the experience dimension refers to subjective religious experiences and emotions. A member told me, for instance, after he prayed for the first time that he became overwhelmed by feelings of joy and tranquillity. Fourthly, the intellectual dimension involves acquiring knowledge about the fundamental tenets of the Islamic faith. For example, the basis of a member's actions is restricted to the *Hukm Shariah* (divine ruling) and therefore no action is performed until its ruling is known. Finally, the consequential dimension relates to the interaction with other people, and the effect religious beliefs and attitudes have on everyday life. Clearly, no comprehensive list can be crafted that correctly documents religiosity, as religious experiences are unique and complex. However, I have used these generic markers to identify a general pattern, which will help me analyse the commitment and development of members' religious beliefs and practices.

Tracking Religiosity among HT Members

Trying to locate a period in time when members became religious is central to my investigation. I wanted to gather data on the importance of religion during childhood: whether the members were religious, and, if so, what role it played in their family and social lives.

The overwhelming majority of members became involved with, and committed to, religious beliefs at university. What is greatly striking about the religious experiences of members is the lack of parental influence, which appears non-existent. If this is true, then how did a lack of religious background affect their conception of themselves? Firstly, it is relatively clear that parents played a marginal role in religious transference. For example, most parents failed to teach their children how to pray. However, trying to understand this phenomenon is not easy, especially since research on working class Muslims has shown that family members are primary influencing agents for religious matters (Modood and Werbner, 1997; Kucukcan, 1999). Most theorists acknowledge young people's beliefs and practices are principally determined by parental religiosity (Hood et al., 2009). Moreover, beliefs and practices are usually transmitted through modelling of parents' behaviours. Therefore, if parents are not religious, then it is

---

3   The five dimensions of religiosity include: the belief dimension, religious practice dimension, experience dimension, the intellectual dimension, and the consequential dimension.

Table 7.11   Location of Religiosity

Influence(s) for religiosity?	Male Members	Female Members	Members	Average (%)
Parents	0	1	1	0.5
Siblings	17	11	28	15.1
School/College	6	3	9	4.8
University	72	76	148	79.6
Work	0	0	0	0
Private experience	0	0	0	0
Total	**95**	**91**	**186**	**100**

Table 7.12   Prayer

How old were you when you learnt to pray?	Male Members	Female Members	Members	Average (%)
Under 10	3	4	7	3.8
10-15	2	1	3	1.6
15-18	19	24	43	23.1
18-21	64	59	123	66.1
Above 21	7	3	10	5.4
Total	**95**	**91**	**186**	**100**

fair to assume that their children's religious values, or lack of, will resemble their parents' non-religious dispositions.

Focusing on the effects of non-religious parents is of course highly complex and not easy for a survey of this kind to elicit information on. So, I tried to ask several members questions about these matters. Most members suggested that during their upbringing they never gave much thought to religion, as their parents were very secular and Western orientated. As a result, religion was not considered important to their identity. Thus, it is important for us to focus on the context or situation in which the members became religious. It is clear that the role of parents in the transmission of religious beliefs and practices was extremely limited. This means religious socialisation took place outside the family setting, in most cases at university through peer influence. In contrast, working class Muslims tend to acquire their religious values from family socialisation, usually in the early formative years. This allows them to categorise and identify themselves with the wider Muslim community. As McGown (1999, p. 98) points out about working class Somali Muslims in London:

It [Islam] provided an oasis of tranquillity amid the dislocation of refugee straits and the turmoil of adjusting to a new culture, trying to learn a new language, and attempting to find jobs What was valuable about it was the very ritual of stepping outside the daily struggle, five times over the course of the day, to concentrate on the prayers that never alter, in rhythmic language that linked them to a community of believers that was theirs no matter where in the world they were.

The results of the survey strongly suggest that members' religious growth and change occurred mainly at university.

Social Triggers

This section will look at the main ways in which experiences have, over the years, affected members' expectations and understandings of other people. As Abdul pointed out, 'I might have a British passport, but that means nothing when people judge you by your skin colour'. The problem this poses, which was noted in passing in previous chapters, is that if social triggers have an effect on identity formation, then can these be identified and do other HT members experience them? There are many social conditions and triggers that could account for changes in a member's behaviour. For instance, family breakdown can have a deep psychological impact (Minuchin, 1974). Tracking all the possible triggers across a large population is extremely difficult, and thus I needed to isolate the most common triggers among the members. After several discussions, I noticed that members cited racism as a major childhood experience. Therefore, I quickly realised that despite minor differences in content and emphasis, racism could be singled out as a key social trigger. Although, racism was widely experienced, it mainly occurred during childhood (see Table 1.13). In accord with the current social situation, it was not surprising to discover that religious discrimination, or Islamophobia, became a central issue for most members in adulthood. This would indicate that when members construct their identities, they are trying to connect their present experiences to what has gone before, rendering past experiences with meaning. Therefore, in this section, I want to focus on the effects of racial and religious prejudice.

The Effects of Racism

It is extremely difficult to document the many ways in which racism impacted the lives of members, because it is a highly personal experience. In the course of my interviews, most members cited experiencing direct forms of racism – like verbal and physical abuse – principally during their upbringing. Other more subtle forms of racism were cited in adulthood, often in relation to employment opportunities and accessing social resources (housing, health care etc.). These experiences

Table 7.13   Social Triggers during Childhood

Types of Triggers (Childhood)	Male Members	Female Members	Members	Average (%)
Racism				
Victim	93	68	161	86.6
Non-victim	2	23	25	13.4
Islamophobia				
Victim	0	3	3	1.6
Non-victim	95	88	183	98.4
Total	**95**	**91**	**186**	**100**

Table 7.14   Social Triggers during Adulthood

Types of Triggers (Adulthood)	Male Members	Female Members	Members	Average (%)
Racism				
Victim	28	19	47	25.3
Non-victim	67	72	139	74.7
Islamophobia				
Victim	53	71	124	66.7
Non-victim	42	20	62	33.3
Total	**95**	**91**	**186**	**100**

took place during the most formative periods of the members' lives, which had a decisive effect on their development. As Sanchez-Hucles (1998) points out, young people who are exposed to adverse experiences, like racism, tend to carry the effects into adulthood. In chapter five, I realised victims of racism had a tendency to internalise the distorted images that racism promotes. Consequently, the impulse to join radical movements often grows from losing one's 'sense of social belonging' (Parkin, 1968, p. 4). The weakening of social ties is usually triggered by events that cannot be controlled, like racism. This inability to influence events can stimulate the growth of isolation from the wider society, making some more susceptible to HT. I am not alone in this view. One of the key issues to be drawn from the literature on mass movements was the recurrence of alienation and the lack of integration as significant features for recruitment into such organisations (Hoffer, 1982; Parkin, 1968).

The empirical data collected from my own research has shown that most members felt victimised by racism. Consequently, this experience damaged their ties with wider society, leaving most of them feeling socially isolated. Parkin (1968,

p. 11) describes such individuals as 'socially unanchored and adrift in the world'. Therefore, it is assumed this isolation and lack of integration made these young Muslims more receptive to HT. Racial victimisation, for example, has a negative effect as it triggers a host of frustrations. HT deliberately uses this agitation to direct young Muslim anger towards the dominant culture while promoting its own subculture, which participants begin to identify with and gain acceptance from. This subculture is built on similar identities, drawing individuals to a single collective organisation that brings together like-minded people. This specific subculture formed when the larger culture failed to meet the social needs of a particular group of people, i.e. young middle class Asians. Thus, HT provides socially detached individuals access to new social ties and a meaningful way to gain self-identity. As Kornhauser (1959, p. 33) argues, the alienated are more inclined towards fringe movements, 'because they provide occasions for expressing resentment against what is, as well as promises of a totally different world'.

The Effects of Islamophobia

It is somewhat unusual to see a discrepancy between racial and religious discrimination. Although both variables have high representation, racial discrimination is seen as a more vivid form of discrimination, especially during childhood. On the other hand, Islamophobia is much harder to describe. Some social theorists, namely Poynting and Mason (2007, p. 61), argue Islamophobia is a form of 'anti-Muslim racism'. In France, for example, a Muslim cemetery was desecrated. This act was described as Islamophobic. The Runnymede Trust (1997, p. 1) defined Islamophobia as acts of exclusion and discrimination based on an irrational 'dislike of Muslims'. For many HT members, this is undoubtedly a persuasive argument. For example, many members argue banning the *hijaab* is an example of Islamophobia. So, it is not surprising to see such a high percentage of alleged Islamophobic incidents. Consequently, I would treat these claims with a degree of caution since HT exploits a skewed definition of Islamophobia. I was somewhat surprised by the relatively low number of instances of Islamophobia cited during childhood. This might suggest that Islamophobia emerged more vividly in the wake of the 2001 terror attacks (Benn and Jawad, 2004). More significantly, Islamophobia cannot be singled out or attributed to HT radicalisation, because the vast majority of members only cited incidents post-radicalisation.

Sources of Recruitment

Recruitment into HT occurs through a multitude of sources: family and friendship networks, peer groups, universities and mosques are some of the most common examples. Although recruitment sources can be highly diverse, it still entails a process of locating, screening and selecting people to join HT. Despite widespread interest in HT, there is limited empirical data that explains why certain social spaces are more productive in recruitment. Since my research has two interconnected goals, namely to figure out the causes of radicalisation within HT from both an individual and a group perspective, I need to look at recruitment from this dual perspective as well.

Table 7.15   Sources of Recruitment

Location(s) of Recruitment	Male Members	Female Members	Members	Average (%)
University	81	65	146	78.5
College	5	4	9	4.9
School	0	0	0	0
Mosque	0	0	0	0
Work	1	0	1	0.5
Community (clubs/centres)	2	0	2	1
Home (family relations)	6	22	28	15.1
Other	0	0	0	0
Total	**95**	**91**	**186**	**100**

It is clear that one unchangeable characteristic of HT success has been its ability to mobilise and recruit students behind its radical mission, a fact often singled out by many social commentators (Taji-Farouki, 1996). During the early 1990s, the party gained notoriety for attracting young Muslims to its cause, which was something of a new phenomenon on university campuses. Given this picture of youth activism, I need to try and identify why a sub-section of the Muslim student population became inclined to HT. One of the most obvious explanations for the emergence of HT radicalism among a homogenous group of Muslim students is social isolation. Once in higher education, ethnic minorities tend to find themselves more alienated and excluded. Several case studies, for instance, in the previous chapter, showed that alienation and exposure to unsettling social environments at university made the respondents more susceptible to form peer friendships with HT activists. Thus, it is important to ask, who participates in these peer groups and why?

University Peer Group and Deviant Subculture Formation

To begin, it is worth first trying to tackle one key question: Why are middle class Asian students more inclined to join HT at university? Some social theorists attribute deviant group formation to an absence of social alternatives. As Lemert

(1967, p. 336) suggested, these groups usually form 'because there is nothing else to do'. Although this may be the case for many working class gangs, it is harder to apply this reasoning to HT. This is because, as the data has shown, recruitment mainly takes place within a university setting. Most universities provide open access to countless social activities and clubs, giving students an opportunity to find a place for themselves. Yet, as I learned from my interviews and case studies, in the previous chapters, most members failed to adjust to the social realities of university life. It was quite apparent members were unable to come to terms with feeling socially isolated. Thus, soon after arriving at university, most members began to seek out peers that matched their social backgrounds – young middle class Asians. They started spending much of their spare time with the peer group, constituting a major outlet for social activity.

There is, then, a fairly strong argument to suggest joining HT occurs in part as a psychological response to loneliness and social alienation. As a result, the participant's desire for companionship allowed HT peers to socialise them into their deviant subculture. Members cannot be thought of as being unwilling participants within HT subculture, because psychological need appears to be a key social trigger. I was, therefore, greatly interested to discover the emerging features of HT's subculture. HT subculture formed when the larger culture fell short in meeting the needs of some young middle class Asians. In addition, this homogenous group failed to develop a proper connection with their own communities. They were unable to expressively relate themselves to their families, leading to their withdrawal from society. As a result of this lack of social integration, they became highly susceptible to the radical values of HT, which differed strongly from the prevailing set of social and political norms. As Brake (1985, p. 10) explains, subcultures are 'meaning systems, modes of expression or life styles developed by groups' in order to distinguish themselves from the population at large.

In the case of HT, these meaning systems are believed to emerge through resistance, providing structured solutions to the perceived contradictions rising from the wider societal context. In this respect, a subculture inevitably involves membership of a class culture, and the subculture may be an extension of, or in opposition to, the class culture. Juvenile gangs, for instance, provide working class youths with an alternative source of self-esteem (Cohen, 1980). Miller (1958) discovered the values of youth subculture merely reiterated, in a distorted fashion, the focal concerns of the adult working class population.

Trying to understand why middle class Asians are the most receptive demographic to HT's radical message is very tricky. To start, I need to locate the features of HT middle class radicalism that serve to distinguish it from the radicalism of the working class. Many social theorists argue that working class radicalism is firmly based upon their perception of, and place within, the social structure (Parkin, 1968). In other words, it is assumed the hub of working class activism is orientated around economic and material change, while middle class radicalism is believed to be influenced by more moralistic features. After speaking to several working class Muslims, non-HT affiliated, I was able to gain a better picture of the class divide. One activist asserted that HT is too idealistic, as he explained: 'the Muslim community is the most deprived, we have huge unemployment and there is a big drug problem with the youth … HT doesn't address these issues'. Most working class Muslim activists engage in interest-group politics – such as lobbying for equal rights, better working conditions and equal employment opportunities – that is fundamentally designed to provide benefits to the working classes. By contrast to this, HT, with its middle class roots, is not orientated to achieve material gain for its members. They are more typically concerned with issues of an ideological or spiritual nature, which offers no particular benefit to those involved. As one member insisted, 'we [HT] are doing Allah's [God's] work'. Abdul (HT, member) described the feelings of performing actions for HT as a 'spiritual buzz'.

During my interview with Omar Bakri, former leader of the UK branch, I made it a point to ask him why so many young middle class Asians were attracted to HT. He attributes this phenomenon to a 'clash between cultures and values' (Omar Bakri, Interview 26 March 2004). In some respect, this is true since a subculture tends to develop in response to the prevailing culture, acting in opposition, as it seeks to differentiate itself from the mainstream. In this context, the term culture is perceived as a separate entity within the larger society, and one with which the larger society must contend (Cote, 1996). Theorists who purport subcultures form through resistance often state that members are always striving against dominant classes and the older generations. They seek to find ways to disrupt the social position of the dominant actors, so as to create spaces for themselves. In this respect, HT members are counterpoised against the first generation, opposing their culture, language and ideals. This loathing was directed towards the first generation for importing sectarian and ethnic characteristics from their previous domiciles. In contrast, working class young people tend to have closer interaction with their parents, demonstrating less intent on being different (Cohen, 1980). In comparison, middle-class young people display greater tendencies to associate with a subculture group so as to reinforce their independence. These young people are also given more disposable income with which they form their subcultures around themselves, engaging in a greater diversity of pursuits.

The sociological data collected from HT has found that the membership is disproportionately represented. This unbalanced stratification allowed HT members to group together in accordance with their social status, facilitating a subculture that was determined by class, ethnicity and age. At university, for example, most members experienced social isolation. This, Bakri believes, facilitated the rise of an 'identity crisis', pushing them to interact with people similar to them (Omar Bakri, Interview 26 March 2004).

Brake (1985) points out youth subculture are formed from more than one particular identity, moving from different types and even mixing identities. Exposure to HT subculture, initially through peer groups, opened up a new social world, comprised of Muslims who emerged from similar family, class and ethnic backgrounds. HT offered disaffected middle class Asians a homogenous social space to gain acceptance and belonging. The rise of an oppositional subculture among the Muslim middle class, inspired by common experiences, became personified by the life-cycle identity change. In this respect, age played a central factor, because the types of individuals who became radicalised within HT were those who were young, well-educated and had been raised in a middle class household. Many disaffected middle class Asian youths found comfort and belonging within HT's subculture because it gave them a sense of purpose. This middle class radicalism offered its participants access to identity options outside of the constrained family and community structures.

Summary

In this chapter, I have searched for common characteristics and trends in HT member behaviour, in order to better understand why some young Muslims join the group. However, many concepts that are relevant to this question cannot be measured readily by single variables. In fact, I have discovered that the relationships between members and their environments are 'mutually shaping' (Bronfenbrenner, 1979, p. 22). In other words, I had to look at social interactions across connected systems – namely family, university and peer-group friendships. Increased religiosity, for example, did not take place in a family setting, rather in most cases it originated from peer interactions at university. Peer group relations are a very important, and recurring, feature of the data collected. This social space allowed members to find solidarity with other Asian students who emerged from similar experiences and social backgrounds. Every HT member is marked by the stages of social life, each providing a set of experiences that get internalised into psychological expectations. Firstly, during early socialisation, it was observed that most members endured some form of racial discrimination. These negative encounters reflect not only the development of frustrations but also the influence of shared disaffection and anger towards the larger culture. This enabled HT to bombard the novice with ideas about how to deal with these perceived problems, providing a sense of belonging.

Let me return to the main themes of the chapter to summarise what my analysis has revealed about the common characteristics of a typical HT member in Britain. Firstly, the most instantly recognisable trait of HT radicalism is its success in mobilising young people. Thus, it was not surprising to find that most members were recruited at a similar age. Secondly, recruitment generally takes place within the same social space, namely university campuses. Thirdly, and perhaps most importantly, I discovered that HT membership is firmly rooted within the ranks of the educated middle classes. There are deep cultural and socio-political divisions amongst the working and middle classes within the Muslim community, to such an extent that lifestyle and orientation has created two very different sub-groups. Consequently, HT has struggled to gain support among the fairly large and heterogeneous working class population, forcing it to narrow its recruitment pool to middle class students. Fourthly, early childhood experiences left members feeling isolated and disconnected, which in most cases created a predilection to become involved with HT, and that these experiences were rooted in racial discrimination. HHHSome theorists argue that exposure to social instability during one's childhood can dramatically increase the chances of exhibiting deviant behaviour in adulthood (Chansky, 2001; Howe, 2010). Therefore, HT members exist within a small homogenous group, which may be narrowed down and defined as young middle class Asians.

Chapter 8
A Conveyor Belt for Terrorism?

The call to proscribe HT has received significant attention in the aftermath of the 7 July London bombings. The British media has portrayed the group as dangerous and uncompromising, making it worthy of proscription. David Cameron, the leader of the Conservative Party, added his voice to the growing body demanding to ban HT, prompting greater scrutiny of its subversive activities and extremist ideology (*BBC*, 4 July 2007). Despite this wave of condemnation, HT remains a legal organisation. More significantly, it has been described in a leaked home office report as a 'radical, but to date non-violent Islamist group' (*The Guardian*, 22 July 2005). If this assessment is accurate, then the study of violence in HT requires an approach that focuses on the relationship between radical speech and physical violence. Trying to equate HT with radical violence is extremely problematic. This is because radicalisation is often thought consequential for violence, or at least a natural precursor of violence. The outcome, however, is not necessarily towards more violence. In fact, religious initiatives may either support or help undermine violence, and there is no clear-cut cause and effect to be seen. During my interview with Omar Bakri, he emphatically declared that he was a force for good in British society, as he advocated non-violent activism, which helped young Muslims channel their frustrations away from violence. Although one might question such an assertion, it is crucial to reiterate how HT evolved into one of the most dominant radical youth movements, and whether it has stimulated violence in Britain.

Defining Violence and Radical Speech

In my encounters with HT members, I had countless discussions regarding the nature of its alleged non-violent ideology. The prevailing opinion within the fraternity indicates acts of physical violence are non-existent. HT violence, if in fact such a thing truly exists, cannot be understood independently from the concept of radical speech. In other words, a more fruitful debate would be to understand the synthesis between radical speech and violence. In order to understand the relationship between these two concepts, I must first try to define each term. Although, several attempts have been made to define violence, it still remains a highly ambiguous and divisive term. Steger (2003, p. 12), for example, believes that violence has countless meanings: including 'to force, to injure and to violate'. Honderich (2003, p. 91) narrows his definition of violence to the 'use of physical force' that violates and destroys people or things. Interestingly, both accounts make reference to violence as an act that violates. However, I would caution against restricting a definition of violence to physical force, because a violation can occur without physical force.

Relating violence to 'extreme speech' is an exceedingly difficult exercise, since it raises the question of what type of speech should be made unlawful. From a legal standpoint, speech is rarely considered a crime, unless an overt act is committed (Weinstein and Hare, 2010). In Britain, 'public order' proclamations are used to counteract hate speech in public, but these laws have created a great deal of uncertainty because they are 'unworkable in practice' (Hare and Weinstein 2010, p. 60). As Hare and Weinstein (2010, p. 60) point out, British courts struggle to differentiate between words that 'insult' from those that 'offend, shock or disturb'. Traditionally, the United States requires clear and present danger of an overt act following a speech, before a prosecution can be sought. In other words, a clear line of distinction is usually made between speech and actions. However, an individual who, by speech, provokes an action is then equally culpable with the individual who perpetrates it. More recently, in Sweden a religious minister was prosecuted for a speech he gave to his congregation in which he referred to homosexuality as a perversion. He had violated Sweden's Anti-Hate statute, an act that gives broad protection to individuals and groups from 'verbal violence' (The *Local*, 29 November 2005).

In the UK such a law does not exist, the introduction of anti-terror laws has ignited debate about acceptable speech. In particular, in the aftermath of 7/7, there was a concerted effort to criminalise speech under the Terrorism Act 2006 (Malik 2010, p. 96). This Act gave extensive powers to detain and charge individuals who glorify acts of terror and incite others to carry out such attacks. Tony Blair, the former Prime Minister, insisted the law was passed to take stronger measures against those who 'don't just directly engage in terrorism but indirectly incite it' (*The Guardian*, 10 November 2005). The glorification laws were brought into immediate effect in the aftermath of the London terror attacks to clamp down on radical speech. However, the newly introduced measures were widely condemned for their ambiguity. Dominic Grieve, the Conservative legal affairs spokesman, pointed out that the laws would not be properly understood by juries when prosecutions were eventually brought (House of Commons research paper, 16 June 2005). His concerns were realised in the trial of the first person to be prosecuted under the act, Samina Malik, the self-dubbed lyrical terrorist (The *Guardian*, 6 December 2007). The jury struggled to understand what crime they were prosecuting, that is, her poetry or downloading terrorist material.

Despite the many shortcomings of the terrorism legislation, it does offer legal insight into the relationship between radical speech and violence. The courts have upheld convictions even for remote tendencies to violence as proper grounds for punishing mere speech. Omar Brooks, a member of Al-Ghurabaa, and several others were prosecuted for speeches they gave at Regents Park Mosque in which they allegedly incited young followers to commit acts of violence (BBC, 17 April 2008). The reformatted statutes identify acts not deemed punishable a decade ago as worthy of prosecution today, mere utterances of beliefs and even membership in groups holding radical opinions are potential for incarceration. It may be argued that any such discussion of where to draw the line for criminalisation of radical speech is not relevant to my research, since no cases directly involving violence have been brought against any UK HT member. Despite this truth, the proscription of HT is still under review by the Home Office, making it essential to track its activism in the light of their willingness to advocate violence against others.

Campus Wars

By the start of the 1990s, HT had shifted its emphasis to public activism, with the intent to bring about social and political change. Although freedom of speech allows individuals to oppose the state, it could be argued that HT's aim to overthrow the government cannot be accomplished without force. However, as one member pointed out:

> Our goal is not to establish an Islamic State in Britain … it was never our intention to do so. The party is being deliberately targeted and victimised for policies that were not sanctioned by the central leadership, the misunderstandings of former members (Omar Bakri) should not be used to judge the party … to do so would be a deliberate attempt to distort our true aims.

This may be the case of HT today, but I am trying to track the development of HT. According to Omar Bakri, the type of activism enacted by the group during the 1990s was designed to subvert the system. More interestingly, the above member does not deny this fact. Instead he tries to equate their radical past to Omar Bakri, singling him out as the person responsible for their extremist and combative tendencies. These tendencies towards confrontation earned HT a reputation for being overaggressive and confrontational, particularly when dealing with Muslim and non-Muslim students, which set it on a collision course with university authorities. HT entered university campuses during the placid period of the 1980s, allowing Farid and Bakri to lay the interior platform for activism. Farid Kassim, when asked about the rapid success of HT at universities, candidly proclaimed:

> I think the reason why Islam is so attractive and stimulated so much debate and discussion is precisely that it is an ideology. And it's an ideology that is coming to a society that is devoid of intellectual debate and discussion, a society not interested in intellectual issues (Public Eye BBC 2, 25 July 1995).

This zealous declaration by Kassim stands as confident testimony to the ascendance of HT activism. They surfaced rapidly as a new phenomenon pioneering Islam in the form of intellectual ideas that became the main focal point of discussion across university campuses.

HT gained media notoriety during the 1990s for their overt activity in more than 50 universities across the country. The rise to national prominence, in part, was achieved due to their sheer determination to take full control over university campuses, 'taking over from the beleaguered and defeated socialists' (Kassim, 26 May 2004). The growing rise of HT was closely monitored by the National Union of Students (NUS) for some years, especially as party members infiltrated university clubs and societies, disseminating political and intellectual ideals that were deemed to be anti-Semitic and homophobic. As a result, the NUS sanctioned a generic ban that prevented HT from assembling any kind of organised activity on university campuses. Kassim, in the wake of the NUS proclamation, emphasised his complete indignation at their unjust position, when he stated: '… there is an intellectual storm taking place … it's time for the NUS to acknowledge that and try to construct an appropriate intellectual response to that, instead of banning and censorship' (*Public Eye* BBC 2, 25 July 1995). However, the imposed sanctions forced HT to operate clandestinely under the semblance of duplicate societies. The process of operating under the guise of these surreptitious clubs allowed the party to manoeuvre around broad restrictions, despite campus-wide bans for alleged anti-Semitic rhetoric.

Promoting Anti-Semitism on Campus

No sooner had HT emerged than speculation began about its subversive campus activism. From a British Muslim perspective, student radicalism was somewhat unprecedented. Although HT advocated a non-violent approach, it propagated an extremely radical ideology. In particular, outrage rapidly grew against HT for creating an upsurge of hostility towards Jewish students. The question I wish to pose here is whether HT's radical message promoted violence against Jewish students. It is important to emphasise that radical speech and violence are not synonymous. Clearly, not all radical speech promotes violence. For instance, I have surveyed most of HT campus activism and, despite the hysteria; very few violent incidents could be associated to HT directly. In fact, HT activism mainly involved organising public events and debates, most of which passed without incident. However, there were several talks convened by HT under the guise of discreet clubs that are worthy of discussion. To start, a meeting arranged by the Culture Society, at King's College, had to be dispersed by the police, in order to escort Jewish students away from a meeting of the Jewish Society that was taking place in a nearby room.

This incident was eclipsed by the unfolding problems at the School of Oriental and African Studies (SOAS), where the 1924 Committee was operating as a front for HT members. The 1924 committee held a talk, entitled: 'Israel, the Apartheid State'. Faisal Muhammad, a British born Malaysian, was an active member of HT and was the chairman for the meeting. Police were again called in to escort the opposing factions away from the college after the talk. Unsurprisingly, the 1924 committee was found guilty of its association to HT. On 31 October, SOAS issued a statement saying, 'the 1924 Committee had by its action shown itself to be closely aligned to an Islamic fundamentalist group, the Hizb ut-Tahrir' (*The Times Higher Education Supplement*, 4 November 1994). As a result, SOAS banned speakers representing the views of HT from speaking at future meetings of the 1924 Committee. HT members, aggrieved at the decision, felt victimised by the college authorities, and thus quickly adopted a proactive response that sought to expose the fallacy of this incident. The members launched a poster campaign that read:

> SOAS bans Islam. SOAS has finally exposed its long-standing, hidden agenda of deep hatred for Islam by banning speakers invited who present Islam as an ideological alternative. The West and universities such as SOAS espouse ideas such as freedom of speech, but these become redundant when Muslims want to express their views. (*The Times Higher Education Supplement*, 4 November 1994)

The proceeding clampdown on HT continued throughout London campuses, and it was not restricted to meetings. Numerous party leaflets and flyers were generating condemnation for promoting anti-Semitic extremism. In particular, a leaflet advertising a meeting at which Farid spoke was entitled: 'Peace with Israel – a crime against Islam'. Outrage was directed at an inflammatory quote in the leaflet, which read: 'The last hour would not come unless the Muslims will fight against the Jews and the Muslims would kill them, until the Jews would hide themselves behind a stone or a tree, and a stone or a tree would say: Muslim, or the servant of Allah, there is a Jew behind me; come and kill him'. Even though this provocative extract was a direct reference to a *Hadith* (saying of Muhammad), it did not safeguard the group from criticism. Kassim definitely rejected these claims, when he stated: 'The vast majority of our leaflets are political and intellectual, that's the main focus of our activity … if we put a gun on a poster then we're immediately called extremists, but Sinn Féin for example, at the University of North London have been doing it for some time' (*Public Eye*, BBC 2).

However, this did not prevent the suspension of the Islamic Society of Brunel University for three months after holding a meeting judged to be illegal by the university authorities. A debate entitled, '*Hands off Muslim Land or* Jihad', had resulted in the cancellation of the event, as the university authorities believed it did not promote respect and tolerance for opposing views. Firdaus Miah, a British born Bangladeshi, was the president of the society and a member of HT. As a result of the incident, Firdaus Miah was subjected to disciplinary action for alleged activities that were deemed to be in breach of the university's disciplinary code. Universities became the central battleground between Jewish students and HT. It was necessary for HT to contest the continuing claims of their alleged anti-Semitism. The party felt a deliberate campaign of misinformation was being spearheaded by vociferous elements, designed to prevent debate about the legality of Israel. HT elaborated their statement of innocence in a six-point declaration that defined the position of HT. It stated:

1. Jews are to be accorded the protected status of *dhimmi* provided that the trust placed in them is not betrayed.
2. The Muslims of Palestine are entitled to fight in self-defence of their lands which are under occupation. This disposition does not extend outside of Muslim lands and thus does not include any 'battlefield' in Britain.
3. Muslims living in non-Muslim countries are to live according to the commands of God and to refrain from harming, betraying or cheating non-Muslims. They are to seek to invite non-Muslims to embrace Islam.
4. The killing of innocent people, including hijacking aeroplanes, is forbidden in Islam.
5. The Qur'anic verses referring to adultery, fornication, stealing and homosexuality are clear but the punishments prescribed apply only to an Islamic State.
6. There is a concerted effort by the media to limit the effectiveness of Islamic proclamation on university campuses. (Extract from *Daily Awaz*, 7 March 1994)

The situation did not change, even though HT published their opinions, which sought to clarify the misunderstandings. However, articles in the national press continued to vilify HT activity at universities in an attempt to prevent the party expansion. The *Daily Mirror* described HT as a 'fanatical group of Muslim extremists... stirring up hatred in Britain against Jews' (The *Daily Mirror*, 4 March 1994). A similar article to those noted appeared in *The Observer*, under the provocative headline: 'Hitler's Heirs Incite Islamic Students' (*The Observer*, 13 March 1994).

As a result of the frenzied assault on HT by the national press, the NUS, at their annual conference in Blackpool, singled HT out for its alleged anti-Semitic and racist pronouncements. Kassim dismissed these allegations, as he expressed his outrage at the NUS, claiming:

> The great crime is that the National Union of Students has been taken over by people that are involved in a conspiracy, if you will, an anti-Islam conspiracy to mute the voices of Muslim students at university campuses ... We are well aware that the NUS is controlled by forces that have their own hidden political agenda, and Islam is a convenient way in which they can enact their agenda. (*Public Eye*, BBC 2)

This emotional statement illustrated the frustration Kassim and party officials felt at the imbalance of the NUS rules and regulations that were intended to limit HT activity. Therefore, HT utilised this attack to condemn the concept of free speech as a 'Western myth'. It became evident that anti-Semitism and anti-Zionism were being quantified as the same thing, and as a result Muslim students who protested against Zionism and the activities of the State of Israel were branded as anti-Semitic and thus condemned by the policies of the NUS (Kassim, 26 May 2004). The decision to publicly condemn HT was seen as a calculated act of provocation. Kassim responded by saying, 'It doesn't deter us because we believe all the prophets were vilified by their own people...We believe intellectual thought changes human beings and we must discuss things in order to change society' (*Public Eye*, BBC 2). This rather polemical rant was overshadowed by an address made by Kassim in which he said, 'it will be better for the Jews to become Muslims if they want to live in peace in the land of Muslims' (*The Guardian*, 7 February 1994). Inevitably, this provoked many sections of the Jewish population into action, and was widely condemned for its anti-Semitic rhetoric.

I have presented a small selection of examples of HT anti-Semitic rhetoric and activity. On the basis of available evidence it is difficult to equate HT activism with increased violence towards Jewish students. Although the rhetoric of HT is unpalatable to most, it does not warrant proscribing. Many contemporary theorists and law makers have struggled to correctly identify radical speech in terms of violence, and this makes it problematic when studying HT. There are at least two distinct ways of conceptualising HT's radical speech related to Jews. Firstly, on a personal level, no case has to date been presented against any HT member concerning speeches deemed unlawful. Despite objections to the anti-Semitic speeches and leaflets attributed to HT, no legal action has been taken. However, with the widening of terror laws, its inflammatory material if replicated today would surely warrant greater sanction. Secondly, the organisation, as I will show in latter sections, has undergone significant change. In particular, its speech towards Jews has been toned down, especially after the departure of Omar Bakri. According to Home Office documents, released to the party under the Freedom of Information Act, 'HT's activities centre on intellectual reasoning, logical arguments and political lobbying' (HT Britain website, 1 June 2005). With respect to anti-Semitic speech, HT denied stirring up hostility towards British Jews. In fact, they believe a deliberate campaign of misinformation was waged against them in an attempt to subvert the group from propagating the Islamic ruling about the state of Israel (*The Daily Awaz*, 7 March 1994). Even though this may be partially correct, HT's attempts to undermine the legitimacy of the Jewish state created a combative environment in which many Jewish students felt intimidated.

From a historical perspective, university authorities were totally unprepared to deal with the rise of HT on university campuses. As a result, the NUS set up a 24-hour hotline for students to ring in with fears of intimidation on university campuses because of continued HT activity. HT was particularly identified as a source of concern by the NUS president, as he attested: 'It is the single biggest extremist threat in the UK at the moment' (*The Times*, 31 October 1995). The results of calls in 1995 were published in an NUS report entitled 'Campuswatch'. This revealed that threats and harassment were twice more likely to be blamed on extreme Islamic groups than on ultra-right-wing organisations (*The Times*, 31

October 1995). Furthermore, 'there were more than 100 reports of distribution of offensive material by Islamic extremists, primarily Hizb ut-Tahrir, and 50 reports of offensive meetings, 47 threats of violence and 31 acts of physical intimidation or harassment' (*The Guardian*, 31 October 1995). In all, there were 271 complaints about Islamic extremists as opposed to 91 against the British National Party (BNP). The report boldly proclaimed that freedom of speech, though fundamental to campus life, did 'not include the right to make propaganda which incites violence' (*The Times Higher Education*, 16 August 1996). The question that needs to be posed here is did HT speeches intimidate, or incite violence against, Jewish students? From a legal perspective, intimidation and violence can be classified differently, as intimidation does not necessarily entail the use of physical force (Lumpkin, 1999). Verbal intimidation, for example, is often used without inflicting physical injury. More significantly, intimidation is a subjective act (Shields, 1999). Radical HT speeches that reject the legitimacy of Israel, for example, need to be seen from two sides. HT activists believe equating violence to their speeches ignores the intellectual nature of their talks and message. In contrast, Jewish students perceive such speeches as intimidating, as they contribute to a feeling of fear. Thus, there is no evidence to suggest that radical speeches attributed to HT resulted in acts of violence. After a relatively lengthy search, I was able to catalogue most of the campus speeches given by HT related to Jewish themes. Although, some of the speeches had anti-Semitic undertones, no violence could be attributed in the aftermath of such events to HT members. Even the charge of anti-Semitism is not definitively provable. Apart from a few leaflets, no radical speech was directly equated to anti-Semitism.

Promoting Militancy

During the 1990s, it became common to describe HT campus activism as militant. BBC 2, for example, broadcasted a documentary about HT entitled: 'Islam's Militant Tendency'. Although militancy is often used to depict violent activism, it can refer to a person who engages in non-violent confrontation. In order to understand the relationship between HT radical speech and violence, I need to focus on more overt instances of violence attributed to HT. An article in *The Guardian*, for example, alleged HT had written an inflammatory leaflet sanctioning violent terrorism: 'Do something to prove that on your shoulders there stands a head not a piece of cheese. Throw a stone, trigger a bomb, plant a mine, hijack a plane, and do not ask how' (*The Guardian*, 7 February 1994). Kassim mentioned his absolute disgust at such articles, as purporting false allegations from questionable sources; he strongly condemned the media for its partial coverage, which was unwilling to engage HT intellectually. The alleged HT leaflet was distributed outside Regents Park Mosque. More significantly, the printed allegations were not accredited to any published HT articles, diminishing the integrity of the accusations.

HT militancy was placed under greater scrutiny after the fatal stabbing of Tundi Obanubi, an African student at Newham College. It was alleged that Bakri's speech, given days earlier, had stirred up militancy among the largely Muslim student population. Ed Hussain (2007) felt the incident was a direct result of HT infiltration into the college. Relating HT activism to this intentional act of violence is appealing to some, but there appears to be an underlying problem with any attempt to equate violence to an HT radical speech. Firstly, as Bakri suggested, the culprit responsible for this unlawful killing had no affiliation to HT. 'I propagate Islam peacefully ... so it is untrue. My members cannot do such a thing' (Bakri, interview). Indeed, Saeed Nur, the man charged with the murder, had a longstanding relationship with Jihadist organisations (*Q News*, 24 March 1995). His radicalisation into militancy had taken place over several years, and thus his act cannot be attributed to HT speech. Secondly, as mentioned Omar Bakri strongly denied these allegations, he even demanded that HT members cooperate with the authorities. As he said: 'I have asked my people to help the police to find the killers because this was pure murder. In Islam this behaviour is really disgraceful' (*Q News*, 10 March 1995).

This incident once again underscores the need to work out the connection between violence and radical speech. The media has condemned HT for radicalising Muslim youth, forcing the authorities to protect young people from radical influences. The key question that needs to be considered here is how much influence does a speech have on an individual? The tragic death of Tundi Obanubi has been used to charge HT with culpability for actions committed by Saeed Nur. Does this constitute a case for incited violence that HT is responsible for? In fact, it is usual for criminal courts to accept diminished responsibility for imitative violence caused by radical speech, because it is nearly impossible to establish in a court of law the existence of a provable link between speech and violence. Obviously, if the speech demands violence against a stated party, then a credible link can be drawn. Indeed, no HT member has been charged with inciting violence. Let us look at another example, at West Thames College.

HT activity was not restricted to university campuses, as a race riot occurred at the West Thames Further Education College in Isleworth, which saw mass fighting between Sikh and Muslim students. The disturbances erupted after a Muslim student was attacked by a group of Sikh men. The following day saw around one hundred HT affiliates gather at the college to hold a demonstration. However, the police were warned of a pending disturbance, and fighting broke out between the respective sides, leading to 20 arrests. HT mobilised a further hundred affiliates to hold a protest outside Chiswick police station where some of the demonstrators were being held. Fifteen of the young HT affiliates who were arrested were brought before magistrates in Feltham on 10 January 1995 and charged with public order offences. They were remanded on bail until 24 January. However, the charges against the men were formally dropped due to a lack of evidence.

This incident is actually very complex. HT had infiltrated the college, over a sustained period, taking over the Islamic society. This gave them a strong presence on campus. It was alleged HT had stimulated a renewed sense of religious association among Muslim students. This greatly undermined existing identity affiliations. For example, a sustained campaign was launched against 'Asianism'. Before HT gained access to college grounds, most Asian students coexisted together. Indeed, Asian students shared similar values, which united them culturally. However, religious violence was inevitable. HT instigated the revival of religious identities across the campus, which in effect led other religious groups to renew their identities. Thus, the rise of Sikh and Hindu fundamentalism were firmly rooted in reactionary trends against the emergence of radical Islam, as pioneered by HT. Clearly, HT activism increased the appeal of religion among Muslim students, but is this sufficient ground to claim they were responsible for a full-scale riot at West Thames College? In short, it is difficult to equate this episode to HT, because they did not instigate the outbreak of violence. The root of the riot was attributed to a group of Sikh men who attacked a Muslim student.

Departure of Omar Bakri (1996): Decline in HT Radicalism?

The mid-1990s were a golden period in which HT grew beyond any predictable parameters. They were dubbed 'Europe's fastest-growing Muslim group' by the national press (*The Observer*, 13 August 1995). This popularity allowed HT to enjoy a period of unrivalled success in the recruitment of young Muslims. According to Bakri (Ibid., 2 June 2004), the group was attracting a growing following among students across the country. This golden era came to a resounding end, however, after the departure of Omar Bakri. Very little is known about the rapid decline HT underwent during this rocky period. In particular, I was greatly surprised by the negative standpoint most HT members have towards Bakri. One member suggested he was responsible for infusing HT with militancy and extremist rhetoric. This raises a variety of very important questions: Did Bakri influence HT's militant disposition? If so, how did he contribute to it? What effect did his departure have on HT's radical disposition? In order to answer these key questions I will need to look at the followings issues: (1) the type of activism sanctioned by Bakri as the UK leader of HT; (2) the change in radical orientation HT underwent after he departed and formed Al-Muhajiroun; (3) the reforms HT mandated after Bakri left.

Bakri's HT

Omar Bakri, even in exile, remains a highly controversial figure. He has caused countless media storms with his radical rhetoric and activism. In the aftermath of the London terror attacks, he boldly declared that the only people he blamed for the bombings were the British government and public. Naturally, he was seen as a preacher of hate by the media, and widely condemned by the Muslim community. Before his notoriety, he led the UK branch of HT for over a decade.

Trying to understand his legacy as UK leader is not an easy task, because HT has openly condemned his affiliation with the group. In reality, this negative backlash is politically orientated towards undermining his role as one of the groups most popular and influential leaders. So, to what degree did he influence HT? The best sources for assessing the role that Bakri played in turning ordinary students to activism are the members themselves. In order to avoid the skewed views of current members who tend to condemn Bakri's involvement with HT, I interviewed several ex-HT members to discuss the roots of their activism and Bakri's influence. Firstly, the predominant opinion among the members suggested that he did not play a significant role in their joining HT. However, they all agreed Bakri was a key figure in reconstituting HT activism in the UK.[1] Bakri, as an experienced radical activist, changed the focus of party activism to local settings and realities. His goal was to engage in a radical, albeit non-violent, struggle with the state and to bring about an Islamic revolution. As Ferdous asserted, this agenda was at odds with traditional HT ideology. The aim of HT is to revive the Islamic way of life, and thus its primary focus is to re-establish the Islamic state somewhere in the Muslim world. More importantly, as Khalid explained, Bakri operated independently from HT's central leadership. This gave him free rein to carry out activism as he saw fit.

Unlike the indigenous recruits, Bakri had a firm grounding in Islamic teachings, specialising in Islamic Jurisprudence. This enabled him to interpret the need for greater Islamic awareness, focusing on political Islam. Notably, he drew upon the experiences of the Muslims who migrated from Mecca to Abyssinia, which provided a source of guidance to Muslim activity in Britain. Bakri stated: 'Muslims went to Abyssinia, and their focus of discussion was with society and the Abyssinian King' (Bakri, 2 June 2004). In contrast, British Muslims upon migration had become politically and culturally isolated, concerned only with economic survival. Yet, in Abyssinia Bakri proclaimed Muslims 'started to talk about what is Islam' and they rejected those practices that contradicted Islam, as they 'had their own personality and way of life' (Bakri, 2 June 2004). The comparison with Abyssinia was important for Omar Bakri because it provided a standard for organising activity in a non-Muslim country. As Bakri explained:

> ... the Prophet consented to live in non-Muslim society, to speak out and to speak the truth wherever you are, and not to fear the consequences, commanding the good and forbidding the evil, wherever they are ... so the message of Hizb ut-Tahrir is political, therefore when people accept Islam, intellectually and politically, then they start to know more and more about Islam and change their own personalities. (Bakri, 2 June 2004)

---

1   I interviewed 34 ex-HT members about a range of issues related to their radicalisation and why they left HT. 88.2 per cent of ex-members suggested that Omar Bakri had little influence in them joining the group, but 94.1 per cent believed Bakri was a key figure in HT success and expansion during the 1990s.

As a result, Bakri immediately enacted a plan to culture British Muslims. One important issue emerges from this discussion. As Kahlid pointed out, 'OBM (Omar Bakri) is a scholar, and as such he was our reference point'. Bakri gave the indigenous members a way to integrate a wider array of Islamic principles into their daily lives. One ex-member looked back upon this introduction to Islamic ideas as a liberating experience, as he stated: 'Bakri turned on the light'. Thus, as the UK leader, Bakri certainly facilitated the militant disposition of HT in the UK.

Omar Bakri post HT

When the shocking announcement of Bakri's removal filtered down to the fraternity, it caused widespread dissention and discord. Most members struggled to digest the news of their leader's departure. Publicly Bakri declared that his resignation was influenced by HT's new policy, which was 'very heavy in terms of administrative do's and don't do's', putting restrictions on *dawah* (*Muslim News*, 16 February 1996). Although, his resignation sent shockwaves across the UK fraternity, it only had small repercussions. Those loyal to Bakri left HT and joined him, as he established Al-Muhajiroun (ALM). The majority of members, however, remained faithful to HT ideology and denounced Bakri. The division caused deep resentment between the two ranks that became further inflamed when ALM became active. Highly agitated Jewish groups were concerned that HT's change of tactics, which coincided with the departure of Bakri, could herald a new wave of anti-Semitic activity on Britain's university campuses (*The Observer*, 2 February 1996). This hysteria was not found to be justified, as HT was simply attempting to recover from this shock and the reason for its departure from public activity was to implement wide-ranging reforms to its structure.

New Wave of Public Activism

Bakri, now leader of ALM, launched a new wave of bold public activity. Bakri intended to replicate university activity with his new group, using similar styles to those he had pioneered with HT. As he stated: 'They will not be able to ban peace and human societies ... If they do, it will only backfire...We will use other people' (*The Guardian*, 23 August 1996). ALM was starting to gain significant ground on HT, who was still abstaining from public activity, and thus Bakri felt it was time to hold a large public rally. Bakri was, however, totally unprepared for the media and government backlash that soon followed. The Algerian Foreign Ministry in particular urged the UK government to ban the rally, believing it would be 'attended by the paymasters, the ideologists, the financiers and the zealots of international terrorism' (*Weekly Telegraph*, 4 September 1996). In a similar move, the Egyptian government threatened to break off diplomatic relations if the rally were to go ahead. Bakri was under growing pressure to cancel the rally because adverse publicity meant increased security costs at the London Arena, placing the venue outside the scope of his planned budget (Omar Bakri Mohammed., 2 June 2004). Although the rally was cancelled, Bakri claimed the event was a 'success because of the publicity boosting the Islamic cause' (Ibid., 2 June 2004). It is difficult to accept this view; for example, the capacity of the venue was 14,000 but only 3,000 tickets had been sold, and the video messages from Islamic leaders worldwide had not turned up. The cancellation of the event actually averted a disaster in terms of finance and publicity.

There was significant media focus on Bakri and ALM, which he used to condemn what he described as a deliberate attempt by the British government to 'demonise Muslims' (*Asian Age*, 9 September 1996). In the aftermath of such controversy, it was somewhat surprising that ALM was given permission to hold a rally in Trafalgar Square a year later. Bakri decided to invite a host of Islamic scholars, jurists and activists to give evidence against Muslim governments that he deemed guilty of oppression against Islam (Ibid., 2 June 2004). The '*Rally against Oppression*', as it was entitled by Bakri, was held without any major incident on 3 August 1997. ALM was, however, struggling to hold events as local councils continued to ban their activities. ALM, for example, acting under the guise 'The Society of Converts to Islam', booked the Southall Community Centre to hold a rally against Israel. The event was subsequently cancelled as it breached rules regarding the incitement of religious and racial hatred. According to Suleiman Keeler, ALM member and organiser of the rally:

> If some people misinterpret our intentions as violent then that is not our fault. We want people to boycott Jewish businesses, not talk to Jews, but we do not instruct followers to physically attack Jews. Just because the subject matter is a little bit hot it does not mean this event is not going to be a fun day. It is for all the family and there will be book and clothes stalls and a series of lectures. If it is banned I will be annoyed but we will find somewhere else to stage it. (Southall Gazette, 17 October 1997)

Following the banning of the meeting, ALM staged a highly controversial protest outside Ealing Town Hall. The protesters displayed banners and slogans such as: 'The hour will never come until the Muslims fight the Jews and kill them' (*Ealing and Acton Gazette*, 24 October 1997). Unperturbed, ALM continued to hold a variety of events and activities across the country, such as: '*Drink and Drugs, Public Enemy No. 1*'. As a result, the focus on public activity allowed ALM to increase their national profile.

'Tottenham Ayatollah'

Bakri was gaining noticeable media coverage, and, as a result, he agreed to participate in a Channel 4 documentary (1997). The 'Tottenham Ayatollah' was a documentary about a year in the life of Omar Bakri. When Bakri discovered the nature of the programme, he immediately contacted the press to lodge a complaint about the content of the broadcast. He was particularly disgruntled about the way in which the research was conducted and, in a letter to the producers, he threatened to sue the filmmakers and Channel 4 (Ibid., 2 June 2004). According to Abdul Haq (ALM member), 'the programme was a vicious attack on Islam and the Sheikh … it distorted the truth, but what do you expect from the *Kufr* [non-Muslims]?' Similarly, Makbool Javaid (ALM member) suggested 'the general thrust of the programme was the demonisation of Omar Bakri, and not the representation of his Islamic principles and ideology, as he was led to believe' (*Asian Age*, 10 April 1997). The broadcast had raised a number of real concerns regarding Bakri's rhetoric and activities. In particular, his views concerning women, homosexuality and Western society were brought under scrutiny. Homosexuality, for instance, was publicly condemned by Bakri as a perversion and immoral act. Despite grounding these speeches within the framework of religious scripture, they still appear to be motivated by hate and dislike. Moreover, these public declarations created a 'threatening' and 'intimidating' atmosphere in which homophobia was encouraged and endorsed (Leigh 2010, p. 377).

Support of Terrorism and Jihad

After Bakri was able to distance himself from HT, he promptly sought to propagate more extremist views. Jihad, for example, was reinterpreted as '*Fard al-Kafiayh* [individual duty]' (Ibid., 2 June 2004). Using this somewhat literal interpretation he advocated that Muslims should seek military training and fight jihad in those areas under occupation. The fallout of his views, as broadcasted on the television documentary, 'Tottenham Ayatollah,' resulted in the Crawley Council cancelling the lease on a hut rented by ALM. It was alleged that it was being used as a 'training camp to mould militants into Islamic warriors' (*Crawley Observer*, 16 April 1997). Although Bakri denied any involvement in organising jihad training camps in Britain, it was clear that some volunteers from ALM were leaving to fight in Chechnya. As Bakri confirmed:

> The military wing of the IIF is run by Osama bin Laden. Volunteers from Britain are travelling abroad to join camps run by the IIF and other organisations. Once they are there they receive military training or take part in Jihad. Last week we sent 38 people to Chechnya. Our volunteers are not terrorists. They are not targeting civilians and they do not target people in Britain. (*The Sunday Telegraph*, 7 November 1999)

Further concerns were raised regarding fundraising for terrorist activities. Bakri insisted that money raised by ALM to support militants in the Middle East was intended for humanitarian relief and not intended to purchase weapons. He was unwilling, however, to guarantee said money would not end up in the hands of terrorists (*Enfield Advertiser*, 3 December 1997). It was reported, however, that Bakri was a member of a committee that regularly held meetings to consider appeals for money. Bakri admitted that the committee channelled funds for jihad and often received requests from groups linked to Bin Laden (Ibid., 2 June 2004).

In early 2000 Bakri became embroiled in a local incident that soon escalated to national prominence. A distraught Muslim family from Crawley contacted the local authorities as it emerged that their son, Omar Kyam, had absconded to Pakistan to become a 'holy warrior' after being recruited by members of ALM. The family of Omar Kyam demanded ALM provide information on the disappearance of their son, placing mounting pressure on the organisation. Consequently, Bakri was forced to make a statement to the national press, in which he stated:

> I share the worry of these families, but if my child wanted to go and fight for a noble jihad then I would encourage them. I have received many complaints from families in Crawley and other places but I tell them it is a Muslim's duty to have military training when they reach puberty. These boys go not because of what I tell them to do, or what their mother and fathers say, but as an obligation to God. (*The Times*, 22 January 2000).

Although ALM tried to deny their involvement with Omar Kyam's disappearance, it was apparent he spent time with the organisation. More importantly, it was revealed ALM had been concentrating on university campuses in an effort to encourage young students to engage in jihad in countries abroad like Kosovo, Kashmir and Chechnya. This was not a surprising revelation, as Bakri explained: 'Islam demand[s] you struggle ... I form Al-Muhajiroun for this, so I make two networks. There was [the] *Dawah* network and [the] Jihad network' (Ibid., 2 January 2004). The *Dawah* network, as Bakri described it, would attract young students to ALM from Britain's university campuses, and from there students would be enticed into jihad.

Bakri (Ibid., 2 June 2004) proudly proclaimed that his group had successfully sent 'several hundred British Muslims' abroad to receive training and to fight jihad. In the aftermath of the 11 September terror attacks, however, ALM adjusted their combative style. In order to appease increasing governmental concerns about the link between terrorism and ALM, Bakri maintained Muslims were restricted by 'a covenant of security' (Ibid., 2 June 2004). In spite of this, growing pressure forced Bakri to leave the UK in 2005 in an effort to avoid arrest under obscure treason laws. While in exile, Bakri retracted the covenant of security. He cited two key reasons: Firstly, Bakri declared that the banning of Islamic groups and the unwarranted detention of Muslims under newly-formed anti-terror legislation violated the covenant. Secondly, he believed that the MCB had been recruited to spy on the Muslim community, which would bring harm to Muslims (Jay, ALM member, 2007). After he was contacted by UK members, however, he claimed the 'covenant was back on', as his judgments concerning the activities of the British government did not come to fruition.

HT Post-9/11

The 11 September 2001 terror attacks redefined the approach of HT in Britain. In the immediate aftermath of the attacks, the government increased political pressure on radical Islamist groups it accused of having links to terrorist organisations. More significantly, the government introduced stringent anti-terrorism legislation. As a result, HT suspended all public activity and the leadership held several meetings to discuss events post 9/11. According to Fahim (member), 'the events of 9/11 caught us by surprise, that's why we suspended activity … it was a difficult period and we didn't know how the government would react'. In contrast to the Muslim community, whose response to the attacks was mixed, the great majority of HT members condemned the attacks. According to Ameer (member, 2001), 'killing innocent civilians is not jihad'. Similarly, Aminur (member, 2001) stated: 'As a Muslim, and as a member of Hizb ut-Tahrir, I totally condemn the attacks … 9/11 was *haram* [forbidden]'. Also, I personally recall several meetings in which senior members explained how such attacks were 'un-Islamic' and 'totally condemned'. I was somewhat surprised that even beyond the shadow of the leadership; rank and file members still denounced the attacks. Not surprisingly, some members alleged that the event was staged: a 'US conspiracy', but they were a very small minority.

Despite the great majority of its members condemning the 11 September attacks, some political commentators have described the group as 'soft Jihadists' (Crandall 2008, p. 256). The events of 9/11 precipitated a focus on Islamist groups who preached and engaged in violence. In response, Imran Waheed stated: 'The party considers violence or armed struggle against the regime a violation of the Islamic Sharia' (*World Press*, 12 September 2005). This is supported by a restricted Home Office document that was released to HT under the Freedom of Information Act: 'Hizb ut-Tahrir is an independent political party that is active in many countries across the world … It considers violence or armed struggle against the regime, as a method to re-establish the Islamic State, a violation of the Islamic Shariah' (HT website, extract from 3 October 2005). It is clear HT does not advocate violence; instead it seeks to create social and political change through peaceful activism.

Proscribing HT: Global Crackdown

Since the start of the War on Terror, HT has been forced to counter allegations of supporting terrorism. Imran Waheed, HT media spokesman in the UK, declared that the movement had been engaged in non-violent political activity and since its inception had 'never accepted any form of armed struggle or killing of civilians' despite the killing of party members. In recent years, HT has faced growing calls for its prohibition, making it essential to provide an overview of this debate from various perspectives.

In February 2003, the Russian Supreme Court put HT on a list of banned terrorist organisations. A month before, HT was outlawed in Germany, under newly-formed legislation, for going 'against the concept of international understanding' (Radio Free Europe, 26 October 2004). HT gained notoriety in Germany, after organising a conference against the pending war in Iraq at Berlin's Technical University. The conference was also attended by several members of the extreme right-wing National German Party (NPD). The meeting provoked outrage in the press against 'Islamists and neo-Nazis' uniting to deliver anti-Semitic propaganda (Reuters, 15 January 2003). HT's representative in Germany, Shaker Aasim, rejected these accusations:

> We, the members of Hizb ut-Tahrir, are not anti-Semitic ... We consequently reject that [accusation]. We do not call to kill Jews. Our call is addressed to the Muslim people to defend themselves against the Zionist aggression in Palestine. And they have the right to do so. (Taken from www.islamic-state.org/leaflets/november0402.htm, 4 November 2002)

Interestingly, upon being arrested, on 15 January 2003, Aasim asked the police chief 'why we (HT) were banned in Germany, although in other European countries, like Great Britain, where we are much more active and stronger, no one gives us a second thought' (Radio Free Europe, 26 October 2004). The German official responded by saying, 'we banned you in Germany so that what is happening in England doesn't happen here' (Radio Free Europe, 26 October 2004). Uwe Halbach suggested that 'in Great Britain, Hizb ut-Tahrir is still not banned and has a surprisingly strong field of action – a lot stronger agenda than in Germany ... in fact, in Germany, it all came as a surprise' (Radio Free Europe, 26 October 2004). Subsequently, in a similar move, the Danish and Dutch governments also authorised the prohibition of HT. This has not perturbed the group, as they remain active across Europe. In the United States, conservative politicians have been calling for increased pressure on members of HT. A report by the conservative Heritage Foundation think-tank called HT 'an emerging threat to American interests in Central and South Asia and the Middle East' (*Radio Free Europe*, 26 October 2004). President Karimov of Uzbekistan echoed a similar view, when he criticised what he described as the paradox that 'Hizb ut-Tahrir is banned in Germany but is free to run its international headquarters in London' (*Radio Free Europe*, 26 August 2004). Without any credible evidence of violent intent, however, it is questionable why HT has been subject to such harsh treatment, especially since their presence in these European countries is limited. The bans in Europe therefore appear to be a pre-emptive measure to prevent the progress of HT.

The Proposal to Ban HT in Britain

The horrific terror attacks on London's public transport system placed immense pressure on HT. After 9/11, however, HT's leadership appeared to be undergoing a genuine transition towards a more moderate and mainstream approach. The UK leadership, led by Jalauddin Patel, made a concerted effort to modernise the party ideology, which they saw as outmoded. Imran Waheed, for example, tried to re-conceptualise the goal of HT within a Western ideological framework. As he commented: 'Our aim is to re-establish the Islamic Caliphate in the Muslim world. Our vision of the Islamic Caliphate is one of an independent state with an elected and accountable leader, an independent judiciary, political parties, the rule of law and equal rights for minority groups' (Parajpan 2005, interview with Imran Waheed). The move towards a more moderate position has been met with stern resistance from some members, who believe the new party image is a clear sign of its cultural and ideological decline. According to one member, 'The Hizb has lost its identity and message ... it's been watered down by JP [Jalaudin Patel], Imran Waheed and Abdul Wahid to make it palatable to the *Kufr*, so they don't ban us'. This was somewhat evident in HT's response to the Danish cartoon controversy in which they called for a peaceful demonstration and better education initiatives. More surprisingly, they publicly condemned the acts of Islamist groups, like ALM, for inciting hatred and violent behaviour. The leadership felt it was crucial to gain some distance from Omar Bakri, as his extreme rhetoric post 9/11 was being attributed to the party even though his affiliation ended in 1996.

In the aftermath of the London terror attacks, HT issued a public denunciation of the bombings and reiterated its commitment to peaceful activism. The entire fraternity was noticeably outraged at the atrocity, and it was clear they condemned the killing of innocent civilians under any circumstances. Following the attacks, the party sought to calm the situation, believing ordinary Muslims might be targeted for retribution. Imran Waheed, for example, explained in the wake of the 7 July London bombings that it is irresponsible 'to hold the Muslim community entirely responsible for the actions of a few ... will do little for community relations' (BBC website, 19 July 2005). He explained that mosques were not succeeding in channelling the frustration of young Muslims and urged greater dialogue between opposing viewpoints. In the media, however, HT were being linked to Omar Bakri and his militant fringe group Al-Muhajiroun. HT was portrayed as a militant organisation because of its perceived links to ALM. The historical connection with Bakri was proving to be very destructive, as his inflammatory rhetoric was being linked in the press to HT. Omar Brookes, a spokesman of the newly-formed Al-Ghurabaa, refused to condemn the July 7 attacks. As he explained: 'What I would say about those who do suicide operations or martyrdom operations is they're completely praiseworthy ... I have no allegiance to the Queen whatsoever or to British society; in fact if I see mujahideen attack the UK I am always standing with the Muslims, never against the Muslims' (*The Guardian*, 6 August 2005).

Within this context, it is difficult to understand the proposal to place HT on the Home Office's list of proscribed groups. According to one member, 'the Muslim rulers have placed considerable pressure on Western governments to have the organisation banned', because of its demands for political change in their countries. This view is supported by reports that Pervez Musharraf, the former president of Pakistan, urged Tony Blair to ban HT on the grounds that it 'brainwashes people, and that leads to violent acts' (*The Guardian*, 6 March 2005). More recently, David Cameron, the Conservative Party leader, tried to gain political mileage from this issue by asking newly-appointed Prime Minister Gordon Brown, in his first question-time, why HT had not been banned. Cameron insisted HT were indoctrinating young Muslims with an ideology of hatred but John Reid, former home secretary, stated that his department had examined the case of HT on two separate occasions and there was not sufficient evidence to proscribe the party under British law. Clearly, HT is not involved in committing acts of violence, nor does it provide support for and make statements that glorify violence. Craig Murray, the former British ambassador to Uzbekistan, declared that HT 'is a completely non-violent organisation' (Hizb ut-Tahrir Media Information Pack, p. 5). One might disagree with the views of HT, but unless they espouse violence it is unlikely a ban will occur. Thus, on the basis of available evidence and despite HT being banned in other countries, there appears no clear justification yet for a ban in the UK.

Summary

To date, as my data verifies, I do not know of a single prosecution or case brought against any member of HT for incitement to violence. Not a single act of violence has been proved against a member of HT in this country. However, this has nothing to do with radical propaganda. HT has been denounced for its radical speech, but again it is difficult to equate this speech to violence. HT strongly argues that it does not adopt or advocate violence. Its history of activism in the UK in many ways attests to this claim. According to International Crisis Group, HT advocates: 'the restoration of the Islamic caliphate. It differs from jihadi groups that share this objective in abstaining from violent activity (International Crisis Group, 2 March 2005). In fact, I have not encountered any convincing evidence that HT advocates violence. Apart from HT activism, I looked at key events in the organisation's history. In particular, at the height of their success, they imploded in catastrophic fashion. HT suffered two significant splits that saw Omar Bakri and Farid Kassim, the founding members of the UK branch, leave the group. Consequently, HT re-emerged after its self-imposed isolation with a wave of activism and recruitment in an attempt to rebuild the organisation.

It might be relatively clear that HT does not participate in overt violence, but they have been accused of being a 'gateway' organisation to violence. This concern was highlighted in a recent speech by David Cameron, at the Munich

Security Conference (2011). The Prime Minister talked at length about extremist ideology, he identified Islamic radicals who 'may reject violence' (*number10.gov. uk* 5 February 2011). As he explained:

> As evidence emerges about the backgrounds of those convicted of terrorist offences, it is clear that many of them were initially influenced by what some have called 'non-violent extremists', and they then took those radical beliefs to the next level by embracing violence ... So first, instead of ignoring this extremist ideology, we – as governments and as societies – have got to confront it, in all its forms. And second, instead of encouraging people to live apart, we need a clear sense of shared national identity that is open to everyone (*number10. gov.uk* 5 February 2011).

In other words, HT might not be openly implicated in the quest for Jihad, but they may facilitate and expedite the trajectory of young Muslims into Islamic militancy. This claim of 'conveyor belt' radicalisation appears to be somewhat merited. A by-product of HT activism has been increased radicalism. It is common for young Muslims to start with HT, becoming indoctrinated and radicalised, but often some young Muslims feel HT is not doing enough. As one ex-HT activist stated: 'HT talks a good game but they don't do anything ... Muslims are being killed and sisters are being raped and HT say wait for the Khilafah, this is rubbish ... the answer is simple, its jihad'. This feeling is quite common, but it does illustrate that most young Muslims who are inclined to more militant ideology see HT as a non-violent and passive organisation. However, the culturing process within HT offers young Muslims access to radical ideology, which is very similar to the religious and political principles of Jihadist groups. The HT construction of radical identities and frameworks of political Islam produce carbon copies of radicalised personalities. Also, HT introduces young Muslims to diverse networks with more militant actors and groups, exposing them to the ideology of jihadists. However, further research is required to verify this claim, and my research has not been focused towards ex-members and militant groups. Therefore, it is not surprising to see the group still under the spotlight, despite the fact HT emerged from Bakri's departure as a more moderate entity. However, the UK branch openly and publicly denounces terrorism and condemns the actions of Osama Bin Laden. Yet, its role and impact in radicalising young Muslims is still not clear. In the final chapter, I try to explain this issue in greater detail, bringing all my findings together.

Chapter 9
Demystifying the Schemata of HT Radicalisation

Recent debates concerning young people and radicalisation have generated some interesting insights, but there is considerable disagreement over the exact nature of radicalisation. Speaking broadly, a scholarly consensus on radicalisation is unlikely since it is a highly complex phenomenon that has a wide range of causal factors. Moreover, radicalisation is constantly moving forward into new areas of discussion and debate. The coalition invasion of Iraq, for example, instigated widespread debate about Britain's foreign policy. In particular, military occupation of Muslim countries and real or perceived collaboration with despotic Muslim regimes tend to be treated as causal factors for radicalisation by many British Muslims. The alleged relationship or overlap between foreign policy and radicalisation is often cited in testimonies of violent radicals. Mohammed Bouyeri, the murderer of Theo van Gogh, for example, expressed his deep anger with Western foreign policies in a note which he stabbed with a knife to the body of van Gogh. Although the government explicitly rejects any connection, HT claims Muslim anger towards the West is born out of its illegal war in Muslim lands. As Imran Waheed, spokesman for HT, stated:

> When Westerners get killed, the world cries. But if Muslims get killed in Iraq or Afghanistan, it's the smallest of news. I will condemn what happened in London only after there is the promise from Western leaders to condemn what they have done in Fallujah and other parts of Iraq and in Afghanistan. (*New York Times*, 10 July 2005)

In the course of writing this book, I have spoken to several young Muslims who voiced similar concerns regarding British and US foreign policy, which they claimed acted as a trigger for violent and extremist behaviour. The government has a tendency to divorce foreign policy from extremism, which is rather naïve, but the issues or contexts that lie behind HT radicalisation cannot be reduced solely to foreign policy. In fact, foreign policy did not feature in any of the HT narratives I encountered. So, if foreign policy was not identified as a contributing factor, then what attracts some young people to HT? In the foregoing chapters, I have taken a glimpse into the radicalisation process, but now these diverse strands need to be tied together to produce a relatively complete picture of HT radicalism. This means trying to highlight the findings and integrate them into the wider debates about radicalisation.

In order to go beyond abstract theory, I will need to use the empirical findings to provide an answer to why some British Muslims join HT. I have used many diverse strategies to gather the required data—such as interviews, surveys, focus groups, participant observations, and so on—to ensure that the theories are based on empirical findings. In the introduction, I noted the lack of attention paid to HT members and their backgrounds; a more recent review has seen markedly more focus on HT (Abbas et al., 2007; Lewis, 2008). Even though these noteworthy texts emphasise some interesting developmental issues, they do not claim to provide a clear picture of HT radicalisation. Indeed, as I discovered through the course of this study, any scrutiny of HT radicalisation based on single variables—such as ethnicity, class, or religion—fails to fully explain the causes of radicalisation. The members I observed experienced considerable disorder throughout their life-cycle experiences, making it vital to identify the specific social contextual factors they were exposed to and embedded within. Thus, radicalisation must be measured within a particular social reality, because the relationship between members' experiences and their environments are mutually shaping. Before I sketch out the distinctive features of HT radicalisation, it is first essential to explore the relationship between the social bases of HT membership and radicalisation. A key reason for looking at the social base first, I believe, is that it will allow me to identify and interpret commonalities between HT members, thereby providing a backdrop to radicalisation. HT radicalisation, therefore, has to be placed within a social and cultural context, because this will allow me to single out the types of Muslims who are most susceptible to joining the organisation.

Profiling HT Membership: Young Middle-class Asians

Through undertaking this study, I have gained considerable insight into the inner realities of HT, therefore it seems logical to first identify the social makeup of the fraternity. As I will show, the UK branch of HT is mainly composed of a homogenous group of young middle-class Asians. A number of theories have surfaced about HT in recent years, most of which are restricted by a failure to address adequately the group's social base. This is particularly significant, since HT radicalisation discourses that neglect social structures are unable to provide a picture of the phenomenon. Some social theorists, for example, believe the movement's growth among young people is rooted in frustration at 'the inaction of traditional authority in their communities' (Abbas et al., 2007, p. 157). This claim cannot be properly substantiated, as the findings indicate, because HT members do not emerge from traditional Muslim communities nor are they aligned economically to them. The debate about HT radicalisation has been primarily confined to 'causes', revealing a significant gap in such an approach, since it ignores the analytical importance of the social base. The social structure of HT membership has emerged from similar social experiences and backgrounds, facilitating behaviour and identity changes. In other words, social structures shape members' everyday lives, making it a fundamental aspect of HT radicalisation. Structural forces like religion, class, and ethnicity have been treated as explanatory factors. However, simplifying the concept of identity-formation into these restrictive parameters does not necessarily explain the emergence of generic HT member profiles.

In Chapter 7, I looked at the social structure of HT membership. A generally surprising characteristic and trait of HT membership was its success in mobilising young middle-class South Asian Muslims behind a political ideology and cause. In fact, a recurring feature of HT recruitment is the group's ability to attract homogenous clusters of young people from parallel social worlds. As far as this book is concerned, it seems apparent that HT members are typically drawn from a specific section of the Muslim community: young middle-class Asians. This identity framework provides a 'category of social significance', for belonging to a specific social class and ethnic group enables the members to define their distinctiveness in terms of comparisons with other Muslim sub-groups (Hitch, 1983, p. 118). While these social structures overlap, in a general sense, it becomes necessary to emphasise the homogenous properties of HT membership.

Contemporary theorists are excessively preoccupied with the social conditions of working-class Muslims, creating a tendency to over-exaggerate a link with radicalisation. Traditionally, the political affiliation of the working classes in Britain was often equated with economic disadvantage (Cannadine, 1999). Undoubtedly, the social reality of the Muslim working classes is bound to be affected by unemployment and poverty, as the statistical data verifies (Abbas 2005, p. 9). Beyond the economic dimension, however, there are wider issues directly impacting working-class Muslims. They are firmly embedded, for example, within ethnic and religious cleavages which have been exported from their countries of origin. Significant attention has been paid to these subgroups. In contrast, little focus has been directed to the relatively small minority of middle-class Muslims. In relation to HT, social class is often ignored as membership is characteristically portrayed within a working-class paradigm or equated with 'low social class position' (Abbas et al., 2007, p. 151). In spite of that, once I was able to sketch out a general profile of HT membership, it became clear its recruits were predominately drawn from the ranks of the middle class. Therefore, within an HT context, equating radicalisation to economic deprivation is misplaced.

On the whole, as mentioned, the overwhelming majority of studies dedicated to a better understanding of Muslims in Britain have focused primarily on working-class Muslims. This void in the research meant I could not readily draw upon studies about the Muslim community in Britain, since these are orientated towards working-class communities. As a result, I had to rely heavily upon my own findings in order to identify the differences between the two disparate classes. Identifying these differences became important, as it would provide insight into why middle-class Muslims appear more inclined toward HT. To start with, a large number of HT members were born into middle-class status. This clearly indicates HT members grew up within a social world qualitatively different from that of working-class Muslims. The parents of HT members, for example, did not come to this country in response to the manual labour shortage. Instead, the vast majority of HT parents arrived in this country as professionals—such as doctors, engineers, accountants and so on—giving their progeny an array of advantages. Social class, therefore, was an important factor in the way members narrated their life experiences and made sense of their identities. The importance of the social base means that I have to understand social class in the context of time and place; for instance, how a member's upbringing gave them a sense of who they were and where they came from. So, it was not surprising to hear members talk about where their parents were located in the social hierarchy, making class a very important feature of HT identity.

Unfortunately, most academic research today tends to pigeonhole 'Muslim youth' into a single generic category, shaped strictly by their shared religious traditions. Drawing parallels between working-class and middle-class Muslims ignores the gap in perceptions of social identities that have emerged from these two very diverse social worlds. In previous chapters, I suggested that membership in HT could be interpreted as a partial response to its subculture status. Young (1999, p. 89) believes subcultures tend to provide disconnected youths with joint solutions 'to collectively experienced problems'. Working-class Asians, for example, emerge from sharply contrasting experiences, which can prompt involvement with gangs. Cutting through the bleak social and economic realities of working-class Muslims reveals a unique culture. Firstly, within middle-class HT households, education was seen as an essential commodity. As one member explained, 'the wages of graduates (university) have skyrocketed since the 70s and 80s ... this means education guarantees economic success'. Meanwhile, a high percentage of working-class Muslims have no formal qualifications, restricting their social status and mobility to the bottom of the economic hierarchy. A common problem among working-class Muslims is the prioritisation of employment at the expense of education, reflecting negative economic conditions and realities. As Lareau (2003) noted, working-class parents tend to navigate through parenting by adopting dysfunctional child-rearing procedures, as they are usually forced to contend with adverse social and economic hardships. In contrast, she argued that middle-class parents engage in 'concerted cultivation' (Lareau 2003, p. 2). HT parents, for instance, intensely supervised their children's academic work and pushed them towards after-school leisure activities. Despite these middle class family socialisation techniques, the respondents developed susceptibility to radicalisation. A recurring theme that constantly emerged in the narratives of HT activists concerned 'relative deprivation'. It was clear that significant social problems were encountered during adolescents, especially when navigating through different social settings. As Parkin (198, p. 141) states, 'certain experiences during the most formative period of life tend to be of decisive effect on the development of the individual's political attitudes'. Given this social reality, it seems that most of the respondent's became radicalised in response to the acute experiences of being deprived social acceptance. In fact, the respondent's I spoke to all echoed similar experiences of feeling rejected and excluded from community and society, creating a deep sense of discontent.

This brings us back to the primary issue: the culture gap between working- and middle-class Muslims. The early generations of working-class Muslims found it difficult to build class solidarity with their white counterparts, which led many to retreat into their ethnic cultures (Abbas, 2004). As a result, working-class Muslim communities emerged across the country, forming in economically deprived urban centres. In contrast, HT families consciously shunned these communities in favour of more suburbanised settings, which meant living among the majority white populace. These distinct settings, or social worlds, meant HT members grew up disconnected from their ethnicity and community. Indeed, most members cited encountering Muslims and Asians for the first time at university. Consequently, HT members never developed a proclivity towards their ethnic culture; instead they seemed more inclined towards the majority host culture. This symbolic disassociation with their ethnic origins was partly directed by their parents' own attitudes towards their culture. In fact, most HT parents themselves became wrapped up by the host culture. Given this secular orientation, it is not surprising that minimal space was carved out for their children's religious heritage and development. In some respects, the first generation of working-class Muslims embodied a traditionalist view towards their ethnicity and religion, which they tried to transmit to their offspring. Ironically, both working- and middle-class parents have struggled to transmit their ethnic values to their children. However, in the early stages of development, middle-class parents found it easier to pass on secular attitudes to their children. Thus, HT members emerged from non-ethnically orientated social worlds, while most working-class Muslims are brought up within ethnically centred communities.

Despite emerging from two diverse social worlds, there are still some commonalities between these two groups. In particular, both sets of Muslim youths experienced racism. As Abdul quite rightly pointed out, 'racism is not restricted by class'. However, the racism directed towards HT members during their early childhood is slightly more pronounced. Second-generation working-class Muslims, for example, grew up in segregated communities. This to a degree restricted their interaction with white people, and thus reduced adverse experiences of racism. As several social theorists point out, racism towards minorities usually takes place within a certain space or setting wherein the white majority is more prominent (Miles and Brown, 2003). HT members, for instance, found themselves exposed to social settings in which they were often the only Asian students. By locating these marginalised spaces, it is easier to visualise the consequences of class differences between the two different classes. In other words, HT pathologies were constructed within fixed spaces. In their home lives, members were socialised within a middle-class tradition, which developed identities that correlated with social status. Also, members generally benefited from better and prolonged schooling, allowing them to either maintain their class status or gain more upward mobility. Therefore, I noticed through the interviews and ethnographic observations that HT members carved out a middle-class identity in contrast to the dominant working-class identity of most British Muslims. This created a natural class boundary, which to some extent explains why the HT struggles to recruit working-class Asians.

Many academics within contemporary British society have suggested that class boundaries play a limited role in society (Cannadine, 1999). This may be the case for society itself, but class identification amongst HT members is quite visible and very important. This was rather aptly pointed out by a working-class opponent of HT, whom I met in East London: 'They [HT] can't appreciate the reality of being working class because they're on the other side of the economic spectrum' (Mohammed Khan, 28). Thus, HT membership, which is not exceptionally large, is largely based on individuals with a common middle-class background. This means they are largely unaware of the socio-economic realities of working-class Muslims. Even though HT has managed to recruit a small segment of working-class Muslims, they are still considered outsiders or looked down upon. As Yusuf, an ex-HT activist, explained: 'A postman, like myself, would never be given the chance to do talks because that would distort the image of HT'. This provides some insight into the middle-class culture at play within HT. In bringing into play the issue of class, I found markedly different cultural patterns between HT members and their working-class counterparts. These different strains, at least partly, relate to personal experiences, and thus account for negative HT attitudes towards working-class Muslims. In other words, HT members are generally unable to recruit from the ranks of the working classes, because they are not conscious of the social contexts from which young working-class Muslims emerge and are embedded within.

In the description of a typical HT member, age seems to be a powerful component. The trajectory of HT members, as depicted in chapter five, has shown that age underpins their identity choices. The data revealed most HT activists were recruited during their youth (between the ages of 16 and 21), which is not surprising since young people are more receptive and susceptible to radical ideas. Youth, consequently, is a period in the life-cycle that is greatly affected by recurring and unsettling changes, which impact physical makeup and social position. The female activists, for example, talked about challenging the boundaries of family culture and expectation as they approached adulthood. In order to better understand HT radical identities, the ages that fall broadly within the classification of youth offer the most crucial insight into radicalisation—not least because HT seems to exclusively target and recruit young people. Navigating between childhood and adulthood forms a unique period in a person's life history. Most youth identity is stimulated through participation within a shared social setting, such as a specific youth subculture, which distinguishes it from other age identity experiences. One way of looking at youth subcultures within a British Muslim context is in terms of class identification. Social lives develop at specific times and manifest in certain locales. Working-class Muslims, for instance, spend a lot more time in mosques (Abbas, 2004). In contrast, HT middle-class activists spent little time in their youth in mosques, and thus experienced a secular upbringing and social world.

Ethnicity is another prominent feature of HT's social composition; from the early 1980s a large number of Asian students were attracted to the group. The ethno-religious experiences of working-class Muslims are somewhat removed from the social life of middle-class HT members. In general, the ethno-religious identity of most young Muslims is often shaped by personal and social interactions during childhood. In other words, the members' disassociation from ethno-religious markers relied heavily upon their secular middle-class upbringing and experiences. In this respect, unlike most working-class Muslims, HT members did not inherit a religious tradition from their parents. Therefore, the social realities of HT members differ strongly from working-class Muslims, creating a culturally distinct group that emerged out of the experiences of a middle-class status. Unfortunately, within the bulk of the literature I surveyed, little focus has been given to this homogenous sub-group, making a comparative study between working-class and middle-class Muslims vital. Jacobson (1998), in her study of British Muslim youth in the London borough of Waltham Forest, for example, fails to account for class differences between her subjects. However, if one assumes that the majority of her respondents emerged from working-class households, then her study provides some significant insights. For instance, she argues that young working-class Muslims in Waltham Forest displayed high levels of religious commitment (Jacobson, 1998, p. 126). Furthermore, working-class parents are able to transfer to and maintain religious traditions among their offspring more easily, because their children grow up in very 'close-knit' religious communities (Jacobson, 1998, p. 63). In contrast, as the findings have shown in chapter five, HT members tend to grow up detached from their ethno-religious roots. This, naturally, affects how HT members relate to, and interact with, working-class Asians. Consequently, middle-class HT activists do not share an ethno-religious bond with working-class Muslim youth, providing both groups with distinct and separate frames of reference. Therefore, HT middle-class identity is influenced by the social context from which a member emerges, making it unreliable to look at Muslim youth as a single and unified group.

Causes of HT Radicalisation (why do some young Muslims join HT?)

Before I began writing this book several years ago, I was invited by scholars within the field to talk about my involvement with HT, in an effort to bring about greater insight into radicalisation processes. Although I was not surprised by the overwhelming lack of understanding concerning HT, I became more troubled by the great volume of disjointed theories put forward to provide an explanation for radicalisation. The literature on radicalisation is equally incoherent. However, among the theorists who reflect on radicalisation, there is agreement that more needs to be done to understand the phenomenon. Furthermore, the literature on radicalisation is littered with grand theories that try to unify Muslim behaviour and activism on a general level. This approach is extremely problematic, because, as I have discovered, Muslims emerge from diverse backgrounds and experiences. So, how do I go about understanding why some young Muslims join HT? One approach relied on asking HT members why they joined the group. I listened in earnest to what they said, but what I heard was a torrent of idealistic rhetoric about Islam, which gave me no real insight or answer into why they joined HT. In order to better understand HT membership, I quickly realised, I had to be able to see through the twisted rhetoric to find out what really motivated members.

Another difficulty in dissecting HT radicalisation is merging the statistical data, in Chapter 7, with an understanding of the life trajectory of HT members in Chapters 5 and 6. However, as I will show, there are general patterns and contexts at play from which members emerge, and are embedded within, making them more susceptible to HT radicalism.

A common facet of a member's experience is his or her upbringing. As I commented earlier, a member's early identity is greatly shaped by structural factors like class, ethnicity, and age. However, these identifications usually manifest into boundaries of separation. Unlike working-class Muslims, who generally are more 'physically segregated from the white population', HT members grew up in white middle-class areas (Ansari, 2004, p. 391). This brought them into direct contact with white people and their secular culture, which in most cases was perceived as unwilling to accommodate ethnic and racial differences. Therefore, HT members emerged from their predominantly white surroundings as victims of racism. This rather hazardous exposure to perceived British culture and sensibilities left most members with a variety of challenges. Firstly, they could not revert to their ethnic or religious identity, since they did not inherit an attachment to their families' Asian-Muslim origins. In fact, most HT parents encouraged their children to pursue a distinctly secular path, seeing that a religious heritage was perceived in the Western society as an entirely backward and irrelevant phenomenon. Alongside this religious void, members could not enhance their own sense of ethnicity as they felt culturally British or white. These perceived contradictions helped sustain a feeling of uncertainty among the members, who had grown up in white middle-class suburbia as outsiders. In large part the attraction of HT, especially for its activists, lies in the fact that it gives young Muslims a way of disentangling themselves from the insecurity and quandary of living in contemporary Britain.

The adverse experiences of living, and interacting, with white people drew the members away from British society. The members I spoke to talked about how they started to believe the negative distortions about their race and ethnicity, which left a lasting impression on the way they viewed their place in British society. As they matured, most members could not develop a unified understanding about all the diverse aspects of their life. Religion and ethnicity were disconnected from their social identity, preventing them from establishing a unified identity. Consequently, the members found themselves in a social limbo, rejected by the dominant white culture and unwilling to embrace an ethno-hybrid identity like their working-class Muslim counterparts. The lack of stable and coherent ties linking the members to their ethnic and non-ethnic communities resulted in their being psychologically and socially divorced from the wider society. According to Parkin (1968, p. 11), individuals that fail to integrate or find a place in society are 'highly susceptible to the appeals' of radical and fringe movements. Although the social encounters the members experienced played a significant part in their upbringing, they cannot be attributed as causal features of HT radicalisation. This is because I encountered a small number of HT members who insisted they felt socially connected to their white middle-class communities; they had strong ties with friends and did not differentiate according to ethnicity or race. Despite coming across only a handful of members that claimed to be well adjusted, I had to accommodate their experiences and insights into the theory of HT radicalisation. Consequently, it is very difficult to maintain with absolute certainty a generic set of causes for radicalisation that fit into the life pathologies of every HT member. Therefore, it is better to conceptualise radicalisation in terms of 'social agents and settings'. This allows me to consider the major features of radicalisation that commonly exist across HT's fraternity; in particular, locations of radicalisation, experiences, and group radicalisation have been treated as explanatory factors.

Throughout the course of my interactions with HT activists, it became apparent that despite minor differences in location and experiences the primary trigger in the radicalisation process is HT. The group is the central agent in radicalising young people. During the ethnographic stage, for example, I was able to observe the ways in which members seemed to lose parts of their individuality when they encountered HT. In fact, I noticed several key themes were present during the 'contact' stage of the recruitment process—new social settings, dysfunctional transitions, and peer group associations—appeared frequently in the case histories of HT members. It is therefore argued that recruitment is an integral part of the radicalisation process, because the contact is moving towards joining the group. To start with, recruitment into HT is likely to occur at university or college, as I identified in chapter five. When the members left their homes for the first time they struggled to deal with the transition to a new social and cultural environment. Parsons (1960, p. 293) quite aptly points out that radical movements 'which exploit the generalities and ambiguities' of social situations are able to naturally recruit troubled or alienated individuals. This tendency was set off by perceived social barriers, namely ethnicity and religion, which inhibited the formation of close ties with others. Consequently, this turbulent transition into university life forced members to seek out people who shared the same socially constructed identities as themselves (that is, middle-class Asian-Muslims).

Even though the peer group brought together Muslims who emerged from similar social realities, the one feature that overrides everything else is religiosity. The peer group, made up of HT recruiters, provided a sense of purpose and significance to members' lives by infusing them with religion. This involved rapid socialisation into very intensive religious practices. It seems clear that the advent of a 'religious awakening' was triggered by the formation of powerful religious bonds between members and peer group participants. Religion gave the peer group an opportunity to recruit non-religious students into HT. Most members revealed that they had never considered themselves spiritually connected to a global *ummah* (community) and thus never felt emotionally moved by the plight of Muslims. However, this changed when members were exposed to HT rhetoric, and began to embrace party ideology and belief.

It can be fairly assumed that peer group ties are critical, because new ideas are transmitted through these friendship bonds, allowing new recruits to enter the group setting in familiar surroundings. However, joining HT is not purely a free choice; significant coercion is applied in order to manipulate a potential member into joining. Although there is no physical pressure, the coercion is clear in that if you do not join HT, you will be deemed to be sinful and God will condemn you to the pits of hell for eternity. By virtue of ignorance, one is placed in a state of guilt for not working for the Party's aims, and thus feels compelled to join. Thus, I was not greatly surprised by one member's suggestion that the 'Hizb (group) does not need you, rather you need the Hizb (group)'. What strikes me about this statement is that it underscores the negative impact of group membership. The conditions and experiences of the members are of particular interest to me, since the success of HT is dependent on their ability to isolate identities that display a need for the group. One of the key subjects I will need to consider in this chapter, as I think about group influence and group processes, is what happens to members in the group. When members start to act collectively, for example, does this erode their sense of individual identity?

Joining HT as a novice requires attending a weekly *Halaqah* (study group); this deepens and cements the radicalisation process. It is considered a key stage and an instrumental part of group radicalisation. During this period, intellectual pressure is applied, forcing the novice to bend towards the group's expectations. In particular, the *Mushrif* (teacher) is very keen to establish a joint construction of reality in order to create a new cognitive viewpoint. Developing a new cognitive framework entails changing the way a novice views his or her social surroundings, often by making sense of their past and present experiences. In other words, the reinterpretation of the world around them takes place in the *Halaqah*, eventually leading to the internalisation and manifestation of a radical HT identity. To remove extreme individual differences and independent thought the *Mushrif* forces novices to agree with and accept as their own the ideas presented in *Halaqah*. The novice is seen as intellectually inferior, especially if they display independent thinking. Although this alignment of ideas is consciously arrived at, it does denote the acceptance of influence.

Beyond the setting of the *Halaqah*, I was able to witness group practices that overpowered the member. The norms, roles, and patterns of communication engineered by HT constrain behaviour. As one member explained, 'when the *shab* [novice] is new his *nafsiyya* [behaviour] is in conflict with his concepts so you need to draw him closer to the *Hizb* [group] in order to purify and cleanse his *nafsiyya* [behaviour]'. Indeed, Milgram (1974) makes an important distinction between conformity and obedience that has relevance. He conceptualised conformity as following one's peers in a group setting, while obedience relates to a chain of command (Milgram, 1974). Conformity, if defined as following one's peers, best describes the *Halaqah*. This is because novices are placed amongst their peers within a controlled setting, forcing them to conform. However, obedience is the psychological apparatus that connects a member's action to the collective work of HT. The party rhetoric, as cited in countless publications, has stated that the *Mabda'a* (ideology) itself to the exclusion of anything else is the basis of organising and mobilising the fraternity. In reality, this is not true. HT imposes the ideology onto the members, demanding they obey the commands of the party hierarchy.

When the novice begins to convey the thoughts of HT effectively, as if they were his or her own, then he or she is considered for membership. Even though radicalisation has no definable end point, membership signals the alignment of beliefs between the novice and the group. At this point, members have fully adjusted their sense of identity, their thoughts and behaviours, to match the collectively defined attributes of HT. By developing a sense of 'we-ness', a member is made aware that beyond HT there is a 'they' that constitutes the dominant culture. This distinction from the larger society allows HT to shape members' identities permanently. Consequently, when a novice becomes a member, they essentially belong to HT, deriving their sense of identity, at least in part, from it. This creates a collective mindset. Thus, when a novice has been sufficiently assimilated, membership is offered. According to one ex-member, 'membership is the final stage of radicalisation, because you feel you can't live without them [HT]'. Therefore, those that are attracted to the homogeneity of the group are those individuals that display a predisposition for belonging. Thus departure is unthinkable as re-socialisation into society cannot occur; this is analogous to criminals who spend a lifetime incarcerated.

In the course of this book, I have sought to dissect HT membership, which I have argued embodies a brand of Islamist radicalism that is characteristically South Asian and middle class in nature. In order to gain a deeper sense of HT membership, I decided to hold focus group discussions with ex-members, as I felt this would provide a useful picture of HT appeal through a less idealistic narrative. After speaking to these ex-members, I noticed a common perception of HT radicalism emerge. As Dawud explained, 'they (HT) are a cult'. If this was so, then I wanted to know how HT operated like a cult. Hassan (1988) suggests that 'thought-stopping tactics' and installing an 'us-versus-them' mindset help to coerce people into joining cults. In a similar way, HT use coercive influences to psychologically control their members (for example, like the *Halaqah*). However, Zimbardo (1997, p. 14) believes cult methods of recruiting, indoctrinating and influencing their members are not 'exotic forms of mind control'. Rather, they are more intensely applied tactics of social influence, which are practiced daily by all societal agents of influence. In other words, certain environmental conditions can make people more vulnerable to cult recruitment, such as social alienation, depression and frustration. Within this context, cults often provide a set of life-altering solutions, which are more importantly accompanied by structure, authority, and close social contacts.

From a general perspective, HT clearly exhibits a host of similar characteristics to those found in cults. I have located five comparable features between cults and HT. Firstly, strict adherence to a set of shared beliefs is mandated and, in turn, provides a sense of meaning and purpose to their members. Secondly, group members are intensely motivated by the group-mind, succumbing to group pressure. According to Bion (1980), when individuals function in a group context, their individual judgement and behaviour are strongly influenced by the powerful forces of group dynamics. Thirdly, the group facilitates the psychological need to be part of a group, making the member feel significant, which provides a sense of belonging and security. According to Post (1998), 'belonging' to the group may be the first time they truly belonged, the first time they felt truly 'significant', the first time they felt that what they did 'counted'. Fourthly, recruitment techniques often rely on intense social influence, using coercion and guilt, to force the recruit to agree with the group. Finally, in most cases, it is often extremely difficult to leave the group. These obstacles can come in the form of group pressure, where loyal members will intervene in the case of a member who has doubts about the group and longs for his or her old life, or the obstacles may be psychological.

Recruitment Grounds: The University Link

Another important variable in the radicalisation schemata of HT is location of recruitment. Clearly, as this research has outlined, university campuses are primary recruiting grounds for HT activists. Universities provide a magnet for HT activism and recruitment, as they attract a wide spectrum of young British Muslims from diverse geographical locations and backgrounds. In keeping with the middle-class dimension of HT's social base, universities offer the group access to a large pool of middle class Muslims, who have often moved away from their homes for the first time. This creates a deep feeling of social displacement, making them gravitate towards HT activists who exploit the social commonalities that often exist and the deficit for companionship. As a result, apart from the socio-economic similarities, potential recruits find themselves in vulnerable settings, rendering them more receptive to the allure of HT. Notwithstanding the importance of universities, the peer group associations that are created within this social space are primary factors in the radicalisation process. What is subsequently striking about the location of HT radicalisation is the minimal influence Mosques appear to play in recruitment activity. This is consistent, though, with the research of Muslim middle-class lifestyle and activity. The background and upbringing of the respondents shared the notable lack of religiosity during their youth, manifesting in complete disconnection from religious institutions.

In the mind-set of HT activists, Mosques have become increasingly synonymous with working-class Muslims, and thus offer slim recruitment opportunities

(Kepel, 1997, p. 105). This also reflects the overly secularised nature of the respondent's upbringing. In particular, religious activity played no real role in their daily activity, which meant the mosque lacked any instrumental significance. Therefore, seeing that Mosques have little centrality in the makeup of young middle class Muslims, it is reasonable for HT to target universities at the expense of Mosques. As the early HT pioneers suggested, there is no overtly better location then university campuses in which to encounter young middle class Muslims, especially since they display a heightened receptivity to the radical message of HT. Historically, HT invested significant focus and attention to universities, creating hubs of activity across the country in which large scale recruitment took place. Therefore, the HT infiltration of British university campuses marked a key stage in HT recruitment, and thus the success of the UK branch rests and falls in this critical social space.

De-radicalisation

In recent years, critical questions have been asked about how radicalisation can be tackled or countered. In the UK, in the wake of the London bombings, considerable effort and resources have been assigned to building greater community cohesion. The PREVENT strand of the former government's CONTEST strategy was used to challenge the ideology of violent extremism. More significantly, the government tried to revise its counter-terrorism strategy to widen its definition of extremist behaviour. It drafted a proposal, dubbed CONTEST 2, to broaden the radical net to include activists who: advocate a caliphate (Islamic State), promote Shariah law, argue that Islam bans homosexuality, believe in jihad, and fail to condemn the killing of British soldiers in Iraq or Afghanistan (*The Guardian*, 17 February 2009). Although, this strategy is defunct, there were obvious problems with the rationale behind such an overreaching approach, especially concerning issues of free speech and opinion. Muslims must feel confident in their ability to enjoy and express views in an open environment. Thus, it seems clear now, this redraft aimed to control Muslim thought, forcing them to embrace the Western political system and its core values. Moreover, those who advocate this strategy 'say hard-line Islamist interpretation of the Qur'an leads to views that are the root cause of the terrorism threat Britain faces' (*The Guardian*, 17 February 2009). I have already suggested that radicalisation has no single definable cause. Instead, radicalisation needs to be regarded as a multi-layered phenomenon that has multiple triggers. This would suggest that de-radicalisation strategies need to be case-specific, as generic plans fail to acknowledge the distinct realities of group members. Despite the importance of de-radicalisation, I only have time to analyse the effectiveness of current UK policy, and thus hope in the future to formulate a more precise strategy based upon the findings.

The first, and perhaps most common, strategy concerns proscribing HT. Reworking the legal boundaries to tackle HT radicalisation is very complex and counter-productive. To start with, UK counter-terrorism legislation does not include groups like HT, because they employ a non-violent ideology. This is all very well but HT radicalisation, if deemed a threat, needs to be tackled by formulating a distinct plan that treats the underlying factors of HT radicalism. As Faz, an ex-member from East London explained: 'the government is incapable of tackling HT radicalisation because they don't understand the ethos of the party ... HT is a middle class entity and so you need to tackle middle class radicalism amongst British Muslims'. Also, a generic ban will only drive the group underground, and thus may strengthen its appeal amongst disaffected Muslim youths. Anecdotal evidence suggests that banning radical organisations, like Al-Muhajiroun, tends to have a limited effect, as they still continue to recruit new activists and engage in public events. Therefore, a de-radicalisation strategy cannot rely wholly on legal intervention; rather it needs to tackle the causes of HT radicalisation through social, political and educational strategies.

There is little doubt that bringing young Muslims of different social backgrounds together is an important first step in tackling the problem of radicalisation on a national level, but it seems government strategy fails to understand the nature and complexity of Muslim identities. For instance, assessing young British Muslims as a single homogenous group ignores class and cultural differences. As Ansari (2004, p. 3) points out, 'a Sylheti from Bangladesh, apart from some tenets of faith, is likely to have little in connection with a Mirpuri from Pakistan, let alone a Somali or a Bosnian Muslim'. Such variation means a de-radicalisation strategy, such as CONTEST, is not suitable because its functionality is structured around a set of fixed rules and guidelines. Instead, a more malleable approach is required that can be adapted to fit the various social realities of British Muslims. Rouleau (2001) further elaborates upon this when he writes, 'Islamist parties are quite dissimilar: often they have nothing in common but their references to the Prophet and Islam, which they interpret in a number of conflicting or contradictory ways, and they span the political spectrum from left to far right'. According to Dawud (ex-member), 'a policy that pigeonholes Muslims into a single cluster is doomed to fail ... Look at HT and ALM, on the surface they seem the same, but you and I know that's not the case'. Therefore, a de-radicalisation strategy cannot be homogenous; rather separate initiatives need to be tailored to each form of Islamic group radicalism. Historically, Al-Muhajiroun and HT had very similar aims and ideologies, but their influence and impact was very different. ALM tends to exclusively recruit working-class Muslims, while the vast majority of HT members emerge from middle-class backgrounds. Even though ALM and HT operate from within very similar radical frameworks, the social reality of their recruitment is poles apart. With this in mind, a more group specific strategy is required.

It would seem HT is only able to recruit from the ranks of middle-class Asians, making it in theory possible to formulate a generic de-radicalisation strategy for HT. The evidence I have accumulated in this book shows that HT radicalisation requires a human interface. This is partly due to the context in which radicalisation takes place. First and foremost, HT members often emerge from a homogenous socio-demographic background, which signifies attraction to peers of similar identity and trajectory. This means HT radicalisation initially takes place within a specific social context, usually amongst a group of friends at university. Even though similarity amongst the members breeds connection, it also limits their social interactions with the wider society. As a result, they enter a distinct social world in which the culture they receive, the attitudes they form, and the interactions they experience take place within a closed group environment. The radicalisation process reinforces this state of homogeneity, as it cements social ties between group members, while simultaneously cutting off relations with non-members. Despite the acknowledgment that a range of factors contribute to radicalisation, government strategy continues to hinge on broad policy initiatives such as 'PREVENT' and 'CONTEST'. These broad measures are fairly ineffective against HT as they are designed to counter violent extremism. Moreover, government strategy over-emphasises an approach of criminalisation to radicalisation, which generally allows HT to continue its activism, as they operate legally. Finally, I would suggest that if the government wants to tackle HT radicalisation then it needs to confront the following three issues: (1) Muslim middle-class identity formation (disaffection and cultural exclusion); (2) peer group radicalisation at university; and (3) HT radicalisation practices (tackling HT ideology and indoctrination strategies). These points illustrate HT's social influence over a distinct group of British Muslims, namely young middle-class Asians. By dealing with these issues a more robust and distinct challenge can be mounted against HT.

Throughout the course of writing this book, I have been interested in understanding why some young Muslims join HT, and in doing so provide greater insight into the causal factors of radicalisation. In order to bring this book to a close, one key question remains: what impact has HT radicalisation had on British Muslim identity? If we first consider the British Muslim population as a whole, then HT has had a limited impact. There are several clear reasons for this lack of broad appeal. Firstly, first-generation Muslims tend to interpret and practice their religious beliefs within a rigid framework that sustains the values and traditions of their countries of origin. As a result, HT activists have been unable to dislodge the deep-rooted beliefs of the first generation, making it difficult to gain any support or base amongst this demographic. Secondly, as I have already explained, HT is generally unsuccessful amongst working-class Asians; however, middle-class Asians tend to live and think differently allowing HT to establish a strong foothold in the midst of this social group. Consequently, it would be important in any HT de-radicalisation strategy to categorise this demographic as potentially vulnerable to HT radicalisation.

HT may not have been successful in recruiting across the wider Muslim community, but recruitment is only one facet of impact. From a historical perspective, HT has been operating in the UK for over three decades, and thus it would be unfair and somewhat simplistic, to argue the group has had no real impact on British Muslim identity. HT introduced its radical message into a fresh social environment, like university campuses, which in turn heightened religious identity amongst the placid Muslim populace. During this period, British-born and raised Muslims started to assert their own distinct forms of identity. As mentioned in earlier chapters, charismatic figures like Omar Bakri Mohammed set about formulating an Islamic response to the challenges of living in modern Britain. In this context, HT exploited a gap amongst some young British Muslims, who were stuck between the world their parents migrated from and the world they were living within. Before HT overwhelmed university campuses, the vast majority of Muslim students were drawn to Asianism. This identity united students of South Asian origin together under the banner of their common culture and ethnicity. HT quickly erected ethnic boundaries between British Asians, pointing to a single Muslim identity that excluded other diasporic religious faiths. This redefining of student identity created a platform for HT to promote its political radicalism. By introducing '*Khilafah*' to a politically inactive Muslim student body, HT was able to engage with British society and state in a new and radical fashion. The appeal of HT grew rapidly across universities principally amongst the Asian middle class, who felt socially excluded from their ethnic community and the wider society. In this respect, HT gave some young British Muslims a way to break free from the shackles 'of the Islam of their forefathers' (Ansari, 2004, p. 393). The radical interpretations of HT offered them a way to rediscover their religious identity, which became the sole determinant of their public and cultural life. Thus, HT gave some young Muslims a way to come to terms with their identity.

All this begs the question: does HT have a positive or negative effect on British Muslims? I spoke to several HT members regarding this issue, and to some extent I was surprised by some of their responses. One member argued that HT works within the Muslim community to build better understanding between the West and Islam, which he suggested, would 'help counter terrorism'. Similarly, another member insisted HT was a force for good, as it directed Muslim grievances towards peaceful political activism. Despite its radical rhetoric, HT repeatedly and unequivocally has said the killing of civilians is forbidden. This is not a recent or opportunistic shift in policy since party methodology rejected the use of violence as a means for achieving its ideological goals over 50 years ago. Since the 9/11 terror attacks, HT has tried to counter the growth of Islamic militancy in the Muslim community by articulating a non-violent channel for Muslim anger. According to HT its work is peaceful and positive, as they have stated:

> In the UK our work with the Muslim community is focused on directing Muslims to make a positive contribution to society whilst preserving their Islamic identity … Many of our members have senior roles in IT, economics, medicine, teaching, engineering, and some of our members were involved in treating the victims of the 7th July bombings in London's hospitals (HT media Pack 2008, p. 4).

HT believes they are working towards the betterment of the Muslim community by offering alternative solutions to the dilemmas of British life. Yet, this seemingly noble goal does not quite extend to integrating Muslims within the social fabric of

British society, making it harder to see the group as a symbol for good. However, British Muslims in growing numbers are beginning to question their association with the state. In the poorly constructed counter-terrorism strategy, CONTEST 2, the government sought to establish 'a British version of Islam' that would have artificially compelled Muslims to adhere to British values. This extremely disjointed proposal expected Muslims to adopt shared British values, even though, despite the inescapable undermining of freedom of opinion, these values remain highly ambiguous and undefined. It seems the government was trying to intervene in theological issues, which is surely a matter for the Muslim community to debate and resolve themselves. These proposals, if targeted towards HT, seem counter-productive since they will not pacify their radical activism.

Last Thought

The research presented in this book has concentrated on one of the most controversial Islamist groups in Britain. Although the British media seem fascinated by HT, the academic community has failed to quantify its emergence within a British context. This is partly why I chose to carry out the study. I have discovered HT radicalisation to be a narrow and distinct process with identifiable patterns related to those who are attracted to the organisation. One of the main sets of issues raised for discussion throughout this study has been the phenomenon of HT middle-class radicalism. In recent times, broad strategies have been formulated to counter radicalisation, which assumes radicals do not match a specified demographic or profile. In contrast, not only are the underlying features of HT radicalisation identifiable, but more significantly it is rooted within a homogenous context. Amongst political commentators there is a growing tendency to work out and apply generic causal features of radicalisation to highly diverse Islamic groups and peoples. This ignores the features present in middle-class HT radicalism that serve to distinguish it from the radicalism of working-class Muslims. Clearly, there is a need for more sustained study on this social group, as this demographic has shown strong identification with HT.

The HT members I encountered were not 'abnormal'. They were young middle-class Asian professionals who turned their backs on western society and embraced a radical version of Islam. I set out, therefore, to discover why these young men and women had joined HT. In part, HT radicalisation was conceived as a response to the frustrations experienced during the early life cycle. These included issues of racism, social deprivation and alienation, cultural marginalisation, identity crisis and psychological unsettlement. HT radicalisation became a means to express their reaction against these frustrations, and the white majority's alleged failure to live up to certain professed ideals, such as social egalitarianism. Despite their high educational and professional success, HT members were characterised by their social vulnerability, which facilitated a propensity for the radical politics of HT. This is perhaps a measure to the extent adverse social experiences can have upon the identity construction of some young British Muslims. Those who joined the ranks of HT felt a deep sense of social and political displacement within society. Accordingly, HT provided a safe social space to reconstruct identity, which gave the recruits a sense of belonging and acceptance. Based on the foregoing discussion on HT, a clear picture has been sketched out that provides a comprehensive investigation of the roots – political, social, cultural and psychological – of HT radicalisation in Britain. By identifying the context in which HT radicalisation takes place, and through penetrating the clandestine veil of the organisation, an important step forward has been made in 'demystifying' HT radical behaviour and ideology.

Bibliography

Abbas, T. (2007) *Islamic Political Radicalism: A European Perspective* (Edinburgh: Edinburgh University Press).

Adler, A. (2006) *The Collected Clinical Works of Alfred Adler, Volume 1: The Neurotic Character* (New York: The Alfred Alder Institute).

AIVD (2006) *Violent Jihad in the Netherlands: Current Trends in the Islamist Terrorist Threat* (Ministry of the Interior and Kingdom Relations).

Al-Nabhani, Taqi al-Din. (1950) *Inqadh Filastin (Saving Palestine)* (Damascus: Matba'at Ibn Zaydum).

Al-Nabhani, Taqi al-Din (2002a) *Islamic State* (London: Al-Khilafah Publications).

Al-Nabhani, Taqi al-Din (2002b) *Al-Takattul al-Hizbi* (London: Al-Khilafah Publications).

Al-Nabhani, Taqi al-Din (2002c) *Nidham al-Islam* (London: Al-Khilafah Publications). Anderson, L. (1997) 'Fulfilling Prophecies: State Policy and Islamist Radicalism', in *Political Islam: Revolution, Radicalism, or Reform?*, edited by J. Esposito (Boulder, CO: Lynne Rienner).

Anon. (2002) *Hizb ut-Tahrir* (London: Al-Khilafah Publications).

Ansari, H. (2004). *The Infidel Within: Muslims in Britain since 1800* (London: Hurst).

Anwar, M. (1976) 'Young Asians between two cultures', *New Society*, 38, 16.

Argyle, M. (1992) *The Social Psychology of Everyday Life* (London: Routledge).

Armstrong, K. (2001) *Battle for God: Fundamentalism* (London: HarperCollins).

Asher, S.R. and Coie, J.D. (1990) *Peer Rejection in Childhood* (Cambridge: Cambridge University Press).

Ayubi, N.M. (1991) *Political Islam: Religion and Politics in the Arab World* (London: Routledge).

Bakker, E. (2006) 'Jihadi terrorists in Europe', *Clingendael Security Paper* No. 2 (Netherlands Institute of International Relations).

Ballard, R. (1996) 'The Pakistanis: Stability and Introspection', in *The Ethnic Minority Populations of Great Britain: Ethnicity in the 1991 Census*, vol. 2, edited by C. Peach (London: Central Statistical Office).

Bandura, A. (1977) *Social Learning Theory* (New York: General Learning Press).

Banks, M. (1996) *Ethnicity: Anthropological Constructions* (New York: Routledge).

Barth, F. (1982) *Ethnic Groups and Boundaries* (Boston, MA: Little Brown).

Bean, J.P. (1985) 'Interaction Effects Based on Class Level in an Explanatory Model of College Student Dropout Syndrome', *American Educational Research Journal*, 22(1).

Bell, S. and Coleman, S. (1999) *The Anthropology of Friendship* (Oxford: Berg Publications).

Benn, T. and Jawad, H. (2004) *Muslim Women in the United Kingdom and Beyond: Experiences and Images* (Boston, MA: Brill).

Berryman, C. (1999) 'Theories of Autobiography', *Mosaic* (Winnipeg), 32.

Bion, W. (1980) *Experiences in Groups* (London: Routledge).

Bloch, M. (1986) *From Blessing to Violence: History and Ideology* (Cambridge: Cambridge University Press).

Bowles, G. and Klein, R. (1983) *Theories of Women's Studies* (London: Routledge).

Brake, M. (1985) *Comparative Youth Culture: The Sociology of Youth Culture and Youth Subcultures in America, Britain and Canada* (New York: Routledge).

Bronfenbrenner, U. (1979) *The Ecology of Human Development: Experiments by Nature and Design* (Cambridge, MA: Harvard University Press).

Campbell, D. and Hooper, J. (2005) 'Second Bomb Suspect was seen in Rome' (*The Guardian*, 1 August).

Cannadine, D. (1999) *The Rise and Fall of Class in Britain* (New York: Columbia University Press).

Chansky, T.E. (2001) *Freeing Your Child from Obsessive-Compulsive Disorder: A Powerful, Practical Program for Parents of Children and Adolescents* (London: Three Rivers Press).

Chibucos, T.R. (2005) *Readings in Family Theory* (Ohio: Sage Publications).

Cohen, S. (1980) *Folk Devils and Moral Panics: The Creation of the Mods and Rockers* (New York: St. Martin's Press)

Cooper, J. (1979) *Class: A View from Middle England* (London: Eyre Methuen)

Coleman, J.C. (1968) *Studies in Ethnomethodology*, in *Review Symposium: Harold Garfinkel*, edited by J.C. Coleman, G.E. Swanson and A.F.C. Wallace (American Sociological Review, 122-30).

Cote, J.E. (1996) 'Sociological Perspectives on Identity Formation: The Culture-Identity Link and Identity Capital', *Journal of Adolescence*, 19.

Crandall, R. (2008) *Islam: The Enemy* (Oxford: Blackwell), p. 256.

Crenshaw, M. (1981). *The Causes of Terrorism* (*Journal of Comparative Politics*, 13, 379-399).

Crenshaw, M. (1992). *Current Research on Terrorism: The Academic Perspective* (Studies in Conflict and Terrorism).

Crenshaw, M. (1985) The Psychology of Political Terrorism, in *Handbook of Political Psychology*, edited by M. Hermann (San Francisco, CA: Jossey-Bass).

Crone, P. (2003) *Slaves on Horses: The Evolution of the Islamic Polity* (Cambridge: Cambridge University Press).

Crone, P. (1989) *Pre-Industrial Societies* (Oxford: Blackwell)

Dabashi, H. (1993) *Theology of Discontent: The Ideological Foundations of the Islamic* (New York: New York University Press).

David, B. and Turner, J.C. (1999) Studies in self-categorization and minority conversion: The ingroup minority in intragroup and intergroup contexts. *British Journal of Social Psychology*, 38.

Davis, K. and W.E. Moore. (1970) 'Some Principles of Stratification'. *American Sociological Review*, 10(2), 242-9.

Della Porta, D. and Diani, M. (2006) *Social Movements: An Introduction* (Oxford: Blackwell)

Dekmejian, H. (1995) *Islam in Revolution: Fundamentalism in the Arab World* (2nd edition rev.) (Syracuse: Syracuse University Press).

Devji, F. (2005) *Landscapes of the Jihad: Militancy, Morality and Modernity* (London: C Hurst & Co Publishers).

Durkheim, E. (1984) *The Division of Labour in Society* (London: Macmillan).

Dwyer, C. (2000) 'Negotiating diasporic identities: Young British South Asian Muslim women', *Women's Studies International Forum*, 23(4), 475-86.

Eliade, M. (ed.) (1987) *Encyclopedia of Religion* (New York: Macmillan).

Erikson, E. (1950) *Childhood and Society* (New York: W.W. Norton and Company).

Esposito, J. (ed). (1997) *Political Islam: Revolution, Radicalism or Reform?* (London: Lynne Rienner Publishers).

Esposito, J. (1983a) *Voices of Resurgent Islam* (New York: Oxford University Press).

Esposito, J. (1983b) *The Islamic Threat: Myth or Reality* (Oxford University Press).

Esposito, J.L. and J.O. Voll (1996) *Islam and Democracy* (New York: Oxford University Press).

Fanon, F. (1968) *The Wretched of the Earth* (New York: Grove Press Incorporated)

Flew, A. (1972) 'Indoctrination and Doctrines', in *Concept of Indoctrination*, edited by I. Snook (Bolton: RKP).

Ford, D.F., Quash, B. and Soskice, J.M. (2005) *Fields of Faith: Theology and Religious Studies for the Twenty-first Century* (Cambridge: Cambridge University Press).

Furseth, I. and Repstad, P. (2006) *An Introduction to the Sociology of Religion: Classical and Contemporary Perspectives* (Farnham: Ashgate Publishing).

Galvin, D.M. (1983) 'The Female Terrorist: A Socio-Psychological Perspective', *Behavioral Science and the Law*, 1, 19-32.

Garfinkel, H. (1991) 'Respecification: Evidence for Locally Produced, Naturally Accountable Phenomena of Order, Logic, Reason, Meaning, Method', in *Ethnomethodology and the Human Sciences*, edited by G. Button (Cambridge: Cambridge University Press).

Gardner, K. and Shuker, A. (1994) 'I'm Bengali, I'm Asian and I'm Living Here: The Changing Identity of British Bengalis', in *Desh Pardesh: The South Asian Presence in Britain*, edited by R. Ballard (London: Hurst & Company).

Geaves, R. (1996) *Sectarian Influences within Islam in Britain: With Reference to the Concept of Ummah and Community* (Department of Theology and Religious Studies, University of Leeds).

Gill, P. (2007) 'A Multi-Dimensional Approach to Suicide Bombing'. *International Journal of Conflict and Violence*, 1(2), 142-59.

Glynn, S. (2002) 'Bengali Muslims: The new East End radicals?' 25(6) *Ethnic and Racial Studies*, 969, 975.

Goldthorpe, J.H., Llewllyn, C. and Payne, C. (1987) *Social Mobility and Class Structure in Modern Britain* (Oxford: Clarendon Press).

Graham, S. and Juvonen, J. (eds) (1998) 'Peer harassment in school: The plight of the vulnerable and victimized', *Journal of Educational Psychology*, 92.

Halliday, F. (1996) *Islam and the Myth of Confrontation* (London: I.B. Tauris).

Halliday, F. (1999) 'Islamophobia' reconsidered, *Ethnic and Racial Studies*, 22(5), September, 892-902.

Hare, I. and Weinstein, J. (eds) (2010) *Extreme Speech and Democracy* (Oxford: Oxford University Press).

Hartup, W.W. (1983) 'Peer Relations', in *Handbook of Child Psychology, Socialization, Personality and Social Development,* edited by E.M. Hetherington (New York: Wiley & Sons).

Hassan, S. (1988) *Guide to Protection, Rescue, and Recovery from Destructive Cults* (Somerville, MA: Freedom of Mind Press).

Hassan, S. (2001) *Releasing the Bonds: Empowering People to Think for Themselves.* (Somerville, MA: Freedom of Mind Press)

Hitch, P. (1983) 'Social identity and the half-Asian child', in *Threatened Identities*, edited by G.M. Breakwell (New York: John Wiley & Sons).

Hourani, A. (1998) *Arabic Thought in the Liberal Age 1798-1939* (Cambridge: Cambridge University Press).

Hood, R.W., Hill, P.C. and Spilka, B. (2009) *The Psychology of Religion: An Empirical Approach* (Guilford Press: New York).

Hoffer, E. (1982) *Between the Devil and the Dragon: The Best Essays and Aphorisms of Eric Hoffer* (Harper & Row).

Hoffman, B. (1998). *Inside Terrorism* (New York: University of Columbia Press).

Hogg, M.A. and Vaughan, G.M. (2002) *Introduction to Social Psychology* (Prentice Hall).

Honderich, T. (2003) *After the Terror* (Edinburgh University Press).

Howe, C. (2010) *Peer Groups and Children's Development* (Wiley-Blackwell).

Huntington, S.P. (1996). *The Clash of Civilisations* (London: Touchstone Books).

Hutnik, N. (1985) 'Aspects of Identity in a Multi-Ethnic Society' *New Community*, 12(2), 298.

Hymel, J.E. and Williams, G.A. (1990) 'Peer rejection and loneliness in childhood', in *Peer Rejection in Childhood*, edited by Asher and Coie (Cambridge: Cambridge University Press).

Ismail, S. (2006) *Rethinking Islamist Politics: Culture, the State and Islamism* (Cambridge: Blackwell).

Jackson, R.H. and Hudman, L.E. (1986) *World Regional Geography: Issues for Today* (Wiley Publications).

Jacobson, J. (1998) *Islam in Transition* (London: Routledge).

James, A. and James, A.L. (2004) *Constructing Childhood: Theory, Policy, and Social Practice* (Basingstoke: Palgrave Macmillan).

Jenkins, R. (2004) *Social Identity* (New York: Routledge).

Jennings, J. and Kemp-Welch, A. (1997) *Intellectuals in Politics: From the Dreyfus Affair to the Rushdie Affair* (London: Routledge).

Kellaghan, T. (1993) *The Home Environment and School Learning: Promoting Parental* (San Francisco, CA: Jossey-Bass).

Kelly, J. and Nicholson, N. (1980) The causation of strikes: A review of theoretical approaches and the potential contribution of social psychology. *Human Relations*, 33(12), 853-83.

Kepel, G. (2005) *The Roots of Radical Islam* (London: Saqi).

Keniston, K. (1967) 'The sources of student dissent', *Journal of Social Issues*, 23.

Komarovsky, M. (2004) *Women in College: Shaping New Feminine Identities* (Washington D.C: Rowman Altamira Press).

Kornhauser, W. (1959) *The Politics of Mass Society* (Glencoe, IL: Free Press of Glencoe).

Knowles, J.P. and Cole, E. (1990) *Motherhood: A Feminist Perspective* (London: Haworth Press).

Knutson, J.N. (1973) *Handbook of Political Psychology* (San Francisco, CA: Jossey-Bass).

Kucukcan, T. (1999) *Politics of Ethnicity, Identity and Religion: Turkish Muslims in Britain* (Aldershot: Ashgate).

Kurtz, L.R. and Turpin, J. (1999) *Encyclopaedia of Violence, Peace and Conflict* (New York: Elsevier Academic Press).

Lareau, A. (2003) *Unequal Childhoods: Class, Race and Family Life.* (Los Angles: University of California Press)

Laursen, B.P. (1993) *Close Friendships in Adolescence* (San Francisco, CA: Jossey-Bass).

Leigh, I. (2010) 'Homophobic Speech, Equality Denial, and Religious Expression', in *Extreme Speech and Democracy*, edited by I. Hare and J. Weinstein (Oxford University Press).

Lemert, E.M. (1967) *Human Deviance, Social Problems and Social Control* (Englewood Cliffs, NJ: Prentice Hall).

Levitz, R. and Noel, L. (1989) 'Connecting students to institutions: Keys to retention and success', in *The Freshman Year Experience*, edited by M.L. Upcraft and J.N. Gardner (San Francisco, CA: Jossey-Bass Publishers).

Lewis, B. (1988) *The Political Language of Islam* (Chicago, IL: University of Chicago Press)

Lewis, B. (1990) *Race and Slavery in the Middle East* (Oxford: Oxford University Press)

Lewis, B. (2004) *The Crisis of Islam: Holy War and Unholy Terror* (Pennsylvania: Random House).

Lewis, P. (2002) *Islamic Britain: Religion, Politics and Identity among British Muslims* (London: I.B.Tauris).

Lewis, P. (2008) *Young, British and Muslim* (London: Continuum Publications).

Lifton, R.J. (1989) *Thought Reform and the Psychology of Totalism: A Study of Brainwashing in China* (University of North Carolina Press).

Lyman, O. and Longnecker, M. (2008) *An Introduction to Statistical Methods and Data Analysis* (Brooks-Cole: Macmillan Publishers).

MacDonald, E. (1992) 'The memory: Women in the Italian underground organizations', *International Social Movement Research*, 4.

Malik, M. (2010) 'Extreme Speech and Liberalism', in *Extreme Speech and Democracy*, edited by I. Hare and J. Weinstein (Oxford University Press).

Mannheim, K. (1936) *Ideology and Utopia* (London: Routledge).

Marcia, J.E. (1993) *Ego Identity: A Handbook for Psychosocial Research* (Springer-Verlag).

McGown, R.B. (1999) *Muslims in the Diaspora: The Somali Communities of London and Toronto* (Toronto: University of Toronto Press).

McLoughlin, S. (2002) *Representing Muslims: Ethnicity, Religion and the Politics of Identity* (London: Pluto Press).

Mead, G. (1934) *Mind, Self and Society* (Chicago, IL: University of Chicago Press).

Mies, M. (1983) 'Towards a methodology for feminist research', in *Theories of Women's Studies*, edited by G. Bowles and R. Duelli Klein (London: Routledge and Kegan Paul), 117-40.

Miles, R. and Brown, M. (2003) *Racism* (London: Routledge).

Miller, W.B. (1958) 'Lower class culture as a generating milieu of gang delinquency' *Journal of Social Issues* 14:5-19.

Milton-Edwards, B. (2006) *Contemporary Politics in the Middle East* (Cambridge: Polity Press).

Minuchin, S. (1974) *Families and Family Therapy* (Boston, MA: Harvard University Press).

Modood, T. (2005) *Multicultural Politics: Racism, Ethnicity and Muslims in Britain* (Edinburgh: Edinburgh University Press).

Modood, T. and Werbner, P. (1997) *The Politics of Multiculturalism in the New Europe: Racism* (Basingstoke: Palgrave Macmillan).

Mollica, K.A., Gray, B. and Trevino, L.K. (2003) 'Racial homophily and its persistence in newcomers social networks', *Organization Science*, 14:2.

Moore, B. (1970) *Social Origins of Dictatorship and Democracy: Lord and Peasant in the Making of the Modern World* (Boston, MA: Beacon Press).

Newcomb, T.M. (1943) *Personality and Social Change* (New York: Dryden Press).

Newcomb, T.M. and Swanson, G.E. (ed.) (1952) *Readings in Social Psychology* (New York: Rinehart and Winston).

Newcomb, T.M. and Feldman, K.A. (1994) *The Impact of College on Students* (Piscataway, NJ: Transaction Books).

Paraipan, M. (2005) 'Our aim is to reestablish the Islamic Caliphate in the Muslim world' (World Security Network), 8 September.

Pargeter, A. (2006) 'North African Immigrants in Europe and Political Violence' *Studies on Conflict and Terrorism*, 29, 731.

Parkin, F. (1968) *Middle Class Radicalism* (Manchester: Manchester University Press).

Paul, E.L. and Kelleher, M. (1995) 'Pre-college concerns about losing and making friends in college: Implications for friendship satisfaction and self-esteem during the college transition', *Journal of College Student Development*, 36(6), 513-21.

Peel, J.D.Y. (1977) 'Conversion and Tradition in Two African Societies: Ijebu and Buganda', *Past and Present* 77, 108-41.

Piscacek, V. and Golub, M. (1973). Children of interracial marriages, in *Interracial Marriage: Expectations and Realities*, edited by Stuart and Abt (New York: Grossman).

Popplestone, J.A. and McPherson, M.W. (1988) *Dictionary of Concepts in General Psychology* (New York: Greenwood Press).

Post, J.M. (1986) 'The Group Dynamics of Terrorist Behaviour', *International Journal of Group Psychotherapy*, 36(2).

Post, J.M. (1990) 'It's us against them: The group dynamics of political terrorism', *Terrorism*, 10.

Post, J.M. (1998) 'Terrorist Psycho-Logic: Terrorist Behaviour as a Product of Psychological Forces', in *Origins of Terrorism: Psychologies, Ideologies, Theologies, States of Mind*, edited by W. Reich (Cambridge: Cambridge University Press), pp. 25-40.

Poynting, S. and Mason, V. (2007) 'The resistible rise of Islamophobia', *Journal of Sociology*, 43(1), 61-86.

Reich, W. (1948) *Listen Little Man* (Harmondsworth: Penguin).

Reich, W. (ed.) (1990) *Origins of Terrorism: Psychologies, Ideologies, Theologies, States of Mind* (Cambridge: Cambridge University Press).

Roberts, K., Cook, F.G., Clark, S.C. and Semeonoff, E. (1977) *The Fragmentary Class Structure* (London: Heinemann).

Robinson, F. (1988) 'Varieties of South Asian Islam' *Research Paper no. 8* (University of Warwick).

Rom, H. and Lamb, R. (eds) (1986) *The Dictionary of Personality and Social Psychology.* (Massachusetts: MIT Press).

Roof, C.R. (1979) 'Concept and Indicators of Religious Commitment: A Critical Review', in *The Religious Dimension. New Directions in Quantitative Research*, edited by R. Wuthnow (New York: Academic Press).

Rosenthal, D.A. and Feldman, S.S. (1992) 'The nature and stability of ethnic identity in Chinese youth: Effects of length of residence in two cultural contexts'. *Journal of Cross-Cultural Psychology*, 23(2), 214-27.

Rouleau, E. (2001) 'Terrorism and Islamism' (article) *Le Monde diplomatique*, November).

Roy, O. (2004). *Globalized Islam* (New York: Columbia University Press).

Russell, C.A. and B.H. Miller. (1977) 'Profile of a Terrorist', *Terrorism: An International Journal*, 1(1), 17-34.

Saeed, A. Blain N. and Forbes, D. (1999) 'New ethnic and national questions in Scotland: post-British identities among Glasgow Pakistani teenagers' *Ethnic and Racial Studies*, 2(5), 821-44.

Sageman, M. (2005) *Understanding Terror Networks* (Philadelphia: University of Pennsylvania Press).

Samad, Y. (1996) 'The Politics of Islamic Identity among Bangladeshis and Pakistanis in Britain', in *Culture Identity and Politics: Ethnic Minorities in Britain*, edited by T. Ranger, Y. Samad and O. Stuart (Aldershot: Avebury).

Samad, Y. (2004) 'Muslim Youth Britain: Ethnic to Religious Identity' (Paper presented at the International Conference Muslim Youth in Europe. Typologies of religious belonging and sociocultural dynamics, *Edoardo Agnelli Centre for Comparative Religious Studies, Turin, 11th June*).

Sanchez-Hucles, J.V. (1998) 'Racism: Emotional abusiveness and psychological trauma for ethnic minorities'. *Journal of Emotional Abuse*, 1(2), pp. 69-87.

Shaw, E.D. (1986) Political Terrorists: Dangers of Diagnosis and an Alternative to the Psychopathology Model, *International Journal of Law and Psychiatry*, 8, 359-68.

Sherif, M. and Sherif, C.W. (1969) *Social Psychology* (Int. Rev. Ed.). New York: Harper & Row.

Shupe, A. and Hadden, J.K. (eds) (1988) *The Politics of Religion and Social Change* (New York: Paragon House).

Silber, M.D. and Bhatt, A. (2007) 'Radicalisation in the West: The Homegrown Threat', The New York City Police Department.

Singer, M.T. and Lalich, J. (1995) *Cults in our Midst* (San Francisco, CA: Jossey-Bass).

Skocpol, T. and Campbell, J.L. (1995) *American Society and Politics: Institutional, Historical, and Theoretical Perspectives: A Reader* (Princeton, NJ: McGraw-Hill).

Smith, B. (1997) *Mothers and Sons: The Truth about Mother–Son Relationships* (London: Allen & Unwin).

Snook, I.A. (1972) *Concepts of Indoctrination: Philosophical Essays* (London: Routledge).

Snow, D.A., E.B. Rochford, Jr., S.K. Wordon and R.D. Benford (1986) Frame Alignment Processes, Micromobilization, and Movement Participation, *American Sociological Review* 51, 464-81.

Stack, J.F.J. (1986) 'Ethnic mobilization in world politics: The primordial perspective', in *The Primordial Challenge: Ethnicity in the Contemporary World*, edited by J.F.J. Stack (New York: Greenwood Press).

Stark, R. and Bainbridge, W.S. (1980) Networks of Faith: Interpersonal Bonds and Recruitment to Cults and Sects, *American Journal of Sociology*, 85(6), 1376-95.

Stark, R. and Glock, C. (1968). *American Piety: The Nature of Religious Commitment* (Berkeley, CA: University of California Press).

Stratham, P. (2003) 'New Conflicts about Integration and Cultural Diversity in Britain', in *The Challenge of Diversity: European Social Democracy Facing Migration, Integration, and Multiculturalism*, edited by R. Cuperus, K.A. Duffeck and J. Kandel (Innsbruck: Studienverlag).

Steger, M.B. (2003) *Judging Nonviolence: The Dispute between Realists and Idealists* (Routledge: New York).

Storr, A. (2005) *Solitude: A Return to the Self* (London: Simon & Schuster).

Taji-Farouki, S. (1996) *A Fundamental Quest* (London: Grey Seal).

Tajfel, H. (1981) *Human Groups and Social Categories* (Studies in Social Psychology) (Cambridge: Cambridge University Press).

Tajfel, H. and Turner, J.C. (1979) 'An Integrative Theory of Inter-group Conflict', in *The Social Psychology of Inter-group Relations*, edited by W.G. Austin and S. Worchel (Monterey, CA: Brooks).

Parsons, T. (1960) *Structures and Process in Modern Societies* (Chicago, IL: The University of Chicago Press).

Tilly, C. (1978) *From Mobilization to Revolution* (New York: Random House).

Thompson, E. (1978) *The Making of the English Working Class* (London: Merlin Press).

Thompson, W. and Hickey, J. (2005) *Society in Focus* (Boston, MA: Pearson).

Thompson, K. (1988) *Under Siege: Racial Violence in Britain* (London: Penguin).

Triandis, H.C. (1989) The Self and Social behaviour in differing cultural contexts, *Psychological Review*, 96, 506-20.

Turner, J.C. (1991) *Social Influence* (Milton Keynes: Open University Press).

Turner, J.C., Hogg, M.A., Oakes, P.J., Reicher, S.D. and Wetherell, M.S. (1987) *Rediscovering the Social Group: A Self-categorization Theory* (Oxford: Blackwell).

Van Gennep, Arnold. (1960) *The Rites of Passage* (Chicago, IL: University of Chicago Press).

Vigil, J.D. (2002) *A Rainbow of Gangs: Street Cultures in the Mega-city* (Austin, Texas: University of Texas Press).

Voll, J.O. (1982) *Islam: Continuity & Change in the Modern World* (Syracuse, NY: Syracuse University Press).

Wade, B. and Souter, P. (1992) *Continuing to Think: The British Asian Girl* (an Exploratory Study), Multilingual Matters.

Waters, M. (1995) *Globalisation* (London and New York: Routledge).

Warner, W.L. (1949) *What Social Class is in America* (Chicago: Bobbs-Merrill).

Way, N. and Hamm, J. (2005) *The Experience of Close Friendships in Adolescence* (San Fransisco, CA: Jossey-Bass).

Wetherell, M. (1987) 'Social identity and group polarization', in *Rediscovering the Social Group: A Self-Categorization Theory*, edited by J.C. Turner, M.A. Hogg, P.J. Oakes, S.D. Reicher and M.S. Wetherell (Oxford: Blackwell).

Wilson, A. (1987) *Mixed Race Children: A Study of Identity* (Boston, MA: Allen & Unwin).

Wilson, J. (1972) 'Indoctrination and Rationality', in *Concept of Indoctrination*, edited by I. Snook (Lancashire: RKP).

Wiktorowicz, Q. (2004) *Islamic Activism: A Social Movement Theory Approach* (Bloomington, IN: Indiana University Press).

Wiktorowicz, Q. (2005) *Radical Islam Rising: Muslim Extremism in the West* (Oxford: Rowman & Littlefield).

Zimbardo, P. (1997) 'What messages are behind today's cults?' *American Psychological Association Monitor*, May.

Newspaper

Times Magazine (1972) 'Behaviour: Male & Female: Differences Between Them', 20 March.

The *Guardian* (1994) Taken from *BMMS* 7 February Vol. II, No. 2, pp. 3/4.

The *Observer* (1994) 'Hitler's Heirs Incite Islamic Students', 13 March.

The *Daily Mirror* (1994) Taken from *BMMS* 4 March Vol. II, No. 3, pp. 7-9.

The *Daily Awaz* (1994) Taken from *BMMS* 7 March Vol. II, No. 3, pp. 7-9.

Sanders, Claire (1994) 'Islamic group accuses SOAS of cowardice', *The Times Higher Education Supplement*, 4 November).

BBC2 (1995) 'Islam's Militant Tendencies' *Public Eye*, 25 July.

The *Observer* (1995) Taken from *BMMS* 13 August Vol. III, No. 8, p. 3-5.

Weekly Telegraph (1996) 'Cancellation of Rally for Revival', 4 September.

Asian Age (1996) (BMMS 9 September Vol. IV, No. 9, p. 1/2).

'Al-Muhajiroun ban' (1997) *Southall Gazette*, 17 October.

'Al-Muhajiroun ban' (1997) *Ealing and Acton Gazette*, 24 October.

'Tottenham Ayatollah' (1997) *Asian Age* (BMMS 10 April Vol. V, No. 4, p. 3/4).

'Tottenham Ayatollah' (1997) *Crawley Observer* (BMMS 16 April Vol. V, No. 4, p. 3/4).

'Cash for terrorism?' (1997), *Enfield Advertiser* (BMMS 3 December Vol. V, No. 12, p. 9).

'Fundamentalists receive training in Britain' (7 November 1999), *The Sunday Telegraph*.

'Fears for boy recruited for 'jihad' (2000), *The Times*, BMMS 22 January Vol. VIII, No. 1, p. 8].

www.islamic-state.org/leaflets/november0402.htm, 4 November 2002.

Reuters, 15 January 2003.

Lambroschini, S. (26 October 2004) 'Germany: Court Appeal by Hizb ut-Tahrir Highlights Balancing act between actions, intentions', *Radio Free Europe.*

Lambroschini, S. (26 October 2004), 'Russian Supreme Court Bans Hizb ut-Tahrir', *Radio Free Europe.*

Grieve, D. (2005) speech (in House of Commons Research Paper (5/48): 'The Racial and Religious Hatred Bill', *Parliament and Constitution Centre* (House of Commons Library), 16 June.

Paraipan, M. (2005) 'Hizb ut-tahrir: An interview with Imran Waheed' The *worldpress.org*, 12 September.

The Local (2005) 'Åke Green cleared over gay sermon', 29 November.

Tempest, M. (2005) 'Blair defiant as pressure mounts', *The Guardian*, 10 November.

Grice, A. (2005) 'Cabinet rallies to defiant Blair as criticism mounts', *The Independent*, 11 November.

Sciolino, E. (10 July 2005) 'For a Decade, London Thrived as a Busy Crossroads of Terror', *New York Times*.

Malik, M. (2006) The Veil Fixation is doing Muslim Women no Favours, The *Guardian*, 25 October.

Truscott, C. (2007) "Lyrical terrorist' sentenced over extremist poetry', The *Guardian*, 6 December.

BBC (2008), 'Arrogant Muslim preacher jailed', 17 April (news.bbc.co.uk/1/hi/uk/7354397.stm).

Baker, Peter (2006) 'Bush Tells Group he sees a 'Third Awakening', The *Washington Post*, (13 September).

Tony Blair, Speech, cited by BBC, 19 November 2006.

Wilson, G. (2007) 'Cameron attacks Muslim hardliners', *The Telegraph*, 31 January.

Paraipan, M. and Romania, A. (2005) 'Hizb ut Tahrir: An Interview with Imran Waheed' (World Press), 12 September.

Radio Free Europe, 26 August 2004.

Dodd, V. (2009) 'Anti-terror code 'would alienate most Muslims', The *Guardian*, 17 February.

Miller, G. (2010) 'CIA acts on fear of Al-Qaeda plot to hit in Europe', The *Washington Post*, 29 September.

Dodd, V. (02 November 2010) 'Profile: Roshonara Choudhry', The *Guardian*.

Home Office Report (2005). 'Report of the Official Account of the Bombings in London on 7th July 2005', *London: The Stationary Office*.

Index